Pyzdek's Guide to SPC
Volume Two
Applications and Special Topics

Thomas Pyzdek

Quality Consultant

Published by:

ASQC-Quality Press *Milwaukee, Wisconsin*
Quality Publishing, Inc. *Tucson, Arizona*

Pyzdek, Thomas
    Pyzdek's Guide to SPC: Vol. 2, Applications and Special Topics
    (Pyzdek's Guide to SPC; Vol. 2)
    1. Quality control. I. Title. II. Series: Pyzdek's Guide to SPC; v. 2.
Library of Congress Catalog Card Number: 89-92170
ISBN 0-930011-04-x

Quality Publishing, Inc.
2405 N Avenida Sorgo, Tucson, Arizona 85749-9305

Current printing (last digit)
10 9 8 7 6 5 4 3 2 1

Table of Contents

Pyzdek's Guide to SPC
Volume Two
Applications and Special Topics

CHAPTER 11

SPC IMPLEMENTATION ISSUES

OBJECTIVES:

After completing this section you will:

- Know how to start an SPC effort
- Know how to administer SPC

Introduction

Starting and administering SPC is not a trivial task. Many traps and pitfalls await the unwary. If not handled properly, a number of unproductive situations can result from the attempt, such as

1. *Beauty contest programs.* These are massive displays of control charts, histograms, cause and effect diagrams etc. which serve no useful purpose. These displays are often placed in "war rooms" which are located far away from the processes being monitored. The charts are usually computer generated and the charts are often very colorful and of near-typeset quality. The problem is, the people who can use them either don't ever see them, or see them too late for the results to serve any useful purpose.

2. *My little darling programs.* These are programs started by an individual or small group, usually in the quality department, with little or no active management leadership. Those who start these programs have often recently attended a seminar and learned about the statistical aspects of SPC, but not the management or human relations aspects. Charting and data collection is started before creating a management system and environment for dealing with the problems highlighted by SPC.

3. *"The greatest show on earth!" programs.* These programs are usually launched by training or human resources departments and they usually feature speeches by senior management,suggestion programs (almost always called something cute), buttons, badges, hats, flags and other paraphernalia, etc.. Everyone is told the obvious ("quality is important to our cus-

1

tomer, and to us!") and asked to give 110% to the cause of quality without ever being told exactly what that means. SPC is implemented on a hit-and-miss basis and everyone is expected to understand SPC with little training or guidance. These programs never die, rather, like old soldiers, they simply fade away.

4. *Drill instructor* programs. These programs are started by autocratic upper managers who have, by god, had it with the rubbish being produced by the "troops." You *will* implement SPC, you *will* produce quality! Of course, once the proclamation has been made, the leader retires from the scene to let someone else handle all of the details. When the smoke clears and no progress has been made, heads may roll. But effective quality improvement is highly improbable.

5. *Potpourri.* This sort of SPC consists of a melange of statistical and pseudo-statistical tools splattered about. Over here we have a "control chart" with control limits that are really the engineering specifications. Over there is a chart with no limits of any kind, put in place to "help people get used to the idea of plotting data." Somewhere else, Mil-Std-105E is being applied and the results plotted on a p-chart. Such an approach results in total chaos, but management can be easily duped into thinking that they are witnessing a truly sophisticated rendition of SPC.

6. *The island of excellence.* This is the immortal pilot SPC project. It was originally started to "get a feel for how SPC can be used here at XYZ Corp.," but expansion never quite got off of the ground. Nevertheless, management was quick to see the PR value of the effort and they refused to let it die. The main purpose becomes eyewash for guests, especially customers who want to see tangible evidence that you are serious about quality improvement.

The list can be extended ad nauseam, but you get the idea. The important lesson here is that successful SPC is no accident. To assure success SPC must be carefully planned and it must receive the active attention of every level of management, from top management on down.

Getting SPC Started

There are as many different approaches to starting SPC as there are companies trying to do it. If you want advice on how to proceed under your particular set of circumstances, you will probably need the services of a consultant. However, I will describe an approach that has been used successfully in the past. The system described includes all of the elements of success except one: your commitment. The style of the material that follows is that of a consultant reporting to a client. Your hypothetical company, Superiority Corporation, has just received a report from a quality consultant. The report provides recommendations on how you should structure your quality improvement program in general, and how Superiority Corporation should start SPC in particular. You should have little difficulty modifying this report to your own company.

Superiority Corporation manufactures a proprietary electronic subsystem for use by commercial and government customers. It is produced at a single manufacturing facility. Superiority is a small company managed by the original founder, who has a strong personal commitment to quality. The manufacturing operations include complete assembly of printed circuit boards, soldering, systems assembly, and testing. The company also has marketing, design engineering, sales and all of the other departments found in a modern firm. Although you informed the consultant that you wanted him to limit the scope of his report to manufacturing SPC activities, he felt that it was in your best interest to consider the global issues of quality improvement as well.

Consultant's Report to Superiority Corporation

Management organization

I recommend that Superiority Corporation senior management actively lead the quality effort, including SPC activities, through the creation of an Executive Steering Committee. Management leadership activities should include, at a minimum

- Training the management team in quality improvement philosophies and methodologies.

- Provide a long-term quality plan for all of Superiority Corporation. The plan should indicate just where the manufacturing SPC activity fits into the overall Superiority Corporation quality effort.

- Oversee an SPC pilot project on the board assembly line. Oversight activities include chartering the pilot project team (the Core Team), setting goals for the project, monitoring the progress of the team, and removing obstacles encountered by the Core Team.

- Oversee full-scale implementation of SPC and other quality improvement activities. Full-scale implementation should include the remainder of the board assembly line, the remainder of manufacturing, non-manufacturing areas, and suppliers.

The services of a qualified statistician will be of tremendous value. Because of the small size of Superiority Corporation, I recommend they consider the use of a consultant rather than a full-time staff member. Candidate statistical consultants may be found at the state university. Be certain that the statistical consultant has extensive practical experience as well as theoretical expertise. He or she should be compatible with the team-orientation of the Superiority Corporation.

Full-scale implementation

Management should view the SPC pilot project as an effort to create a new and better Superiority Corporation, in microcosm. By learning how to make big quality and productivity gains in the pilot project area, Superiority Corporation will create a model or prototype for improved performance throughout the company. A study of the differences between the pilot project area and other areas of Superiority Corporation will provide insights regarding how management systems can be changed for the better. A study of the problems encountered in setting up the pilot project will be useful in planning for full-scale quality improvement.

Strategic quality planning[1]

It is important that a strategic quality plan be developed for Superiority Corporation. The strategic quality plan describes how the company integrates quality improvement planning into overall business planning. The plan should include both short-term (1-2 years) and longer term goals. The plan should address in detail how the company will pursue market leadership through providing exceptional quality products and services and through improving the effectiveness of all operations of the company. In addition to stating the goals, the quality plan should include principal strategies for achieving those goals.

Short-term plans should summarize key requirements and performance indicators deployed to work units and suppliers; and resources committed accomplish the key requirements.

Longer term plans should include two- to five-year projections of significant changes in the company's most important quality indicators levels. It should also compare these quality levels to those of key competitors over this time period.

---

1   material in this section is based on the 1991 application guidelines for the Malcolm Baldrige National Quality Award, section 3.0

Manufacturing Implementation

While the Executive Steering Committee works *on* the management system, manufacturing personnel must work *within* the current system to improve quality and implement SPC. The objective of SPC is quality improvement through reduction of variation. The improvement will come from two sources:

1. Reducing process variation which is the result of special causes.
2. Reducing process variation which is the result of common causes.

Control charts

Control charts will be used to operationally define a special cause of variation. Thus, everyone involved with the SPC effort must understand control charts and their purpose.

When the control chart indicates that a special cause is present, a well defined series of actions should be taken to identify the special cause. These actions should be determined by the SPC team and communicated to the people who are responsible for the process. Provision should be made for situations when the special cause can't be found. A formal written procedure should be developed and kept at the process. When the control chart indicates that common causes are responsible for economically significant variation, action will be taken by SPC teams, working with management, to improve the process. The term "process" should be understood to mean the entire system of inputs, actions and outputs which interact to create a product or service; the process is more than just a machine. Superiority Corporation can, in fact, be viewed as a system of processes. Quality improvement will result from people improving their processes and from management improving the system.

Control charts can be thought of as tools that measure the amount of ignorance that exists about a process. The control limits are a measure of ignorance since they define the limit to which you can improve by solving problems due to special causes. The only way to improve beyond the control limits is to develop a better understanding of the common causes of variation; in other words, to reduce your ignorance about the process.

Core team

The foundation of the manufacturing SPC effort is the Core SPC Team. This team should consist of individuals who will champion SPC throughout manufacturing. The members will all be directly involved with the pilot project. Upon completion of the pilot project phase, at least one Core Team member will become a member of subsequent SPC teams. In this way the training and experience acquired from the pilot project will be used to maximum advantage.

Core team training

Core Team members should receive training in the following subjects:

- SPC and problem solving methods (sixteen hours minimum)
- Group dynamics (four hours minimum)
- Project management (two hours minimum)

It is likely that Superiority Corporation already has one or more people who can provide this training. If not, training can be obtained from a wide variety of sources such as community colleges, professional societies, correspondence courses or consultants.

Core team membership

Based on my brief visit to Superiority Corporation, I do not feel qualified to make recommendations for membership on the Core Team. However,your SPC

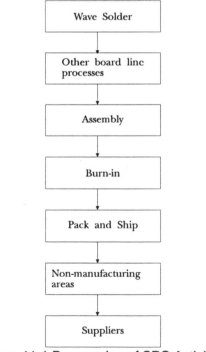

Figure 11-1 Progression of SPC Activities

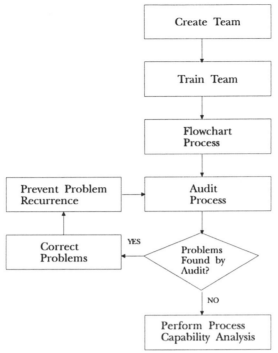

Figure 11-2 Typical SPC Startup Activities

coordinator seems to be an obvious candidate based on her training in SPC and her enthusiasm for the SPC effort. The manufacturing manager's position in the organization makes his membership almost mandatory; he should also be a member of the Executive Steering Committee. Other members should be chosen based on their enthusiasm, importance to the success of the pilot project, and their ability to help expand SPC to other areas of manufacturing. I recommend that the size of the Core Team be restricted to a maximum of ten members. Team members should be individuals, not "representatives" of an area. Effective teamwork is based on interpersonal trust, which only develops when people work closely together for an extended period of time. Team members are not "interchangeable parts."

Project plan

The first activity of the Core Team should be the creation of an overall plan for the pilot project. The plan should describe the goals for the project, milestones that indicate progress towards the goals, a timetable for reaching the goals and milestones, resources required and individual responsibility for specific tasks. The plan should be reviewed with the Executive Steering Committee.

Pilot project

The pilot project area, tentatively selected during my visit, is the wave solder process. From this process, the likely progression to other areas is as indicated in figure 11.1.

Regardless of where SPC is implemented, the standard approach shown in figure 11.2 is recommended. These activities are designed to identify important process control items already known to the team and to assure that these items are acceptable. Items in poor repair are corrected before actual collection of data. The lessons learned here will be helpful later in planning the control chart and preparing the process control plan.

Process capability analysis

Once the wave solder process is in reasonably good operating condition, a process capability analysis (PCA) can be undertaken (see chapter 13). PCAs consist of two stages:

Stage One   Identify and remove special causes of variation.

Stage Two   Determine the ability of the process to meet requirements when only common causes are present.

PCAs involve several activities:

- Evaluate the measurement system (see chapter 12)
- Provide a control system
- Gather and analyze data with control charts
- Identify and remove special causes of variation
- Estimate the process capability
- Establish a quality maintenance and improvement plan for the variable

Once a stable process state has been attained steps should be taken to maintain it and, hopefully, improve upon it. SPC is one means of doing this. Far more important than the particular approach taken is a company environment that makes continuous improvement a normal part of the daily routine for everyone.

When the quality maintenance plan includes the use of control charts, a control chart plan should be prepared. The plan should include

✓ A statement of the objective of the chart
✓ Selecting the type of control chart to be used
✓ Setting the sampling interval, subgroup size, and sample selection method
✓ Description of the measurement method
✓ Listing of most likely special causes to be investigated when out-of-control situations are encountered

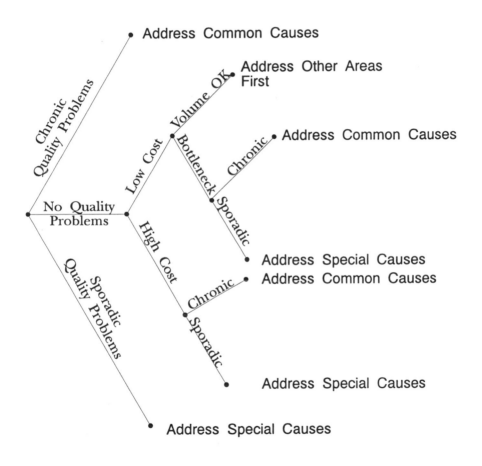

Figure 11-3 Guide to Choosing SPC Application Areas

✓ Listing of course of action to be taken when out-of-control situations are encountered

✓ Description of how the chart will be maintained (and by whom) and who is responsible for action when the chart indicates the need for action

✓ Schedule for off-line analysis of the data by the SPC team

Management Review

Progress on the pilot project should be periodically reviewed by the Executive Steering Committee. I recommend formal monthly reviews. Upon completion of the pilot project, both the Core Team and the Executive Steering Committee should review their long-range plans. The chances are excellent that the lessons learned on the pilot project will require extensive modification of all plans.

As discussed earlier, management should consider the pilot project area as a prototype of the new Superiority Corporation. By focusing intense management attention, and other corporate resources, on the area you should see dramatic improvement in both quality and productivity within six to twelve months. The question this poses to management is: *"what is different about this area?"* The answer to this question provides valuable information about how Superiority Corporation's systems can be improved. Once this information is known, plans can be made for company-wide quality improvement.

In choosing areas where SPC methods are likely to be beneficial, consider the possible impact of SPC on quality, costs, or deliveries. The decision tree shown in figure 11.3 can be used as a guide.

Selecting performance indicators

Variables versus attributes performance indicators

SPC involves monitoring one or more indicators of process performance. The indicator selected should provide information about the state of the process as it relates to quality. It may be an attribute performance indicator or a continuous variable. Attribute performance indicators are based on counts, such as the number of changes on an engineering drawing, the number of customers who rate your service as better than your competitor, or the number of parts that don't conform to requirements. Continuous variables are usually physical measurements such as size, volume, temperature, weight, etc..

Attributes and continuous variables are monitored with different SPC tools. Usually, continuous variables are preferred because they provide much more information per measurement than attributes. For example, a go/not-go gage can

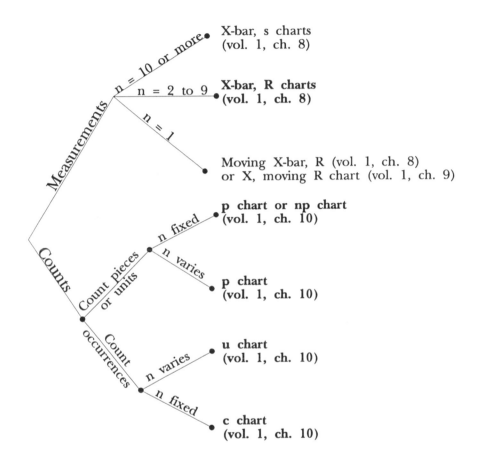

Figure 11-4 Guide to Choosing SPC Tools

tell you whether a part meets the size requirement but an actual measurement will tell you exactly how close the part is to its target value. Because of the limited information content of attributes data, attribute SPC charts usually require a much larger sample size than variables SPC charts for the same sensitivity. The diagram in figure 11.4 provides a guide for selecting an SPC tool (Munoz and Nielson, 1991.)

Guidelines for selecting process control indicators[2]

The objective of SPC is to control all *process factors* which cause variation in *product features*.

> *Please read the above sentence again, it is important.*

There are many ways to determine which process factors cause variation in product features. Sophisticated statistical procedures such as regression analysis, principal components analysis and cluster analysis can be performed by a statistician if reliable data is available. However, I don't recommend this approach at the start of an SPC program because the reliability of data is unknown. I have been involved in many SPC projects where, at the start, process controls didn't function as they were supposed to -- which would wreak havoc on conclusions from studies using advanced statistical methods. Also, these techniques require help from professional statisticians and a lot of up-front planning to collect the necessary information and data. Statistical analysis of data that just happens to be available is *very* risky. Also, any sophisticated statistical analysis should always be supplemented with easily understood graphics that can be evaluated by people who can relate the conclusions to the process; people who may lack training in advanced statistical analysis.

I have found that SPC teams with a good understanding of their process area can do a competent job of choosing control indicators if they follow certain guidelines. Furthermore, SPC has a built-in self-correcting mechanism: if you make poor choices you won't make progress, and your SPC data will make the lack of progress obvious quite quickly. With this in mind, I offer the following guidelines in a form that can be used as a checklist.

❑ The indicator should be closely related to cost or product quality.

❑ The indicator should be easy to measure economically.

❑ The indicator should show measurable variation. A control chart of a number that seldom changes doesn't provide any information. However, these

---

2   see chapter 22 for additional information on this subject.

indicators can be monitored with periodic audits to verify that they haven't changed.

❏ The indicator should have a high information content, i.e., pick an indicator that provides information on other indicators as well as itself. For example, do you need to check every pad on a screen printed pattern with fifty pads, or do a few pads adequately describe the entire pattern?

❏ Reality test: does the control chart for this indicator actually help improve quality?

These questions should be addressed one-by-one by the SPC team. The team should reach a consensus answer to each question. It will often be necessary to collect and analyze data from management reports and a variety of other sources to answer these questions. The team should ask "Who is the customer for this process?" The customer's input should be used in deciding which process control indicators to use. Remember, there are customers inside the company as well as outside the company.

As a rule, use the smallest possible number of control indicators. There is a tendency for SPC teams to set up separate control charts for every part number, this is poor practice. Remember, the objective of SPC is to change the real world to make it more consistent. If there are differences observed between quality levels of different part numbers, the team should ask how the process and/or the parts could be changed to make the differences smaller. Even though it is easier to bring control charts into control by setting up many charts, it misses the point.

Guidelines for implementing SPC using variables data

Variables data are obtained from variables measured on a continuous scale. Examples include temperature, weight, pH, flux density, pad height, and viscosity. The other type of SPC data is attribute data. Attribute data are based on counts, not measurements. Examples of attributes data are solder defects, number of missing components or the number of misoriented components. This section provide guidelines for variables data. Guidelines for attributes data are provided later in this chapter.

The preferred or "default" SPC method for variables data is the averages, or $\overline{X}$ chart. The $\overline{X}$ chart shows the central tendency of the measured process variable. It is accompanied by a chart which shows the process spread or variability, usually a range or standard deviation chart. For the purpose of computing averages and ranges or standard deviations, subgroups are formed by taking consecutive units from the process. Care is taken to assure that all units in the subgroup were produced under essentially the same conditions.

There are many advantages to using the $\overline{X}$ chart. If sample sizes of four or larger are used, the distribution of the averages will be approximately normal even if the underlying distribution is not normal. This fact makes it possible to apply sensitive "run tests" to detect process changes that would otherwise be missed. By increasing the sample size, the $\overline{X}$ chart can be made more sensitive to process changes. Creating subgroups from consecutive units makes it possible to detect process cycles and trends that are often missed by other SPC methods, such as individuals charts. $\overline{X}$ charts dampen the effect of measurement error on control chart validity. $\overline{X}$ charts are described in chapter 8 of volume one. As good as they are, it is not always possible to use $\overline{X}$ charts. The following items make the use of $\overline{X}$ charts inadvisable.

- Within subgroup variability is too small to be measured. This condition will result in a large number of subgroups with a range or standard deviation at or near zero. When this happens, any non-zero range or standard deviation will cause an out-of-control indication on the R or sigma chart. Also, since the control limits for the $\overline{X}$ control chart are based on the average of the range or standard deviation chart, the $\overline{X}$ chart will be out-of-control almost continuously. This situation will also occur if the subgroup size is too large.

- Cost-per-measurement is very high. An $\overline{X}$ chart consists of one plotted point per subgroup of n values. If the cost of getting the plotted point is higher than the value obtained, then smaller and/or less frequent samples are indicated. When the subgroup size is less than two, it is not possible to use $\overline{X}$ charts.

- Normal process changes occur as cycles that last several sample periods. An example of this is a batch chemical processes that change gradually as the contents of a tank change. At Superiority Corporation this might occur with such variables as solder temperature, solder chemistry or solder flux density. Standard $\overline{X}$ charts are only valid if the process is supposed to maintain a constant level, so processes that have inherent cycles or drift $\overline{X}$ charts would show normal process changes to be special causes of variation. However, if the inherent process patterns are from causes that are "built into the process," there are SPC techniques that can be used to monitor the process. See chapters 17 and 20 for two SPC tools that can be used with such processes. Chapter 18 describes a method of adjusting the sampling interval in such a way that standard X control charts can be used with processes that have data that are serially correlated.

- Process changes occur sporadically and there is a high cost associated with running in an out-of-control condition. When this occurs it is advisable to sample frequently, but $\overline{X}$ charts tend to have a high cost-per-plotted point which precludes frequent sampling.

When one or more of the above conditions are present, the options listed below should be considered.[3]

Option A: Moving $\overline{X}$ charts

These control charts, discussed in volume one, chapter 8, are created by forming subgroups from grouping individual measurements collected at different points in time. For example, you might measure the thickness of a circuit board. A moving $\overline{X}$ chart would create the first subgroup with boards 1, 2, 3, 4 and 5; the second subgroup would be from boards 2, 3, 4, 5 and 6 and so on. Each new subgroup would replace the oldest data point with the new data point. After the first subgroup, the moving $\overline{X}$ chart will have a plotted point for every observation. However, unlike ordinary $\overline{X}$ charts, the plotted points will not be independent. The lack of independence results in deceiving patterns on the moving $\overline{X}$ chart, so run tests are not applied. However, the resulting chart retains many of the other benefits of a standard $\overline{X}$ chart, such as the approximately normal distribution of averages, adjustable sensitivity, etc..

Option B: Individuals charts (X charts)

These charts, discussed in volume one, chapter 9, are created by plotting the actual measurement values instead of statistics computed from the measurements. They provide the minimum inspection cost per plotted point; note that this is not always the minimum *total* cost. Individuals charts have a number of advantages over the methods discussed so far:

- The control limits can be compared directly to the specifications.

- These charts are usually the easiest for untrained personnel to understand.

- No calculations are needed.

- An independent plotting point is obtained for every measurement.

There are also some disadvantages to using these charts:

---

3   These options apply to ordinary processes, for SPC tools that apply to special situations see chapters 15-21.

- They are less sensitive to process changes than the other charts discussed so far.

- They won't work well unless the underlying distribution is at least approximately normal.

Individuals charts can be used when ranges within subgroups are zero. Since, the sampling interval can be extended until measurements are independent, they can also be used for processes that have "built-in" cycles or trends. When using X charts, the process spread is usually measured by computing the ranges based on the difference between consecutive measurements.

Option C: Median control charts

Median control charts, discussed in chapter 14, combine some of the advantages of $\overline{X}$ charts and individuals charts. Like $\overline{X}$ charts, the sensitivity of median charts can be increased by increasing the subgroup size; the subgroup range can also be measured. Like individuals charts, median charts can be designed so that no calculations are involved. However, median charts are statistically less efficient than $\overline{X}$ charts with the same sample size. Also, median charts require at least two measurements per subgroup so they always involve more sampling than individuals charts. The recommended subgroup size for median charts is 3, 5 or 7. Odd subgroup sizes mean that the median is the middle value of the data set so no calculations are necessary. Smaller subgroup sizes are recommended because medians become less and less efficient as larger subgroup sizes are used.

Guidelines for choosing an SPC method for attributes data

Control charts for attributes are discussed in volume one, chapter 10. Attributes data are obtained by counting. The count is usually the occurrence or non-occurrence of some product feature. Most often, the count is the number of defects or the number of units with one or more defects. The count may be plotted directly, as with c charts or np charts, or it may be mathematically transformed, as with u charts or p charts. Table 11.1, reproduced from volume one, provides guidelines for selecting one of these "standard" attribute SPC methods.

Process sampling

Sampling to determine process control is more an art form than a science. The objective is to select subgroups such that the variation of measurements or counts within the subgroup will be produced by only common causes. The

Table 11-1 Attribute Charts and Their Usage

Attribute Chart	Usage
np chart	Control of performance measures that involve unit counts. Usually the units counted posess some attribute, such as a flaw or an error. The subgroup size must be constant. Examples: sample 100 invoices each week and count the number of invoices with errors; check 50 drilled holes each hour with a go/not-go gage and tally the number of holes that fail.
p chart	Same as np charts except that proportions are used instead of actual counts and sample sizes can vary.
c chart	Control of performance measures that involve occurrence per unit counts. The unit can be a number of items, a time peroid, or any opportunity for the occurrence to appear. The number of units per subgroup must be constant. Examples: accidents per 100,000 labor hours; defects per square yard of carpet; pieces made per tool; machine breakdowns per day.
u chart	Same as c charts except the number of units per subgroup can vary. The number plotted is the number of occurrences divided by the number of units in the subgroup.

spread of the control limits will be based on only within-subgroup variation. Thus, any additional variation will cause the production of subgroup statistics which fall beyond the control limits, signalling a special cause of variation.

I have always found it helpful to think about the process as a bowl of blue chips with numbers written on them. A controlled process is one where the same bowl of chips is sampled time-after-time. If the chips in the bowl have different numbers on them, there will be variation in the sample. However, since the bowl doesn't change, the variation will be relatively consistent from one sample to the next. After sampling the bowl numerous times we will become more and more comfortable setting up some limits on the variation we expect to see in future samples from the same bowl. The bowl represents a controlled process, a predictable process.

Now let's say that there are two bowls, one with blue chips and one with green chips. Assume further that the numbers written on the blue chips are quite different than those written on the green chips. Furthermore, let's say that you don't get to see the chips themselves; all you know is the numbers you obtained. Sometimes your sample is taken from the blue chips and sometimes from the green chips. Could you tell the difference?

The answer depends a great deal on the way you formed your subgroups. If your subgroups were formed from a mixture of blue and green chips, then the process is neither blue nor green; the process is blue+green. The subgroup variation would include the variation from both the blue *and* the green *and* the difference between them. For example, if the blue chips varied from 10 to 50 and the green varied from 60 to 100, a mixed sample of both blue and green would vary from 10 to 100. Control limits based on the mixed sample would show a greater spread, and your estimate of the process capability would indicate a less capable process than either the blue or the green alone. In other words, you would probably conclude that the blue+green process was "in control and capable of holding a tolerance of 10 to 100."

The objective of forming rational subgroups is to identify the underlying process so that departures from the underlying process can be quickly detected and corrected. The underlying process can be thought of as the performance that could be attained if all special causes of variation were eliminated and the process was operating at its best. To do this you must plan carefully to avoid mixing processes from different cause systems, which is comparable to mixing the blue chips and the green chips.

Here's a more down-to-earth example. An o-ring is made in a mold with fifty cavities. It is known that there is a substantial difference between the cavities. It would be a mistake to form a subgroup using o-rings from cavities known to be different because the cavity-to-cavity variation would mask the variation caused by other factors such as material, temperature, etc.. SPC methods useful for this type of data are presented in chapter 21. However, taking a longer-term perspective, you should try to modify the mold so that there is less variation between the different cavities. Eventually you would like to get the molding process so consistent that the o-rings are all alike regardless of which cavity in the mold produced them. That is the ultimate goal of SPC, to change the real world for the better *not* to make a control chart look better.

Subgroups with too little variation

Many people have difficulty understanding how a subgroup can have too little variation. After all, isn't reduced variation the objective of SPC? Well, yes and no. The objective of SPC, as stated above, is to change the real world for the better; and, to be sure, reducing variation is part of that. However, what I am talking about here is not too little *actual variation*. I am talking about too little *apparent variation* due to problems in the way subgroups are formed.

A control chart with too little variation will exhibit a range or sigma chart that is largely in-control, but the $\overline{X}$ chart will be largely out-of-control. The average of the range or sigma chart will be very small, and the ranges may "jump" from one level to the next in discrete chunks. Many subgroup ranges or standard deviations may be zero. There are many reasons why this might occur, here are some of the most common.

Capricious batching	When output from continuous processes or quasi-continuous processes is arbitrarily divided into discrete units, it is known as capricious batching. A continuous process is one that produces product in an unbroken stream; for example a process producing an industrial gas that is placed in small bottles. A quasi-continuous process is one that produces product in very large batches for delivery in smaller batches; for example the production of bars of soap from vats which hold enough to produce tens of thousands of bars. If subgroups are formed by taking consecutive (or very near consecutive) bottles of industrial gas or bars of soap, capricious batching has occurred. See chapter 17 for information on applying SPC to continuous and batch processes.

Sampling of batch processes	When a process produces output in uniform batches, samples taken from the same batch will be similar in most respects. For example, a process that produces uniform vats of printing ink that are shipped in tank cars. If the tank car holds several vats of ink, the samples should be taken from the individual vats. It would be a mistake to take, say, five samples from a vat to plot an $\overline{X}$ and R chart. It would be a bigger mistake to take five samples from the tank car. See chapter 17 for information on applying SPC to continuous and batch processes.
Gage resolution	Too little variation is a symptom of a measurement system that can't discriminate between different units from a process. This happens because the process varies in a range too small for the gage to detect. For example, it would be unwise to use a tape measure to control a precision machining operation. Poor gage resolution often appears on a control chart as discrete "jumps" in the data. See chapter 12 for additional information on analyzing measurement error.
Serial correlation	Standard control charts assume that the observations from a process are independent from one another. This means that knowing one measurement tells you nothing about what the next measurement will be. A good analogy is throwing two dice, knowing the number of spots on the first die tells you nothing about what the second die will be. However, the assumption of independence often fails in SPC of real-world processes. Many processes tend to drift from one level to another for reasons that are inherent to the process rather than from special causes, e.g., tool wear or consumption of a catalyst. See chapters 17, 18 and 20 for additional information.

Detecting subgrouping problems

A poor choice of subgroups results in a number of distinctive patterns on control charts and histograms. If the subgroups include a number of different sources of variation (e.g., the multiple-cavity mold described earlier), the range chart will often show a distinct absence of ranges below $\overline{R}$ and the $\overline{X}$s will be clustered near the center of the chart.

Histograms are often useful in detecting subgrouping problems. Most processes will produce histograms with only one peak or mode. Histograms of large data sets (at least 100 observations) that have more than one mode usually indicate a mixture of more than one source of variation. Multi-modal histograms should be investigated.

Automated versus manual sampling

It is often possible to sample a process either using automated test equipment or a manual method. The decision as to which is best is an economic one, based on the cost of sampling with each method. However, whichever method is used, decisions regarding the state of the process (i.e., is the process in or out of control?) must be based on valid statistical methods. With automated sampling it is often possible to measure every unit of product, or to take thousands of process samples in a short time interval. This often leads to serially correlated data and other problems that require special statistical handling. See chapter 18 for additional information.

Even if automated testing is used, it is often necessary to verify the results with manual methods. Scatter plots (see volume one, chapter 6) can be used to compare the results from the two methods.

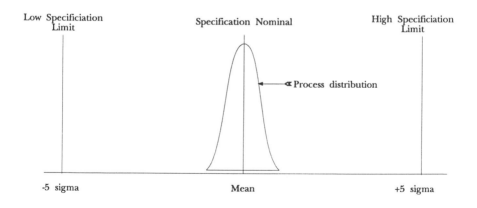

Figure 11-5 Very Capable Process

How many? How often?

There is an extensive literature on the subject of economical control charting (Montgomery, 1980.) In this volume we will discuss simple guidelines that do not require sophisticated mathematical skills.

First, the basics

❑ All processes change constantly. SPC is not supposed to detect *all* changes, only those changes that are important economically. The question of "how many?" affects the sensitivity of the control chart.

❑ You are sampling too few units if your control chart will not detect a change of economic importance fast enough to prevent significant loss.

❑ You are sampling too many units if your control chart goes out of control for changes that are of no economic importance.

❑ You are sampling too often if the cost of sampling and plotting the chart exceeds the economic gain obtained from controlling the process.

❑ You are not sampling often enough if the economic loss that occurs between samples is greater, on the average, than the cost of additional sampling.

Control charts can be made as sensitive as you wish simply by increasing the subgroup size. But the question of how sensitive a control chart *should be* is an

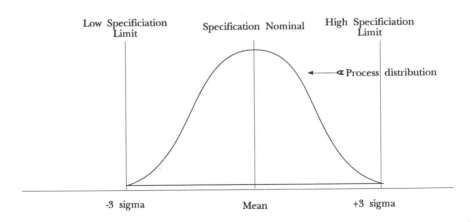

Figure 11-6 Marginal Process

economic question, not a statistical one. Excessive sensitivity exists when it simply doesn't pay to investigate an indication of a special cause. For example, the process shown in figure 11.5 is clearly capable of meeting, even exceeding, the requirements. The economic loss from a change of 1σ or even 3σ is minimal. The sample size required to detect a change of this magnitude is n=1; see volume one, table 8.1. If subgroups of n=5 were used the control chart would detect changes of 1.5σ. If the sampling frequency remained the same, your sampling costs would increase by a factor of five, but you would have little to gain by it. On the other hand, larger subgroups might well be justified for the marginal process shown in figure 11.6; the loss caused by a change in this process will be much larger than that of the process shown in figure 11.5.

The above discussion should not be taken as a suggestion that very capable processes be allowed to drift until production of scrap is imminent. There are other costs associated with variability, often hidden. Most products perform better and for a longer period of time if they are produced at their nominal values, so any deviation from target involves some loss to the customer. What I am saying is that the SPC procedure should not lead to preoccupation with minor process variation of no economic importance.

The question of how often to check the process depends on the stability of the process and the difficulty in finding the special cause if too much time has passed. A process that seldom changes should be sampled less often than one that changes frequently. If the nature of the special cause is unclear it may pay to sample more often so that the investigation of the special cause can begin while there are still "tracks." For example, I once had an experience with a process that changed when a bay door was opened and cold air blew over the process. Since an opening door is not a noteworthy event, its effect wasn't discovered until the process was sampled continuously for several hours. Like many special causes, this one is easy to eliminate once it has been found, e.g., the machine could be moved or a partition installed. Another item to consider is the cost associated with running the process while it is out-of-control. Higher costs justify more frequent process sampling.

Evaluating the effectiveness of SPC

SPC has been a proven success world wide for decades, but that doesn't mean that attaining success is automatic. SPC applications that fail are not at all rare. Many of the causes of failure have already been discussed earlier in this chapter, as well as the keys to success. It is vital that the quality improvement effort, including SPC, be monitored continuously by management. This should include periodic audits by senior management and by sources outside of the company. Firsthand observation through attendance at meetings and time spent in the work area should be a routine management activity.

SPC should also be monitored at the project level by the SPC team. Hard questions should be asked, such as

❑ Are we making progress?
❑ Are the results obtained what we expected? If no, why not?
❑ What are the obstacles to further progress?
❑ Why haven't we made faster progress?

Individual applications of control charts should also be evaluated by the SPC team.

❑ Is the control chart useful?
❑ Should it be modified?
❑ Should it be eliminated?
❑ Is it being properly maintained?
❑ Are the sampling procedures adequate?
❑ Are they being followed properly?

Offline analysis of control charts

When used on line, control charts are tools that provide an operational definition of a special cause of variation on a real-time basis. But they also contain a great deal of additional information that should not be ignored. I recommend that control charts also be evaluated "offline" by SPC teams to extract the additional information for use in continuous improvement.

Control charts are analytic statistical tools, not enumerative statistical tools. An analytic technique is designed to help people increase their understanding of some phenomenon so they can improve its performance in the future. Analytic techniques are applied to dynamic processes.

Enumerative statistical techniques are what nearly everyone is taught in traditional statistics classes. Enumerative techniques are used to study a static situation. The much used sampling urn is an example of a situation where enumerative methods can be used. Since the urn doesn't change we can employ such enumerative concepts as point estimators, tests of hypotheses and confidence intervals to describe the contents of the urn based on samples from the urn. Such concepts not only do not apply to the analytic situations encountered in business, they often get in the way.

An example of how these concepts get in the way is probably in order. Here's an example I actually witnessed.

The process involved a machine that drilled two rows of holes in a part. The manufacturer wished to determine the ability of the machine to place the holes in the correct location. Using enumerative statistics the process engineer determined that a sample of n=100 parts would produce a confidence interval of the desired precision. He obtained a random sample of 100 from inspection records generated over a considerable time interval, computed $\overline{X}$ and sigma (unbiased), and calculated the confidence interval. Using a table of standard normal deviates, he determined the expected process yield. His conclusion: the process mean is acceptable, but the process variance is too large; the process is not capable of meeting the requirement. The conclusion was supported by the fact that this process was a chronic problem and, in fact, the sample data included many out-of-specification measurements. Based on this he recommended the purchase of new equipment at considerable expense.

Next an SPC team applied an analytical technique (and, more importantly, an analytical *approach*) to this situation. Two control charts for individuals were used: one for the location of the first hole and one for the location of the last hole of the pattern. The result is shown in figure 11.7. The SPC team noted that both of the processes were in-control but the first hole was always above the nominal and the last hole was always below the nominal. They brainstormed and discussed several theories regarding the cause of this. Additional data indicated that all of the holes in one row were above nominal and all of the holes drilled in the other row were below nominal. Finally, they discovered that the problem was caused by "play" in the mechanism that positioned the drill head. By replacing the mechanism they brought the process mean to the center of the tolerance and eliminated the difference between the two rows. The end result: the process with the new mechanism was easily capable of meeting the requirement, and a great deal of money in unneeded equipment was saved.

Incidentally, the process engineer who performed the original analysis was a very active member of the SPC team. He went on to become one of the champi-

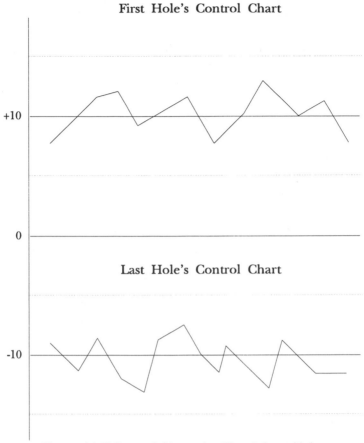

Figure 11-7 Control Charts for First & Last Holes

ons of SPC for his company. A company environment where people are free of fear is vital to success.

Another place where the traditional enumerative techniques fail is in the conceptual model of the process they provide. Most classical texts in statistics picture the control chart as a normal distribution "elongated in time." In other words, they encourage you to think of the process as a static normal distribution with an unchanging mean and variance. The control chart is depicted as the result of taking multiple samples from this unchanging process. Out-of-control points are indications that the process has changed, which is your signal to identify the cause of the change. An in-control process is, by definition, an unchanging process.

Wrong.

The process is always changing. *Always*. And in most cases the reduction in variation achieved by eliminating special causes is only a small fraction of the total variation. The real payoff is in reducing variation from *common causes*. But the mindset of classical, enumerative statistics inhibits this activity. The questioning, probing, exploratory approach combined with analytical tools like the control chart encourage you to find the cause of all of the variation. When evaluating the control chart off-line, forget the control limits. Investigate the chart as a whole, examine the patterns. Relate the data to what the team knows about the process. Place the charts end-to-end on a large table and look for cycles and patterns across several charts.

Brainstorm. Be OH!pen minded. Think!

Ad hoc SPC (The Art of Winging It)

Statistical design of experiments (DOE) is a powerful tool for obtaining a maximum amount of information at a minimum cost. This is accomplished through elaborate planning and execution of controlled experiments. It requires highly trained professionals who are always in very short supply. It involves a tremendous effort and often considerable expense. Thus, formal designed experiments are usually reserved for those few special cases where the immense effort and expense is clearly justified.

Most problems are neither serious enough nor complex enough to warrant the formal DOE approach. For these problems, which represent the vast majority of cases, an informal approach is much better. I recommend an approach which I call "ad hoc SPC" which capitalizes on the skills acquired by SPC teams as part of their SPC training. Ad hoc SPC can be done at a minimal expense by the SPC team members themselves using tools and methods they are already trained to use. However, there will be mistakes. When data is collected and experiments are run those who do so are obtaining objective information which can be evaluated by anyone. This places the team which collected the data at risk. They can be criticized for their less-than-optimal methods or for their lack of careful planning or for their lack of rigor in controlling the experiment. The safest approach is to do nothing, then there is nothing to criticize. This is the legacy of the slogan "do it right the first time," which is, like all slogans, poor advice. When faced with the unknown it is far better to conduct many experiments and learn through trial and error. This is why it is so important that management work to provide an environment that encourages risk-taking behavior. Drive out fear.

Most of what is written about SPC describes the systematic application of a complete system of methods and procedures. However, SPC methods can also be used to tremendous advantage as a "quick and dirty" way of getting sound, factual data in a hurry. Many SPC studies get bogged down on some point or another and, without data, they stay bogged down. Some of the most productive SPC applications I've seen have been spontaneous, off-of-the-cuff exercises. Here are a couple of examples, with discussion.

Wave solder process	The SPC team was concerned about the effect of "lambda" on solder quality. Lambda is a measure of the velocity of the solder wave. Two team members were discussing the issue outside of the meeting room, in fact they were at the wave solder machine itself. One of them suggested an experiment: "...as the board starts across the solder wave, we will begin recording the lambda readings off of the control panel display. It takes about ten seconds for the board to cross the wave, so we will get about five lambda readings per board. Then we can identify the board and determine its quality. Then, during the next SPC team meeting, we can all plot control charts of the lambda readings and we'll have a control chart showing the lambda readings for each board. We can sort the control charts for good and bad quality boards and see if there is any difference due to lambda."

Are these statistically valid sample sizes? Was the study conducted for a sufficient length of time? Were the boards representative samples? The answer to all of these questions is probably no, at least from a theoretical point of view. But from a practical point of view these questions are largely irrelevant to an analytical study like this. If the team had to wait for the services of a professional statistician, plan the formal experiment, and establish the elaborate control systems necessary to be absolutely correct it is likely that nothing would have been done.

The result of the effort was that the data was immensely valuable to the team. They learned that the lambda value changed far more than they expected during the brief time it took a board to cross the wave. Furthermore, there was no real difference in quality between boards crossing a very high velocity wave and a very low velocity wave. These facts were new, and they strongly suggested that the cause of the quality problems was elsewhere. This didn't *prove* that the problem was elsewhere. Proof takes a great deal of planning, effort and expense. Proving anything is extremely difficult. But the ad hoc analysis provided a clear indication of where *not* to spend a lot of time, which the team found to be very useful. Furthermore, because data had been collected, instead of the mere expression of personal opinion, the nature of the team's discussions changed dramatically. Their approach became much more analytical and experimental. New experiments were planned and carried out. The ad hoc experiment broke the mental logjam.

Purchasing process

The SPC team was evaluating the effectiveness of their process, which was purchasing. The team members were buyers for the purchasing department. The team had been trained in SPC techniques and problem solving. A flowchart of the process had been prepared. They had established their overall goal: better service to their internal customers. A system had been established for measuring the level of customer satisfaction and to track such important process indicators as the time required to process purchase orders and errors on purchase orders. The initial data indicated the purchasing process was in statistical control. The team was not sure how they should proceed from this point. It seemed that the team couldn't reach a consensus on which part of the purchasing process needed to be addressed first. Some felt that the requisition procedure needed to be modified, others felt that suppliers should be involved; it seemed each member had a different idea as to where to start.

The breakthrough came when the team decided that they had a shortage of a very valuable commodity: facts. To get the facts they decided to take another look at their customer surveys. A Pareto analysis revealed that the biggest complaint of the customers was the time it took to process their requests. The team decided that they would take a random sample of 100 purchase orders, place them in time sequence, and create control charts (X and R charts with subgroups of four) and histograms of the time it took to process each purchase order through each step of the process. Then they placed the control charts, histograms and the flow chart on a large table in the conference room and evaluated it. The physical arrangement was such that the control chart and histogram for a given process step were placed by the part of the flowchart for that process element. All of the histograms and control charts used the same scale so they could be compared easily. Finally, a control chart and histogram for the total time it took to process the 100 purchase orders was placed at the end of the flowchart. Was the sample truly random? Was random sampling the best choice, or should representative sampling have been used instead? Is 100 too many? Too few? Should the team have used $\overline{X}$ and R charts or some other method? Was it valid to create the control chart for the total process time? Could the team really see differences in the time it took to go through different process stages without a statistical tool, such as ANOVA? Is the histogram pattern meaningful with only 100 observations? These, and many other questions would need to be answered for a formal study. But this isn't a formal study, nor should it have been. In fact, it is difficult to imagine a formal study for this type of process that wouldn't be prohibitively expensive.

The result of this effort was the discovery that the receiving inspection process was responsible for over 50% of the total processing time. Since this was but one step in a process with more than twenty steps, it was deemed to be important. The purchasing team presented their findings to the receiving inspection SPC team, and to management. In addition to merely identifying the biggest problem area, the study also provided a great deal of information on the causes. Copies of the 100 purchase orders were provided to the receiving inspection SPC team for further analysis, such as stratifying the data by what was ordered. At a later meeting the purchasing team decided that the conclusion they had reached based on their original study was incorrect. The problem wasn't with receiving inspection, it generally took longer for purchase orders for manufacturing. Since these orders required receiving inspection and others didn't, they took longer to process. Their customer surveys also revealed that manufacturing customers were the most dissatisfied. Based on this new insight, the SPC team in purchasing decided to repeat their entire study using 100 manufacturing purchase orders.

The team's efforts resulted in a steady improvement in the time it took to process manufacturing purchase orders. Did they do it right the first time? No, but they found a better way to do it the second time. And they will probably continue to find flaws in their approach, their data, and their conclusions. But they will also continue to make improvements. Isn't that the objective?

Computers for SPC

Computers have proliferated to the extent that nearly everyone has a computer on their desk. That is both good news and bad news. If properly used, computers are useful tools that make it possible to do more in less time than ever before. Used improperly, computers become a barrier to understanding the process. Which situation becomes reality is entirely up to you.

Computers are useful in three basic situations:

1. There is a lot of data.
2. The data analysis is complicated or tedious.
3. Extensive or high-quality reporting is required.

Not every application of SPC will benefit from the use of computers. Operators should keep their own charts up-to-date, and their charts should not be complicated. An application where one or two $\overline{X}$ and R charts are being kept does not require a computer. In fact, most operators find computers confusing and intimidating. An SPC team preparing an occasional flowchart or histogram shouldn't need a computer either, although they may want to dress up a few of their charts for a special presentation or report. The majority of day-to-day applications of SPC can get along just fine without the computer. SPC methods are, in general, not all that complicated and should be done by hand if possible. Even experienced statisticians admit that "handling the data" leads to special insights that are not experienced otherwise.

Still, one or more of the three situations described above arise frequently in SPC work, which accounts for the widespread use of computers. People in charge of entire SPC programs, such as SPC coordinators, often find computers useful in reporting capability indices to management or the customer. Computers can efficiently store the data from a large number of different SPC applications. By evaluating large databases with computers it is often possible to see long-term cycles, trends or interrelationships that would otherwise be overlooked. Computers can perform complex analysis that is difficult to do manually, such as adjusting capability indices or control limits for non-normally distributed data. Computerized data bases can be used by several different programs to prepare different reports or to perform different types of analysis, thus reducing the data input requirements. Computers make it easy to use "cut-and-try" methods that explore the data from various perspectives, something so tedious that it is seldom done without computers. Of course, computers eliminate the simple errors of plotting and arithmetic that often occur. If electronic data collection is used, errors of data entry are greatly reduced.

Computers also serve a standardization function, to a limited extent. Many companies select a single SPC software package for use by all departments and divisions. Some companies even insist that their suppliers use the same software as they do; a policy frowned upon by suppliers who often have several customers demanding that they use their "pet software."

SPC for special applications

Chapters 15-21 describe the application of SPC methods for particular industries and applications. In a few cases the "standard" SPC approach is somewhat modified. These SPC methods extend the scope of processes that can be monitored with SPC methods. As quality awareness increases and is expanded to areas where SPC hasn't been traditionally applied, the demand for modified SPC techniques has grown.

References

Munoz, J. and Nielson, C. (1991), "SPC: What data should I collect? What charts should I use?" Quality Progress, January, pp. 50-52.

Montgomery, D.C. (1980), "The economic design of control charts: a review and literature survey", *Journal of Quality Technology*, April, p. 75.

CHAPTER 12

MEASUREMENT ERROR

OBJECTIVES:
After completing this section you will:

- Understand the basic concepts involving measurement error.

- Be able to quantify and evaluate the accuracy, repeatability, reproducibility and stability of measurement error.

Evaluation of measurement error

Definition
Measurement error is the difference between an actual condition and the estimate of that condition based on one or more measurements. In the case of attributes data, measurement error refers to the correctness of classifications, e.g., the percentage of acceptable parts that are rejected or the percentage of unacceptable parts that are accepted.

Usage
Measurement error should be quantified and evaluated with respect to process performance. Effective statistical process control requires data that provide a valid basis for making process control decisions. This applies to attributes or continuous variables. Thus, measurement error evaluation should be performed early in any SPC project.

Definitions

Accuracy
A measurement system is said to be *accurate* if, on the average, the measured value is the same as the true value. The difference between the average measured value and the true value is referred to as *bias*. When applied to attribute inspection, accuracy refers to the ability of the attribute inspection system to produce agreement on inspection standards. Accu-

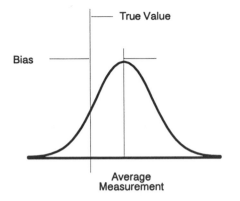

Figure 12.1-Illustration of Accuracy Concept

racy is controlled by *calibration.* The concept of accuracy is illustrated in figure 12.1.

Measurement system: The combination of measurement instruments, environment, person performing the measurement, procedures, items being measured, etc. that result in obtaining an estimate of a condition. Measurement systems are much more than simply gages.

Repeatability (precision): A measurement system is said to be *repeatable* if it always produces the same result when repeatedly measuring the same item. Variation obtained when the measurement system is applied repeatedly under the same conditions is usually caused by conditions inherent in the measurement system. This is sometimes referred to as random variation.

ASQC defines *precision* as (_, 1983) "The closeness of agreement between randomly selected individual measurements or test results. NOTE: The standard deviation of the error of measurement is sometimes called 'imprecision'." This is essentially equivalent to what is called repeatability in this *Guide.* The concept of repeatability is illustrated in figure 12.2.

Reproducibility: If different individuals using the same measurement system get the same results then the results are said to be reproducible. The concept is illustrated in figure 12.3.

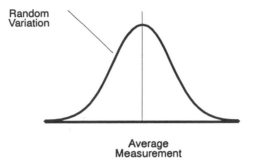

Random
Variation

Average
Measurement

Figure 12.2-Illustration of Repeatability Concept

Resolution   The resolution of a measurement system is the smallest difference it can consistently detect. In other words, if a gage can consistently detect the difference in size between two pins that differ in diameter by 0.0001 inch, then its resolution is at least 0.0001, perhaps better.

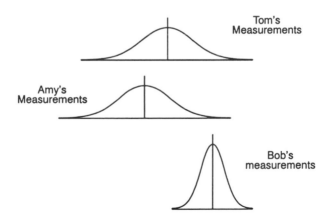

Tom's
Measurements

Amy's
Measurements

Bob's
measurements

Figure 12.3-Illustration of Reproducibility Concept

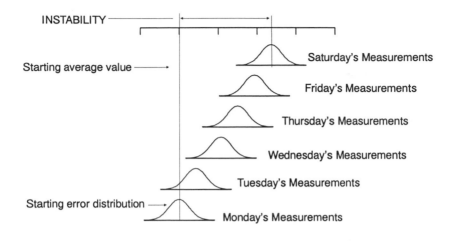

Figure 12.4-Illustration of Instability Concept

Display resolution	The smallest difference the measuring instrument can display. For example, if a digital readout changes in increments of 0.001mm then its display resolution is 0.001 mm. Note that the display resolution of a gage may have nothing to do with its ability to obtain correct measurements. The "correctness" of a measurement is determined by the resolution, accuracy, repeatability, and other performance measures in actual use.
Stability	A system is said to be stable if the results are the same at different points in time. Stability is illustrated in figure 12.4.

Evaluating measurement systems

This section will describe SPC techniques that provide quantitative estimates of the different elements of measurement system performance defined above. Our methods will involve using only those SPC techniques presented in the first part of this *Guide*. These methods have the distinct advantage of producing graphical results that are much easier to interpret. Other methods are in use (___, 1986), however, some apply an enumerative approach to analytic situations.

Evaluating accuracy (calibration)

Gage accuracy can be analyzed by taking several repeat readings on items whose true value (size, weight, etc.) is known. Of course, it is impossible to ever know the true value of any item exactly, but we are concerned with practical matters here and not pure philosophy. Thus, we usually accept a value as being the true value if it has been determined with a measurement system that is much better than we need, usually 2 or more orders of magnitude better. In the typical company gage accuracy is carefully controlled by a *calibration system*. Also, most inspection operations have a *standard* that is used to periodically re-verify the accuracy of the gage. We will describe a procedure that improves the traditional calibration approach by adding valid statistical analysis of the calibration results. To assure valid measurement data all of the procedures described in this chapter must be used. You should be aware that nearly all calibration procedures, including ours, account for only a few of the potential sources of measurement variation. Routine use of control charts will help detect measurement error from sources not dealt with explicitly. However, there will nearly always be some measurement error among the common causes of variation.

When attribute measures are used, calibration is accomplished with *training*. All personnel who will be asked to pass judgement on quality are trained to be able to correctly classify the quality characteristics of items. The accuracy of the classifications can be measured with attribute control charts. Often inspection standards, such as photographs or other visual aids, are provided at the point of inspection so that everyone involved may constantly refer to them and "recalibrate" themselves.

The procedure described below for obtaining a numerical measure of variable measurement accuracy is based on a method originally proposed by Ciminera and Tukey (1989) for charting laboratory instruments.

How to determine accuracy

This section describes a procedure for measuring the *accuracy* of a measurement system. It is followed by a numerical example. The reader is advised to simultaneously read the instructions in this section and verify understanding by referring to the corresponding step in the example.

1. Obtain 50 or more repeat measurements of an item (or as many as is practical) whose true value is known. Maintain the sequence of the readings. If all of the values are exactly equal to the true value, then no further calibration need be performed. If all values are exactly the same but not the same

as the true value, then adjust the measurement instrument to agree with the true value if possible. Otherwise, continue to step 2.

2. Following the procedure described in volume one chapter 9, compute the moving ranges from the measurements.

3. Prepare a frequency tally sheet of the moving ranges, see volume one chapter 6, "How to construct a histogram." For this analysis each cell will equal one "gage increment" and the first cell value will be zero. This type of frequency distribution is known as an ungrouped frequency distribution.

4. Start with the first cell ($R = 0$) and determine the cell frequency. Then continue adding cell frequencies until the cumulative frequency is 50% or more of the total number of ranges. The count of all the remaining cells is called the "remaining count."

5. Compute the cut-off using equation 12.1:

(12.1)

$$cut\text{-}off = \frac{value\ of\ cell\ that\ put\ count\ above\ 50\% + value\ of\ next\ cell}{2}$$

6. Compute the cut-off proportion using equation 12.2:

(12.2)

$$cut\text{-}off\ proportion = \frac{remaining\ count + \frac{1}{6}}{2 \times total\ count + \frac{2}{3}}$$

Where remaining count is defined in step 4.

7. Using table 3 in the appendix, find the Equivalent Gaussian Deviate (EGD) that corresponds to the cutoff proportion.

8. Compute $\hat{\sigma}$ using equation 12.3:

$$\hat{\sigma} = \frac{cutoff}{\sqrt{2}\,EGD}$$

(12.3)

9. Compute the lower control limit and upper control limit for the measurements chart using equations 12.4 and 12.5 respectively.

$$LCL_{bias} = true\ value - 3\hat{\sigma}$$

(12.4)

$$UCL_{bias} = true\ value + 3\hat{\sigma}$$

(12.5)

The center line of the accuracy control chart is the true value. Plot the control chart of the measurements.

Interpretation

If the control chart for individual measurements shows all measurements to be within the control limits, then the *inaccuracy* of the measurement system is due to common causes of variation and probably won't be improved by a calibration adjustment. If the control chart indicates a lack of control relative to only one of the control limits (either the lower or the upper, but not both), it may be beneficial to calibrate the measurement instrument to compensate for the inaccuracy. The difference between the average and the true value provides an estimate of the amount of calibration required. The average of the measurements is computed using equation 5.2. If there are measurements beyond *both* of the control limits, or if the R chart shows a lack of control, then the calibration measurements were not consistent and the special cause of this must be found before calibrating the measurement instrument. Because of the discrete nature of this type of data, run tests are not advised.

Calibration example

A micrometer is used to measure several mechanical dimensions of a pin produced by a machining process. The calibration procedure calls for recalibrating the micrometer every six months using gage pins traceable to a NIST[1] standard. The gage pin's true value is 1 inch. The micrometer's display resolution is 50 millionths of an inch (0.000050 inches). The calibration technician has obtained the 50 repeat readings shown in table 12.1. All readings are deviations from the standard value in millionths of an inch, those readings with a " - " sign are smaller than the standard value. The data in table 12.1 will be analyzed using the calibration procedure described above.

1. The data required in step one are shown in table 12.1. The values are not all exactly equal to 1 inch, nor are they all identical. Thus, we continue to step 2.
2. Table 12.2 contains the ranges between consecutive measurements.
3. Table 12.3 shows an abbreviated frequency table of the ranges in table 12.2.
4. Table 12.3 illustrates finding the cut-off and the remaining count.
5. The cut-off is computed using equation 12.1:

---

1   NIST is an acronym for the National Institute of Standards and Technology, formerly the National Bureau of Standards (NBS).

$$cut-off = \frac{50 + 100}{2} = 75$$

6. The cut-off proportion is found using equation 12.2:

Table 12.1-Calibration Data for Analysis

Reading Number	Measurement	Reading Number	Measurement
1	-50	26	-100
2	50	27	0
3	-50	28	0
4	0	29	-50
5	100	30	-50
6	-50	31	0
7	-100	32	100
8	-100	33	0
9	-100	34	0
10	50	35	-50
11	0	36	-50
12	-50	37	-100
13	0	38	0
14	-100	39	0
15	50	40	0
16	50	41	-150
17	0	42	-100
18	-50	43	-100
19	-50	44	-50
20	-50	45	-50
21	-50	46	0
22	0	47	-50
23	50	48	0
24	-100	49	-100
25	0	50	0

$$cut\text{-}off\,proportion = \frac{17 + \dfrac{1}{6}}{(2 \times 49) + \dfrac{2}{3}} = \frac{17.167}{98.667} = 0.17$$

7. The EGD is found in Table 3 in the appendix. Find the row for the first digit of the cut-off proportion (0.1) and the column for the second digit of the cut-off proportion (0.07); 0.1 + 0.07 = 0.17, the cut-off proportion. The EGD is found as 0.95.

Table 12.2-Moving Ranges of Data in Table 12.1

Reading Number	Range	Reading Number	Range
1	NONE	26	100
2	100	27	100
3	100	28	0
4	50	29	50
5	100	30	0
6	150	31	50
7	50	32	100
8	0	33	100
9	0	34	0
10	150	35	50
11	50	36	0
12	50	37	50
13	50	38	100
14	100	39	0
15	150	40	0
16	0	41	150
17	50	42	50
18	50	43	0
19	0	44	50
20	0	45	0
21	0	46	50
22	50	47	50
23	50	48	50
24	150	49	100
25	100	50	100

Table 12.3-Frequency Table for Ranges in Figure 12.2

Range	Frequency	Cum. Freq.	Cum. Freq. %	
0	14	14	28.6	Cut-off = 75
50	18	32	65.3 > 50.0	
100	12	44	89.8	Remaining count
150	5	49	100.0	= 17

8. $\hat{\sigma}$ is found with equation 12.3:

$$\hat{\sigma} = \frac{75}{\sqrt{2} \times 0.95} = 55.8$$

9. The control limits are found with equations 12.4 and 12.5:

$$LCL_{bias} = 0 - 3 \times 55.8 = -167.4$$

$$UCL_{bias} = 0 + 3 \times 55.8 = 167.4$$

The true value is 0 because the recorded data show *deviations* only. A control chart of the measurements is plotted with a center line of zero and these control limits. The R chart is also plotted, just as described in chapter 9 of Volume One. Figure 12.5 shows the finished control charts.

Interpretation of example

The control chart for individual repeat measurements shows all the points to be within the control limits. Thus, we conclude that the inaccuracy of the measurement system will not be improved by recalibration of the micrometer. In other words, the micrometer is okay as is.

Note that the first reading from the micrometer was 50 millionths below the true value. With traditional methods of calibration the calibration technician would have adjusted the micrometer to read exactly 0 based on this single reading. Our analysis indicates that the effect of these sorts of adjustments would be to increase the bias of the micrometer.

Evaluating repeatability, reproducibility, and stability errors using control charts

The basic concept behind any control chart is simply that limits are computed that define the variation expected from common causes. Any variability beyond these limits is probably due to a special cause of variation. With this in mind, we can use control charts to investigate the potential sources of measurement er-

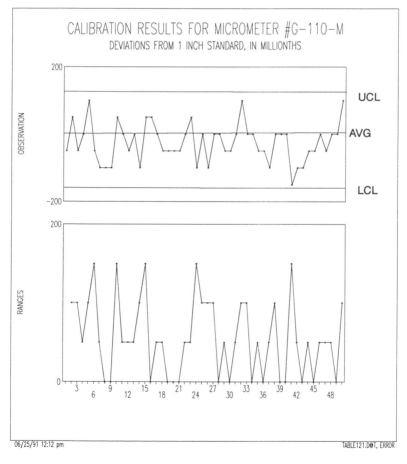

Figure 12.5-Control Chart of Calibration Data

ror as special causes of variation. This is done by carefully planning and organizing the data collection. The procedure is as follows:

1. Select 25 or more items for inspection (in the case of attributes, subgroups of items). As always, the more items used the more expensive your test, but the better your estimates. If you can't get 25, use what you can get.

2. Have each inspector check each item twice. Assign the items to the inspector in random order and take care to conceal his previous inspection results from him. Be sure that each inspector understands and follows the correct inspection procedure. Randomize the order in which the items are checked. For example, if you will be checking 25 items twice, identify each of the 50 readings with a separate "index number;" reading #1 for unit #1 = 1, reading #*1* for unit #2 = 2, ... , reading #2 for unit #25 = 50. Then use a table of random numbers to determine which index number to do first, second, etc..

3. Plot a control chart using the layout shown in figure 12.6 as a guide.

Pointers for using measurement error control charts

- With this layout the range is actually measuring *repeatability.* If repeatability were perfect, every range would be zero, the average range would be zero, and the control limits would have zero spread on both the averages chart and the ranges chart. We can separate the results for individual parts and inspectors. With this arrangement we are comparing the part-to-part and inspector-to-inspector variability to the control limits based on repeatability.

- It should be easy to see that the data need merely be reorganized to measure other types of measurement error. For example, if the columns represented different inspectors then the ranges would be measures of *reproducibility error.* If the columns were two different periods of time then the ranges would be measures of *instability.*

- The range control chart should be in control. The smaller the average range is, the better.

- The ranges for all the inspectors should be in control. If not, then the measurement system is not *reproducible.*

- If the range chart is out of control for a certain part for all inspectors, then find out why that part is so hard to check.

- *The averages control chart should be out of control!* The limits for the averages control chart are based on the average range, and the average range is based on measurement repeatability. However, the part-to-part variation is determined by the process, and the process variation should be much greater than the measurement variation. Since the averages control

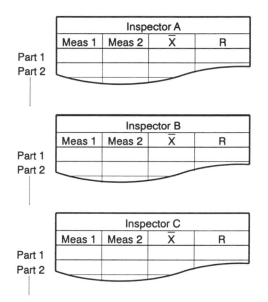

Figure 12.6-Measurement Error Control Chart Layout

chart shows the part-to-part variation, it should be out-of-control. If the averages chart is not out of control, then the measurement system can't tell one part from another and it cannot be used.

- The pattern on the averages chart should match for each inspector.

- The entire study should be repeated periodically. A direct comparison of the results of the different studies over time is a way of evaluating the *stability* of the measurement system. To check stability, plot the results of subsequent studies against the control limits computed from the first set of data. Even if only a part of the study can be done again (e.g., if different inspectors are used) it will provide an indication of stability.

Computing the percent of error

If the range chart is in control, the standard deviation can be estimated from $\bar{R}$ as $\bar{R}/d_2$. When subgroups of 2 are used, as it is here, $\hat{\sigma} = \bar{R}/1.128$. Because of the way we have organized the control chart data, this sigma estimate is an estimate of repeatability error. Equation 5.4 is given in volume one as

$$s = \sqrt{\Sigma(x_i - \bar{x})/(n-1)}$$ (5.4 repeated)

where the sum goes from i=1 to n and n= the number of individual observations. This equation provides a value of sigma that includes both process variability and measurement error, thus we will call it σ_{total}. These two related estimates of σ can be used to estimate the percentage of total variation accounted for by repeatability error. The necessary equations are:

$$\sigma_{total}^2 = \sigma_{process}^2 + \sigma_{error}^2 \qquad (12.6)$$

Where σ_{total}^2 is the square of the value obtained with equation 5.4, and σ_{error}^2 is the square of the value obtained using $\overline{R}/d2$ from the measurement error control chart. The error percentage is computed as:

$$error\ percent = 100 \times \frac{\sigma_{error}^2}{\sigma_{total}^2} \qquad (12.7)$$

Now the percentage error due to the process itself, with the repeatability error factored out, is:

$$process\ percent = 100 - error\ percent \qquad (12.8)$$

Example

The data in table 12.4 are from a measurement error study involving 2 inspectors. The inspectors were asked to inspect the surface finish of 5 parts[2]. Each part was checked twice. The gage used is called a "profilometer" and it records the surface roughness in microinches ($\mu-inches$). It has a digital readout that shows 1 decimal place, thus its display resolution is 0.1 $\mu-inches$.

Based on this data we get, using the procedures described in chapter 8 of volume one, we construct the Range chart and find $\overline{R} = 0.67$ and $UCL_R = 2.19$. An analysis of the Ranges indicates that the R chart is in control for all except part number 5, inspector A. The engineer who conducted the experiment had noted that for the first measurement the inspector had checked the part in a slightly different location than was specified. A recheck showed that this caused the problem. Knowing this we can drop this group, giving a new value of $\overline{R} = 0.49$. The problem indicates a special cause that should be permanently remedied if possible. For example the engineer might design a fixture to make the proper meas-

---

2   In a measurement error study at least 25 parts should be checked, if possible. For this particular study, only 5 pieces were available

urement location fool-proof. With all remaining groups in control (UCL_R = 1.6), we compute the measurement error sigma with equation 9.5 and get:

$$\sigma_{error} = \frac{0.49}{1.128} = 0.4344$$

and the error variance is:

$$\sigma_{error}^2 = 0.4344^2 = 0.1887$$

The process standard deviation can be calculated from equation 12.6. First σ_{total} and σ_{total}^2 are found with equation 5.4 without using the data of the subgroup for part 5, inspector A:

$$\sigma_{total} = 7.491$$

$$\sigma_{total}^2 = 56.115$$

Thus, using equations 12.7 and 12.8, the percentage repeatability error and process error are:

$$repeatability\ error\ percent = 100 \times \frac{0.1887}{56.115} = 0.34\%$$

$$process\ percent = 100 - 0.34 = 99.66\%$$

Clearly, this measurement system is sufficiently repeatable for this process. The repeatability control charts are shown in figure 12.7. Note that the $\overline{X}$ chart is out of control. *This is proper for a measurement error control chart!* The width of

Table 12.4-Measurement Error Data-Repeatability Layout

INSPECTOR A DATA				
PART	**Reading 1**	**Reading 2**	$\overline{X}$	**R**
1	111.9	112.3	112.10	0.4
2	108.1	108.1	108.10	0.0
3	124.9	124.6	124.75	0.3
4	118.6	118.7	118.65	0.1
5	133.0	130.7	131.85	2.3
INSPECTOR B DATA				
1	111.4	112.9	112.15	1.5
2	107.7	108.4	108.05	0.7
3	124.6	124.2	124.40	0.4
4	120.0	119.3	119.65	0.7
5	130.4	130.1	130.25	0.3

the control limits for the $\overline{X}$ chart are based on $\overline{R}$, which is, in turn, based solely on repeatability error. Thus the spread of the control limits on the $\overline{X}$ chart show how much uncertainty is caused by repeatability error. If all points *were* within the control limits it would indicate that the measurement system repeated so poorly that it could not distinguish between the different units produced by the process.

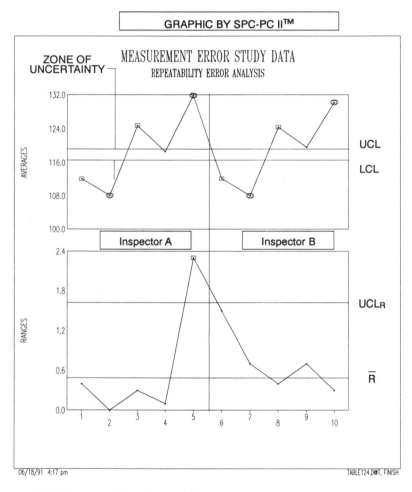

Figure 12.7-Repeatability Control Charts

Figure 12.7 also shows quite clearly that the two inspectors tend to get the same results, the pattern of the measurements of the five parts is a very close match. Thus, the measurement system is also *reproducible*. However, it is possible to rearrange the data and prepare another control chart to get a numerical estimate of the magnitude of the reproducibility error. Table 12.5 shows the new arrangement. Remember that reproducibility measures the "person to person" variability. Note that we have arranged the data so that all four readings of each part represent a single subgroup. Now the R chart will measure the difference due to reproducibility as well as repeatability. Since we already know the magnitude of the repeatability error (0.34%), we can factor out the reproducibility error. In this case, with such a tiny error, we probably would not bother to factor out the reproducibility error. However, sometimes the error is large and this analysis will help us determine how much of it is due to person-to-person variation. Since we already know that part 5 was out of control for repeatability, this part is not included in the analysis.

The reproducibility error control chart of data is shown in figure 12.8. All 4 parts are in control on the R chart. Using the $\bar{R}$ value we can now estimate:

$$\sigma_{repeat + repro} = \frac{\bar{R}}{d_2} = \frac{1.075}{2.059} = 0.522$$

and since we have already estimated $\sigma_{repeat} = 0.4344$ we can easily factor out the repeatability error to find the variance due to reproducibility.

$$\sigma^2_{repeat + repro} = \sigma^2_{repeat} + \sigma^2_{repro}$$

substituting our values gives:

$$(0.522)^2 = (0.4344)^2 + \sigma^2_{repro}$$

Table 12.5-Measurement Error Data-Reproducibility

PART	INSPECTOR A		INSPECTOR B		$\bar{X}$	R
	Reading 1	Reading 2	Reading 1	Reading 2		
1	111.9	112.3	111.4	112.9	112.125	1.5
2	108.1	108.1	107.7	108.4	108.075	0.7
3	124.9	124.6	124.6	124.2	124.575	0.7
4	118.6	118.7	120.0	119.3	119.150	1.4

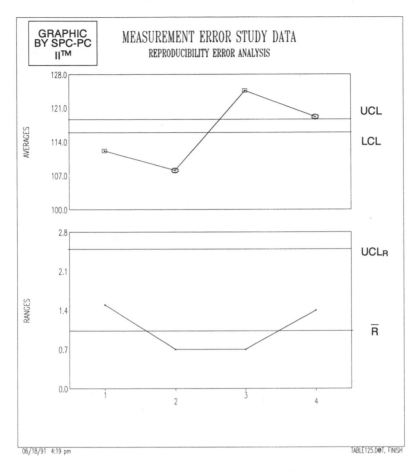

Figure 12.8-Reproducibility/Repeatability Control Chart

thus:

$$\sigma^2_{repro} = (0.522)^2 - (0.4344)^2 = 0.084$$

Obviously, the reproducibility error is a tiny fraction of the observed variability.
The percentage variation due to reproducibility error is:

reproducibility error percent $= 100 \times \dfrac{0.084}{56.115} = 0.15\%$

The entire experiment should be repeated at a future date and compared to these results to determine if the measurement system is also **stable**. Stability can be easily checked by using the control limits obtained during this study and plotting the results of future studies against them.

References

__, 1983, "Glossary and Tables for Statistical Quality Control," ASQC Quality Press, Milwaukee, Wisconsin.

__, (1986), "*Automotive Division Statistical Process Control Manual*," ASQC Automotive Division, ASQC Quality Press, Milwaukee, Wisconsin, pp 3-4 to 3-5.

Ciminera, J.L. and Tukey, J.W., (1989), "Control-charting automated laboratory instruments when many successive differences may be zero," Journal of Quality Technology 21(1), pp. 7-15.

CHAPTER 13

PROCESS CAPABILITY ANALYSIS

OBJECTIVES:

After completing this section you will:

- Understand the basic concepts of capability analysis.

- Be able to undertake process capability studies.

- Be able to compute and interpret capability indices.

- Be able to use normal distribution tables to estimate long term process yields.

- Be able to calculate yields from non-normal distributions, including skewed, folded normal, and true position distributions.

- Be able to use probability paper to predict process yields.

Process capability analysis

Definition   Process capability analysis is a two-stage procedure that involves bringing a process into a state of statistical control for a reasonable period of time and comparing the long-term process performance to management or engineering requirements.

Usage   Process capability analysis can be done with either attribute data or continuous data *if and only if the process is in statistical control and has been for a reasonable period of time.* Two variations on traditional process capability analysis allow use of the statistical approach with limited data: the *potential study* where only 30 consecutive units are checked (Ford Motor Company), and the *mini-capability study* where only 10 consecutive units are checked (General Motors). It is the author's experience that these approaches provide unreliable estimates of long-term performance and that their results should be considered to be "bounds on the process." In other

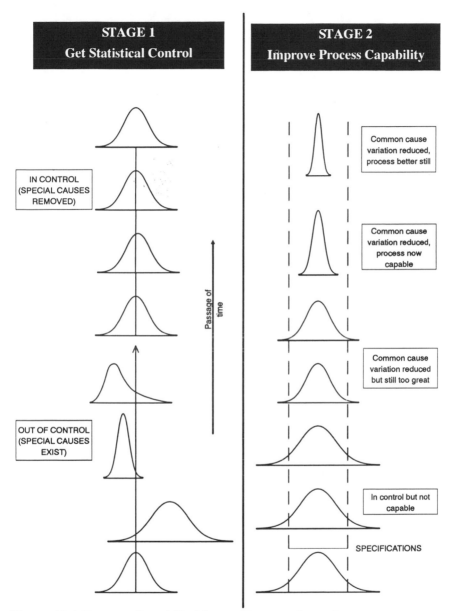

Figure 13.1-Process Capability Versus Process Control

words, the process will do no better than indicated, but it may do **much** worse. Application of process capability methods to processes that are not in statistical control results in even more unreliable estimates of process capability and should never be done. Figure 13.1 illustrates these concepts.

How to perform process capability studies — A 10 step plan

This section presents a step-by-step approach to process capability analysis (Pyzdek, 1985.) The approach makes frequent reference to materials presented elsewhere in this *Guide*.

1 Select a candidate for the study

This step should be institutionalized. A goal of any organization should be on-going process improvement. However, because a company has only a limited resource base and can't solve all problems simultaneously, it must set priorities for its efforts. The tools for this include Pareto analysis and fishbone diagrams. See chapters 1 through 4 of this *Guide* for information on these techniques.

2 Define the process

It is all too easy to slip into the trap of solving the wrong problem. Once the candidate area has been selected in step 1, define the scope of the study. A process is a unique combination of machines, tools, methods, and personnel engaged in production or service. Each element of the process should be identified at this stage. This is not a trivial exercise. The input of many people may be required. There are likely to be a number of conflicting opinions about what the process actually involves. These differences must be resolved into a consensus, see chapter 2 in this *Guide* for a discussion of group dynamics. Finally, when the consensus has been achieved, a flowchart of the process must be prepared, see chapter 4 for information on flowcharting.

3   Procure resources

Process capability studies disrupt normal operations and require significant expenditures of both material and human resources. Since it is a project of major importance, it should be managed as such. All of the usual project management techniques should be brought to bear. This includes planning, scheduling and management status reporting.

4   Evaluate the measurement system

Using the techniques described in Chapter 12, evaluate the measurement system's ability to do the job. Again, be prepared to spend the time necessary to get a valid means of measuring the process before going ahead. See chapter 12 for statistical methods of evaluating measurement systems.

5   Provide a control system

The purpose of the control system is twofold: (1) isolate and control as many important variables as possible and, (2) provide a mechanism for tracking variables that can not be adequately controlled. The object of the capability analysis is to determine what the process can do if it is operated the way it is supposed to be. This means that such obvious sources of *potential* variation as operators and vendors will be controlled while the study is conducted. In other words, a single well trained operator will be used and the material will be from a single vendor. There are usually some variables that are important, but that are not controllable. One example is the ambient environment, such as temperature, barometric pressure or humidity. Certain process variables may degrade as part of the normal operation; for example tools wear and chemicals are used. These variables should still be tracked using logsheets and similar tools. See chapter 3 for information on designing data collection systems.

6   Select a method for the analysis

The SPC method will depend on the decisions made up to this point. If the performance measure is an attribute, one of the attribute charts will be used. Variables charts will be used for process performance measures assessed on a continuous scale. Also considered will be the skill level of the personnel involved, need for sensitivity, and other resources required to collect, record, and analyze the data.

7   Gather and analyze the data

This entire chapter, and much of the rest of this *Guide,* is devoted to techniques to help you perform this step. It is usually advisable to have at least two people go over the data analysis to catch inadvertent errors in transcribing data or performing the analysis.

8   Track down and remove special causes of variation

A special cause of variation may be obvious, or it may take months of painstaking investigation to find it. The effect of the special cause may be good or bad. Removing a special cause that has a bad effect usually involves eliminating the cause itself. For example, if poorly trained operators are causing variability the special cause is the training system (not the operator) and it is eliminated by developing an improved training system or a process that requires less training. However, the removal of a beneficial special cause may actually involve incorporating the special cause into the normal operating procedure. For example, if it is discovered that materials with a particular chemistry produce better product the special cause is the newly discovered material and it can be made a common cause simply by changing the specification to assure that the new chemistry is always used.

9   Estimate process capability

One point can not be overemphasized: *the process capability can not be estimated until a state of statistical control has been achieved.* After this stage has
been reached, the methods described later in this chapter may be used. After the
numerical estimate of process capability has been arrived at it must be compared
to management's goals for the process, or it can be used as an input into economic models. Deming (1986) describes a simple economical model that can be
used to determine if the output from a process should be sorted 100% or shipped
as is. The place of acceptance sampling of production lots, once an accepted
practice, has become quite controversial. For processes in perfect statistical control it can be shown mathematically that acceptance sampling provides no information on the quality of the lot (Mood, 1943). It can also be shown that the
minimum total cost for perfectly controlled processes is always at 0% or 100%
inspection, never at a partial sample. However, there is debate over the practical
application of these principles in the real world (Milligan, 1991). One thing is
certain, acceptance sampling is not an effective *substitute* for SPC.

10   Establish a quality improvement and control plan for the process

Once a stable process state has been attained steps should be taken to maintain
it and, hopefully, improve upon it. SPC is one means of doing this. Others include employee involvement programs, quality circles and quality of work life
programs. Far more important than the particular approach taken is a company
environment that makes continuous improvement a normal part of the daily routine.

Statistical analysis of process capability data

Control chart method: attributes data.

1. Collect samples from 20 or more subgroups of consecutively produced
   units. Use the guidelines presented in chapter 10 in volume one to determine the subgroup size and sampling frequency. Follow the guidelines pre-

sented in the 10 step plan for process capability studies for setting up and conducting the study.

2. Plot the results on the appropriate control chart (np, p, c, or u chart). If all groups are in statistical control, go to the next step. Otherwise identify the special cause of variation and take action to eliminate it.

3. Using the control limits from the previous step (called operation control limits), put the control chart to use controlling the process for a period of time. Once you are satisfied that sufficient time has passed for most special causes to have been identified and eliminated, as verified by the control charts, go to the next step.

4. The process capability for attribute data is estimated as the control chart *centerline*. The centerline on attribute charts is the long-term expected quality level of the process. This is the level created by the *common causes* of process variation.

5. If the process capability doesn't meet management requirements, take immediate action to modify the process for the better. Whether it meets requirements or not, always be on the lookout for possible process improvements. The control charts will provide verification of improvement.

Control chart method: variables data.

1. Collect samples from 20 or more subgroups of consecutively produced units. Use the guidelines presented in chapters 8 or 9 in volume one to determine the subgroup size. Follow the guidelines presented in the 10 step plan for process capability studies to set up and conduct the study.

2. Plot the results on the appropriate control chart ($\bar{X}$, R, median (see chapter 14,) or individuals chart). If all groups are in statistical control, go to the next step. Otherwise identify the special cause of variation and take action to eliminate it.

3. Using the control limits from the previous step (called operation control limits), put the control chart to use for a period of time. Once you are satisfied that sufficient time has passed for most special causes to have been identified and eliminated, as verified by the control charts, go to the next step.

4. The process capability is estimated from the process *average* and *standard deviation*. This is the level created by the common causes of process variation. Estimate the process standard deviation using $\hat{\sigma} = \bar{R}/d2$.

5. After reaching a sustained state of statistical control, the process capability can be compared to engineering requirements. One way of doing this is by calculating "Capability Indices." Table 13.1 presents several popular capability indices.

Table 13.1-Process Capability Index Equations

$$C_p = \frac{engineering\ tolerance}{6\sigma} \tag{13.1}$$

$$C_R = 100 \times \frac{6\sigma}{engineering\ tolerance} \tag{13.2}$$

$$C_m = \frac{engineering\ tolerance}{8\sigma} \tag{13.3}$$

$$Z_U = \frac{upper\ specification - process\ average}{\sigma} \tag{13.4}$$

$$Z_L = \frac{process\ average - lower\ specification}{\sigma} \tag{13.5}$$

$$Z_{Min} = minimum\{Z_L, Z_U\} \tag{13.6}$$

$$C_{pk} = \frac{Z_{min}}{3} \tag{13.7}$$

$$C_{pm} = C_p/\sqrt{1 + (\mu - T)^2/\sigma^2} \tag{13.8}$$

Interpreting capability indices

The discussion below describes the interpretation of the capability indices presented in table 13.1.

INDEX   **INTERPRETATION AND COMMENTS**

C_p This is the most common capability index. The index simply makes a direct comparison of the measured process spread (it was shown in chapter 12 that the measured process spread includes measurement error), to the engineering requirements. Normality is assumed. The process mean is not considered. Both upper and lower specifications are required. Assuming

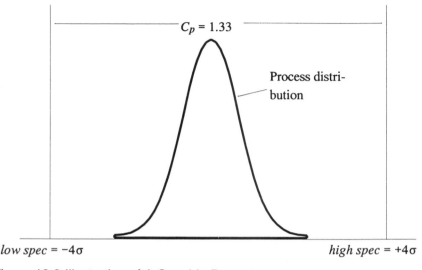

low spec = −4σ   *high spec = +4σ*

Figure 13.2-Illustration of A Capable Process

the process distribution is normal and the process average is exactly centered between the engineering requirements, a C_p index of 1 would give a "marginally capable process." However, to allow a bit of room for process drift, the generally accepted minimum value for C_p is 1.33. This situation is shown in figure 13.2.

In general, the larger C_p is, the better. The C_p index has two major shortcomings. First, it can't be used unless there are both upper and lower specifications. Second, it does not account for process centering. If the process average is not exactly centered relative to the engineering requirements the C_p index will give misleading results.

C_R

The C_R index is equivalent to the C_p index. The index simply makes a direct comparison of the process spread to the engineering requirements. Normality is assumed. The process mean is not considered. Both upper and lower specifications are required. Assuming the process distribution is normal and the process average is exactly centered between the engineering requirements, a C_R index of 100% would give a "marginally capable process." However, to allow a bit of room for process drift, the generally accepted maximum value for C_R is

75%. In general, the smaller C_R is, the better. The C_R index has two major shortcomings. First, it can't be used unless there are both upper and lower specifications. Second, it does not account for process centering. If the process average is not exactly centered relative to the engineering requirements the C_R index will give misleading results.

C_m

C_m is computed just like C_p except using a $\pm 4\sigma$ spread instead of a $\pm 3\sigma$ spread. The difference is that C_m is usually based on a short-term study instead of a sustained period of statistical control, such as the process potential study and the mini-capability study mentioned above. Because of the deficiency of historic data the extra $\pm\sigma$ is added as a "buffer." The idea is that there are additional common causes of variation not seen in the short term that will cause the process to vary more widely. C_m should be viewed as a preliminary estimate only. Normality is assumed. The process mean is not considered. Both an upper specification and a lower specification is required.

Z_U

The Z_U index measures the number of standard deviations between the process mean and the upper specification. If the distribution is normal or only moderately skewed the value of Z_U can be used to determine the percentage above the upper specification. For normal distributions use the first three columns of table 13.2. Yield projections for skewed distributions are described later in this chapter.

Table 13.2-Z Indices and Normal Process Yields					
$\lvert Z_U \rvert$	% Above High Spec		$\lvert Z_L \rvert$	% Below Low Spec.	
	If $Z_U \geq 0$	If $Z_U < 0$		If $Z_L \geq 0$	If $Z_L < 0$
0.0	50.0%	50.0%	0.0	50.0%	50.0%
0.1	46.0	54.0	0.1	46.0	54.0
0.2	42.1	57.9	0.2	42.1	57.9
0.3	38.2	61.8	0.3	38.2	61.8
0.4	34.5	65.5	0.4	34.5	65.5
0.5	30.8	69.2	0.5	30.8	69.2
0.6	27.4	72.6	0.6	27.4	72.6
0.7	24.2	75.8	0.7	24.2	75.8
0.8	21.2	78.8	0.8	21.2	78.8
0.9	18.4	81.6	0.9	18.4	81.6
1.0	15.9	84.1	1.0	15.9	84.1

	Table 13.2-Z Indices and Normal Process Yields				
$|Z_U|$	% Above High Spec		$|Z_L|$	% Below Low Spec.	
	If $Z_U \geq 0$	If $Z_U < 0$		If $Z_L \geq 0$	If $Z_L < 0$
1.1	13.6	86.4	1.1	13.6	86.4
1.2	11.5	88.5	1.2	11.5	88.5
1.3	9.7	90.3	1.3	9.7	90.3
1.4	8.1	91.9	1.4	8.1	91.9
1.5	6.7	93.3	1.5	6.7	93.3
1.6	5.5	94.5	1.6	5.5	94.5
1.7	4.5	95.5	1.7	4.5	95.5
1.8	3.6	96.4	1.8	3.6	96.4
1.9	2.9	97.1	1.9	2.9	97.1
2.0	2.3	97.7	2.0	2.3	97.7
2.1	1.8	98.2	2.1	1.8	98.2
2.2	1.4	98.6	2.2	1.4	98.6
2.3	1.1	98.9	2.3	1.1	98.9
2.4	0.8	99.2	2.4	0.8	99.2
2.5	0.6	99.4	2.5	0.6	99.4
2.6	0.5	99.5	2.6	0.5	99.5
2.7	0.4	99.6	2.7	0.4	99.6
2.8	0.3	99.7	2.8	0.3	99.7
2.9	0.2	99.8	2.9	0.2	99.8
3.0	0.1	99.9	3.0	0.1	99.9
3.1	0.1	99.9	3.1	0.1	99.9
3.2	0.1	99.9	3.2	0.1	99.9
3.3	0.05	99.95	3.3	0.05	99.95
3.4	0.03	99.97	3.4	0.03	99.97
3.5	0.02	99.98	3.5	0.02	99.98
3.6	0.02	99.98	3.6	0.02	99.98
3.7	0.01	99.99	3.7	0.01	99.99
3.8	0.01	99.99	3.8	0.01	99.99
3.9	0.01	99.99	3.9	0.01	99.99
4.0	0.00	100.0	4.0	0.00	100.0

In general, the bigger Z_U is, the better. A value of at least +3 is required to assure yields of 99.9% or better. A value of +4 is generally desired to allow some room for process drift.

Z_L The Z_L index measures the number of standard deviations between the process mean and the lower specification. If the distribution is normal or only moderately skewed the value of Z_L can be used to determine the percentage below the lower requirement. For normal distributions use the last three columns of table 13.2. Yield projections for skewed distributions are described later in this chapter.

                 In general, the bigger Z_L is, the better. A value of at least +3 is required to assure yields of 99.9% or better. A value of +4 is generally desired to allow some room for process drift.

Z_{min} The value of Z_{min} is simply the smaller of the Z_L or the Z_U values. It is an intermediate result to be used in computing C_{pk}.

C_{pk} The value of C_{pk} is simply Z_{min} divided by 3. Normality is assumed. The process mean *is* considered. Only one specification is required, either the upper or the lower specification. Since the smallest value represents the nearest specification, the value of C_{pk} tells you if the process is *truly* capable of meeting requirements. A C_{pk} of at least +1 is required, and +1.33 is preferred. Note that C_{pk} is closely related to C_p, the difference between C_{pk} and C_p represents the potential gain possible from centering the process.

C_{pm} The C_{pm} statistic measures the process performance as it relates to the width of the process, the width of the requirements, and the process centerline relative to its *target value*. The target value can be thought of as the value that provides the minimum total cost of operating the process. The target value may not be the center of the requirements. For example, assume that a nail enamel bottle filling process has requirements of 15 - 20 cc and its control chart shows sustained statistical control with $\sigma = 0.1$cc. The target value is 15.4 cc, 4σ above the lower specification. At this value the amount of product still meets the requirements. Employing table 8.1 we find that a subgroup size of 11 will detect a process drift of $\sigma = 0.1$ *cc* and allow us to correct the process before any out of specification product is produced. If the process mean were 17.5cc, the center of the specification, a great deal of product would be wasted.

Non-normal distributions

Many processes produce output that does not follow a normal distribution. In fact, normality is the exception rather than the rule. If process capability analysis fails to account for the non-normality it may produce inaccurate long-term yield estimates. This section will describe some of the more common types of non-normal distributions and ways of dealing with them. I recommend that the distribution's shape be evaluated by preparing a histogram as described in chapter 6, and using a probability paper as described later in this chapter. The data used to prepare the histogram should be obtained from a process that exhibits statistical control. Determine statistical control using an $\overline{X}$ chart, if possible; the $\overline{X}$ chart will produce valid results even when the process distribution is not normal. Histograms of processes that are not in statistical control are valuable troubleshooting aids, but useless or, worse, misleading when used for evaluating normality.

Skewed distributions

Skewness is one of the most common types of non-normality. A distribution is said to be skewed if the left and right sides of the distribution from a line drawn through the mean have different shapes. Just because a distribution is skewed doesn't mean it is "wrong." Skewness is a natural consequence of many physical and chemical processes. For example, the width of a sheared plate is likely to be skewed because it is constrained by the backstop in one direction but unconstrained in the other direction, it can move away from the backstop an indefinite distance. Another cause of skewness arises from the scale used, for example the pH scale is non-linear and usually pH data are skewed even when an $\overline{X}$ chart of the pH data shows good control. Figure 13.3 illustrates skewed distributions.

Yields of skewed distributions

Tables have been prepared to help evaluate skewed distributions. Two such tables are given here. The tables are used with the Z values described earlier in exactly the same way as the normal tables are used. Table 13.3 is used for data that is positively skewed, table 13.4 is used for data that is negatively skewed. The tables assume that the coefficient of skewness is approximately ±1. This value is computed by most statistical computer programs; however, many of the SPC computer programs ignore the skewness of the distribution and compute the estimated yields as if the distribution were normal. For moderately skewed data this approach is usually acceptable; yield estimates are somewhat robust to departures from the zero skewness assumption. However, for obviously skewed data tables 13.3 and 13.4 (see below) will give more accurate results.

When data becomes extremely skewed, or otherwise non-normal (e.g., truncated), a transformation can be used to make the data more normal. These normalizing transformations are described in many statistical texts, for example Massey and Dixon (1969). Some computer software packages will automatically find the best-fit transformation and use the fitted curve to compute estimated yields and capability indices (Pyzdek, 1990). However, you may be able to use the approach shown here for data that is moderately skewed.

The following procedure can be used to estimate the coefficient of skewness and to determine if you need to use tables for skewed data (Snedecor and Cochran, 1967)

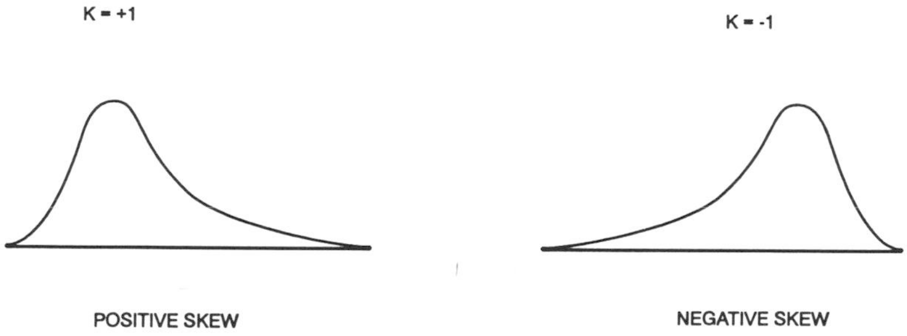

K = +1　　　　　　　　　　　　　　　　　K = -1

POSITIVE SKEW　　　　　　　　　　　NEGATIVE SKEW

Figure 13.3-Skewed Distributions

1. Perform a process capability analysis as described in this chapter using $\overline{X}$ and R charts with subgroups of 4 or more units per subgroup (the central limit theorem will assure that your process control limits are valid even if the underlying process distribution is not normal.) Obtain at least 150 individual observations from the process in a state of statistical control (e.g., 30 subgroups of 5 per subgroup.)

2. Compute $m_3 = \Sigma(X - \overline{X})^3 / n$ and $m_2 = \Sigma(X - \overline{X})^2 / n$ and take

$k = \dfrac{m_3}{m_2 \times \sqrt{m_2}}$, where n is the total number of individual observations and the summation is over the n individual observations, not the subgroup averages.

3. Find $Z = \dfrac{k}{\sqrt{6/n}}$. For normal distributions k has a mean zero and a standard deviation of approximately $\sqrt{6/n}$. If $|Z| < 1.96$, the skewness is not significantly different than zero and you can use the yield table 13.2 for normal distributions. If $|Z| \geq 1.96$ and k is positive, use table 13.3; if $|Z| \geq 1.96$ and k is negative, use table 13.4. If $|k|$ is much larger than 1, say more than $1 + 3 \times \sqrt{6/n}$, you should probably use a normalizing transformation before performing the yield estimates.

Table 13.3-Z Indices and Positively Skewed Process Yields (k=+1)					
$|Z_U|$	% Above High Spec		$|Z_L|$	% Below Low Spec.	
	If $Z_U \geq 0$	If $Z_U < 0$		If $Z_L \geq 0$	If $Z_L < 0$
0.0	43.3%	43.3%	0.0	56.7%	56.7%
0.1	39.4	47.4	0.1	52.6	60.6
0.2	35.8	51.6	0.2	48.4	64.2
0.3	32.5	55.0	0.3	44.6	67.5
0.4	29.3	60.4	0.4	39.6	70.7
0.5	26.4	64.7	0.5	35.3	73.6
0.6	23.8	69.0	0.6	31.0	76.2
0.7	21.5	73.1	0.7	26.9	78.5
0.8	19.4	77.0	0.8	23.0	80.6
0.9	17.4	80.7	0.9	19.3	82.6
1.0	15.8	84.1	1.0	15.9	84.2
1.1	14.3	87.2	1.1	12.8	85.7
1.2	12.9	89.9	1.2	10.1	87.1
1.3	11.6	92.3	1.3	7.7	88.4
1.4	10.4	95.4	1.4	5.6	89.6
1.5	9.3	96.0	1.5	4.0	90.7
1.6	8.3	97.1	1.6	2.9	91.7

Table 13.3-Z Indices and Positively Skewed Process Yields (k=+1)					
$|Z_U|$	% Above High Spec		$|Z_L|$	% Below Low Spec.	
	If $Z_U \geq 0$	If $Z_U < 0$		If $Z_L \geq 0$	If $Z_L < 0$
1.7	7.4	98.5	1.7	1.5	92.6
1.8	6.5	99.3	1.8	0.7	93.5
1.9	5.7	99.9	1.9	0.5	94.3
2.0	4.9	100.0	2.0	0.0	95.1
2.1	4.2	-	2.1	-	95.8
2.2	3.6	-	2.2	-	96.4
2.3	3.1	-	2.3	-	96.9
2.4	2.6	-	2.4	-	97.4
2.5	2.1	-	2.5	-	97.9
2.6	1.7	-	2.6	-	98.3
2.7	1.4	-	2.7	-	98.6
2.8	1.1	-	2.8	-	98.9
2.9	0.9	-	2.9	-	99.1
3.0	0.7	-	3.0	-	99.3
3.1	0.5	-	3.1	-	99.5
3.2	0.4	-	3.2	-	99.6
3.3	0.3	-	3.3	-	99.7
3.4	0.2	-	3.4	-	99.8
3.5	0.2	-	3.5	-	99.8
3.6	0.1	-	3.6	-	99.9
3.7	0.07	-	3.7	-	99.93
3.8	0.03	-	3.8	-	99.97
3.9	0.01	-	3.9	-	99.99
4.0	0.00	-	4.0	-	100.0

	\% Below Low Spec			\% Above High Spec.	
$|Z_L|$	If $Z_L \geq 0$	If $Z_L < 0$	$|Z_U|$	If $Z_U \geq 0$	If $Z_U < 0$
0.0	43.3%	43.3%	0.0	56.7%	56.7%
0.1	39.4	47.4	0.1	52.6	60.6
0.2	35.8	51.6	0.2	48.4	64.2
0.3	32.5	55.0	0.3	44.6	67.5
0.4	29.3	60.4	0.4	39.6	70.7
0.5	26.4	64.7	0.5	35.3	73.6
0.6	23.8	69.0	0.6	31.0	76.2
0.7	21.5	73.1	0.7	26.9	78.5
0.8	19.4	77.0	0.8	23.0	80.6
0.9	17.4	80.7	0.9	19.3	82.6
1.0	15.8	84.1	1.0	15.9	84.2
1.1	14.3	87.2	1.1	12.8	85.7
1.2	12.9	89.9	1.2	10.1	87.1
1.3	11.6	92.3	1.3	7.7	88.4
1.4	10.4	95.4	1.4	5.6	89.6
1.5	9.3	96.0	1.5	4.0	90.7
1.6	8.3	97.1	1.6	2.9	91.7
1.7	7.4	98.5	1.7	1.5	92.6
1.8	6.5	99.3	1.8	0.7	93.5
1.9	5.7	99.9	1.9	0.5	94.3
2.0	4.9	100.0	2.0	0.0	95.1
2.1	4.2	-	2.1	-	95.8
2.2	3.6	-	2.2	-	96.4
2.3	3.1	-	2.3	-	96.9
2.4	2.6	-	2.4	-	97.4
2.5	2.1	-	2.5	-	97.9
2.6	1.7	-	2.6	-	98.3
2.7	1.4	-	2.7	-	98.6
2.8	1.1	-	2.8	-	98.9
2.9	0.9	-	2.9	-	99.1
3.0	0.7	-	3.0	-	99.3
3.1	0.5	-	3.1	-	99.5
3.2	0.4	-	3.2	-	99.6
3.3	0.3	-	3.3	-	99.7
3.4	0.2	-	3.4	-	99.8

Table 13.4-Z Indices and Negative Skewed Process Yields (k = -1)

Table 13.4-Z Indices and Negative Skewed Process Yields (k = -1)					
$\|Z_L\|$	% Below Low Spec		$\|Z_U\|$	% Above High Spec.	
	If $Z_L \geq 0$	If $Z_L < 0$		If $Z_U \geq 0$	If $Z_U < 0$
3.5	0.2	-	3.5	-	99.8
3.6	0.1	-	3.6	-	99.9
3.7	0.07	-	3.7	-	99.93
3.8	0.03	-	3.8	-	99.97
3.9	0.01	-	3.9	-	99.99
4.0	0.00	-	4.0	-	100.0

Folded normal distributions

Another common non-normal distribution is the *folded normal distribution*. The folded normal distribution results when the negative sign of otherwise normal data is "lost." This situation is quite common because of the way in which many dimensions are measured. Here are some examples of features that produce folded normal distributions.

Feature	Discussion
Flatness	Physically flatness can be either concave ("negative flatness") or convex ("positive flatness"). However, flatness data is usually recorded as the difference between the smallest and largest deviations from a reference plane. If the negative signs were included the distribution would be normal. However, the negative flatness readings are folded to positive values, resulting in a folded normal.
Perpendicularity	One surface is perpendicular to another if it is located at a right angle, 90 degrees. However, in practice, an angle of 89 degrees is recorded exactly the same as an angle of 91 degrees; they are both 1 degree from perpendicular. If the actual angle was recorded the result would be a normal distribution. However, when the deviations from perpendicular are used the distribution is a folded normal.

The same logic applies to straightness, roundness, concentricity, angularity, profile of a surface, and many other characteristics. There are two keys features to folded normal data

1. It must be *possible* to get negative values, at least in theory. If negative numbers are not possible, the distribution cannot be a folded normal. For example, a gap can never be negative and the distribution of gap measurements cannot be a folded normal distribution.

2. The negative signs are not used.

Folded normal yields

The procedure for computing yields for folded normal data is as follows:
1. Compute the process mean and process standard deviation from the $\overline{X}$ and R control charts as described in volume one, chapter 8. With folded normal data $\overline{X}$ charts are recommended over individuals charts because averages will tend to be normally distributed due to the central limit theorem. Because folded normal data can not be less than 0, if the lower control limit computes to a value less than 0 it is left off of the control chart. It is always possible to get a lower control limit by increasing the subgroup size. However, the larger subgroup sizes cost more and may lead to control charts that are too sensitive to unimportant changes in the process, i.e., the control chart will show changes of no economic importance.
2. Compute the ratios shown in equations 13.9 and 13.10.

$$process\ ratio = \frac{\mu_f}{\sigma_f} \tag{13.9}$$

$$t_f = \frac{tolerance}{\sigma_f} \tag{13.10}$$

The value μ_f will be the grand average from your process capability analysis, σ_f will be computed as $\overline{R}/d2$, where $\overline{R}$ is from the process capability analysis. The f subscript is used to indicate that the data are folded.
3. Enter table 4 in the appendix with the ratios from equations 13.9 and 13.10. Find the column that comes nearest to the ratio computed with equation 13.9 and go down to the row that is nearest to the ratio computed with equation 13.10. The value in the table is the yield proportion. Multiply this value by 100 to convert it to a percentage yield. For example, if you are measuring flatness then your process data is folded normal. If the process is in control with μ_f = 5 thousandths and σ_f = 2 thousandths and your tolerance is 10 thousandths then, using equations 13.9 and 13.10, you would find that:

$$process\ ratio = \frac{\mu_f}{\sigma_f} = \frac{5}{2} = 2.5$$

$$t_f = \frac{tolerance}{\sigma_f} = \frac{10}{2} = 5.0$$

Entering table 4 in the appendix in the column for 2.5 and the row for 5.0 we find the yield proportion is 0.9934. Multiplying this by 100 gives a yield of 99.34%.

True position

The final non-normal distribution we will consider here is the *Rayleigh distribution*. The Rayleigh distribution results when x and y measurements are converted to radial measurements. The Rayleigh assumes that both x and y are normally distributed with zero mean and equal variances. An approximation to this situation occurs frequently with *true position measurements*. True position is calculated using equation 13.11.

$$true\ position = 2\sqrt{x^2 + y^2} \tag{13.11}$$

In equation 13.11 x is the deviation from nominal in the x direction and y is the deviation from nominal in the y direction. With true position, obviously, no negative values are possible. Thus, there is no lower specification. Table 13.5 shows the percentage above the upper specification based on the value of Z_t where:

$$Z_t = \frac{true\ position\ specification}{\sigma} \tag{13.12}$$

Table 13.5 is only valid if the assumptions mentioned above are correct. As with all capability analysis that uses theoretical curves, be sure to verify that the predicted yields match your actual results.

Table 13.5-Yields for True Position Process Data			
Z_t	% OUT	Z_t	% OUT
0.1	99.88%	4.6	7.10
0.2	99.50	4.7	6.32
0.3	98.88	4.8	5.61
0.4	98.02	4.9	4.97
0.5	96.92	5.0	4.39
0.6	95.60	5.1	3.87
0.7	94.06	5.2	3.40
0.8	92.31	5.3	2.99
0.9	90.37	5.4	2.61
1.0	88.25	5.5	2.28
1.1	85.96	5.6	1.98
1.2	83.53	5.7	1.72
1.3	80.96	5.8	1.49
1.4	78.27	5.9	1.29
1.5	75.48	6.0	1.11
1.6	72.61	6.1	0.95
1.7	69.68	6.2	0.82
1.8	66.70	6.3	0.70
1.9	63.68	6.4	0.60
2.0	60.65	6.5	0.51
2.1	57.62	6.6	0.43
2.2	54.61	6.7	0.37
2.3	51.62	6.8	0.31
2.4	48.68	6.9	0.26
2.5	45.78	7.0	0.22
2.6	42.96	7.1	0.18
2.7	40.20	7.2	0.15
2.8	37.53	7.3	0.13
2.9	34.95	7.4	0.11
3.0	32.47	7.5	0.09
3.1	30.08	7.6	0.07
3.2	27.80	7.7	0.06
3.3	25.63	7.8	0.05
3.4	23.57	7.9	0.04
3.5	21.63	8.0	0.03
3.6	19.79	8.1	0.03
3.7	18.06	8.2	0.02
3.8	16.45	8.3	0.02
3.9	14.94	8.4	0.01
4.0	13.53	8.5	0.01
4.1	12.23	8.6	0.01
4.2	11.03	8.7	0.01
4.3	9.91	8.8	0.01
4.4	8.89	8.9	0.01
4.5	7.96	9.0	0.00

Example

We will now present a numerical example of capability analysis using normally distributed variables data: We will use the sample data that was used in chapter

8 for $\overline{X}$ and R charts. The steps are those described earlier in this chapter in the section entitled "control chart method: variables data."

1. The standard deviation will be computed from the average range using R/d_2. Recall that $\overline{R}$ was 0.2205, from table 1 in the appendix we find d_2 is 2.326 for subgroups of 5. Thus:

$$\sigma = \frac{0.2205}{2.326} = 0.00948$$

2. The average was 0.9983.
3. Before we can analyze process capability, we must know the requirements. For this process the requirements are a lower specification of 0.980 and an upper specification of 1.020 (1.000 ± 0.020). The "target value" is the nominal dimension of 1.000 inches. With this information, plus the knowledge that the process performance has been in statistical control, we can compute the capability indices for this process. Refer to table 13.1 for the equations being used.

$$C_p = \frac{1.020 - 0.980}{6 \times 0.00948} = \frac{0.04}{0.05688} = 0.703$$

$$C_R = 100 \times \frac{0.05688}{0.04} = 142\%$$

$$C_m = \frac{1.020 - 0.980}{8 \times 0.00948} = \frac{0.04}{0.07584} = 0.527$$

$$Z_U = \frac{1.020 - 0.99832}{0.00948} = \frac{0.02168}{0.00948} = 2.3$$

$$Z_L = \frac{0.99832 - 0.980}{0.00948} = \frac{0.01832}{0.00948} = 1.9$$

$$Z_{min} = minimum\{1.9, 2.3\} = 1.9$$

$$C_{pk} = \frac{1.9}{3} = 0.63$$

$$C_{pm} = \frac{0.703}{1.014} = 0.69$$

OK, so what does all of this mean? The answer is found by using the guidelines that follow table 13.1 to interpret the capability indices. Let's look at each of them, one at a time.

INDEX	VALUE	INTERPRETATION
C_p	0.703	Since the minimum acceptable value for this index is 1, the 0.703 result indicates that this process *can not meet the requirements*. Furthermore, since the C_p index assumes the process is exactly centered at nominal we know that the process can not be made acceptable by merely adjusting the process closer to the center of the requirements.
C_R	142%	C_R always gives the same conclusions as the C_p index. The number itself means that the "natural tolerance" of the process uses 142% of the engineering requirement.
C_m	0.527	C_m is computed in the same way as C_p except that it uses 8σ as the acceptable process spread to compensate for limited data. Thus, C_m will always show the process to be less acceptable than C_p. C_m should only be used if the study was performed with limited data, otherwise use C_p.
Z_U	2.3	We desire a Z_U of at least +3, so this value is unacceptable. We can use Z_U to estimate the percentage of production that will exceed the upper specification. Referring to table 13.2 we find that approximately 1.1% of the parts will be oversized.
Z_L	1.9	We desire a Z_L of at least +3, so this value is unacceptable. We can use Z_L to estimate the percentage of production that will be below the lower specification. Referring to table 13.2 we find that approximately 2.9% of the parts will be undersized. To determine the total reject rate we add this to the 1.1% oversized, giving a total reject rate of 4.0%. By subtracting this from 100% we get a projected yield of 96.0% for this process.
Z_{min}	1.9	Obviously, this value will not be acceptable since Z_U and Z_L were not acceptable. In this case, Z_{min} is the Z_L value.

| C_{pk} | 0.63 | The value of C_{pk} is only slightly smaller than that of C_p; Cpk can never be larger than Cp. This indicates that we will not gain much by centering the process. The actual amount we would gain can be calculated by "assuming" the process is exactly centered at 1.000 and recalculating Z_{min}; if you did this you would find the predicted total reject rate drops from 4.0% to 3.6%. |
| C_{pm} | 0.69 | The value of C_{pm} is very close to that of C_p. This indicates that the process is centered quite close to the target value. Since C_{pm} can never be larger than C_p, C_{pm} can never be acceptable unless C_p is also acceptable and this value is clearly too small. |

Based on all of the capability indices we conclude that this process is not capable of meeting the requirements. It is doing about the best it can do and adjusting the process mean will do little to improve its yield performance. The projected long term reject rate is 4%, the projected long term yield is 96%. If the cost of an inspection and the cost of a reject are known, a decision can now be made regarding whether or not the output of this process should be 100% sorted (Deming, 1986, chapter 15).

Probability paper

Probability paper is a simple, graphical alternative to using tables or mathematical equations. This section describes the use of normal probability paper. The procedure for using probability paper for other distributions is identical.

1. Sort the sample data in rank order, from smallest to largest. The smallest value is given a rank of 1, the largest a rank of n, where n is the number of values.
2. Assign a "mean rank" to each value. The mean rank for the value i is found using equation 13.13

$$mean\ rank = 100 \times \frac{i}{n+1} \qquad (13.13)$$

where i is the value's rank and n is the total number of observations in all of the subgroups combined. When plotting data from a histogram or frequency tally sheet, the value is the cell lower boundary and the value's rank i is the cumulative frequency.

Table 13.6-Table 6.7 Modified for Probability Plotting

Upper cell boundary	Cell frequency	Cumulative frequency	Mean rank (% under)
0.9855	8	8	7.9%
0.9895	9	17	16.8
0.9935	17	34	33.7
0.9975	16	50	49.5
1.0015	9	59	58.4
1.0055	19	78	77.2
1.0095	11	89	88.1
1.0135	6	95	94.1
1.0175	3	98	97.0
1.0215	2	100	99.0

3. Using normal probability paper[1], plot the observed values against their mean rank. Note that the mean rank is the probability estimate associated with the value.
4. When using frequency tables, plot the values against the "percent under" scale.

Probability paper example

The use of probability paper will be illustrated using the data in table 6.7. The modified frequency table is shown in table 13.6.

1. Plot the upper cell boundary in column 1 against the mean rank in column 4. Use the percent under scale of the probability paper.
2. Examine the pattern of the points on the probability paper. If the points appear to fall on a relatively straight line, then draw the line that fits the data by eye. If the points obviously don't fall on an approximately straight line, the distribution is probably not normal. If the fit is close, the estimates will probably be acceptable, the average and standard deviation are "robust statistics" that can be used successfully with near-normal distributions. Try different probability papers to determine the correct distribution. King (1971) provides guidelines for using probability paper to evaluate distributions.
3. Estimate the percent over or under any value by drawing a vertical line from the value to the fitted line, then over to get the percent under the value. Figure 13.4 shows the probability plot for the data in table 13.6.

---

1   Blank probability paper for a wide variety of different distributions is available from TEAM, Box 25, Tamworth, NH 03886, (603) 323-8843

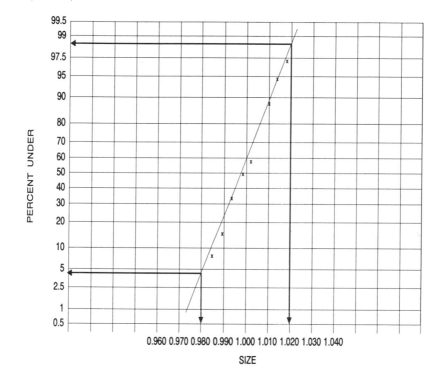

Figure 13.4-Example of Normal Probability Plot

The plotted points fall on an approximately straight line, indicating that the normal curve fits the data. Also, the probability paper estimates that 1.5% would be above the high specification and 3.5% would be below the low specification. This is excellent agreement with the tables where we obtained estimates of 1.1% low and 2.9% high.

Related techniques
Probability paper is the graphic equivalent of the table look up procedure for estimating percentages out of specification.

The pattern of the points on probability paper is closely related to the shapes of histograms. Compare your histograms to your probability plots.

Pointers for using probability plots

- Whenever there are 50 or more points, take advantage of the frequency table method.

- Don't use this method if extreme accuracy is required. Keep in mind that graphical methods are not as accurate as using calculations and tables. However, also remember that sampling and other errors are often far more of a problem than the inaccuracy caused by using probability paper or other graphical methods.

- If there are two or three different sources of variation, such as operators, vendors, etc., plot them with different symbols on the same probability plot to get a direct comparison of their distributions.

References

Deming, W.E. (1986), *"Out of the Crisis,"* MIT press, Cambridge Mass., chapter 15.

King, J.R., (1971),"Probability Charts for Decision Making," TEAM, Tamworth, NH 03886, (603) 323-8843.

Massey, F.J. and Dixon, W.J. (1969), *Introduction to statistical analysis, third edition*, McGraw-Hill, New York, pp. 323 ff.

Milligan, G.W. (1991), "Is sampling really dead?" Quality Progress, April, pp. 77-81.

Mood, A.M. (1943), "On the dependence of sampling inspection plans under population distributions," *Annals of Mathematical Statistics*, Vol. 14, pp. 415-425.

Pyzdek, T. (1985), "A ten-step plan for statistical process control studies," Quality Progress, July, pp. 18-20.

Pyzdek, T. (1990), *SPC-PC: statistical process control for personal computers*, Quality America, Tucson, Arizona.

Snedecor, G.W. and Cochran, W.G. (1967), *Statistical Methods, 6th edition*, Iowa State University Press, Ames, Iowa.

CHAPTER 14

MEDIAN CONTROL CHARTS

OBJECTIVES:

After completing this section you will:

- Be able to prepare, analyze, and interpret control charts for the median.

Introduction

In this chapter we will often use the symbol for the median, $\tilde{x}$. $\tilde{x}$ is simply that value which divides a data set into two equal parts. For example, $\tilde{x}$ of the numbers 1, 2, 3, 4, 5 is 3; there are two numbers below 3 and two numbers above 3. Obviously, like the average $\overline{X}$, $\tilde{x}$ is a measure of *central tendency*. Although $\overline{X}$ has certain mathematical advantages over $\tilde{x}$, there are situations when $\tilde{x}$ has practical advantages.

$\tilde{x}$ control charts are used to fill in a vacuum between individuals charts and $\overline{X}$ charts. As described in volume one, chapter 8, $\overline{X}$ charts, accompanied by either range charts or sigma charts, are the SPC tool of choice for variables data. Their advantages include the normalizing effect of the central limit theorem, sensitivity at whatever level is desired, optimal estimation of process variation through rational subgrouping, graphical control of dispersion, and independence of points on the $\overline{X}$, range or sigma chart. When it is not possible to use $\overline{X}$ charts, individuals charts are usually employed along with the moving range chart. However, sometimes the reasons $\overline{X}$ charts can't be used are purely administrative. For example, perhaps the level of training of the workforce is not yet sufficient for the calculations involved. Under these conditions there is no economic or scientific justification for failing to use $\overline{X}$ charts and they could, in principle, be used. Under the circumstances, $\tilde{x}$ charts offer an alternative that may be preferable to individuals charts. Like $\overline{X}$ charts, $\tilde{x}$ charts can be made more sensitive by increasing the subgroup size. And this chapter presents a scheme for controlling the dispersion of the process using the subgroup ranges that involves no calculations and does not use a range control chart.

Definition $\tilde{x}$ charts are statistical tools used to evaluate the central tendency of a process over time by monitoring subgroup $\tilde{x}$'s.

Usage $\tilde{x}$ charts can be applied to any continuous variable like weight, size, etc.. $\tilde{x}$ charts answer the question "Has a special cause of variation caused the central tendency of this process to change over the time period observed?" To control the dispersion of the process, $\tilde{x}$ charts are sometimes supplemented by a "range control card." $\tilde{x}$ is statistically less efficient than X for process control, and it gets worse as the subgroup size increases. Therefore, use of $\tilde{x}$ control charts must be justified by some practical need, such as the need to avoid the calculations required for averages and ranges charts. To accomplish this the subgroup size for $\tilde{x}$ charts must be an odd number and small subgroups should be used.

How to prepare and analyze $\tilde{x}$ charts

This procedure is based on an approach developed by Barry Griffin (Griffin, 1986.)

1. Determine the subgroup size and sampling frequency. Typically, subgroups of 3, 5, or 7 units are used and subgroups of 5 are most common. Odd sized subgroups are usually selected because no calculations are necessary when the subgroup size is odd. The subgroup size affects the sensitivity of the control chart. Smaller subgroups give a control chart that is less sensitive to changes in the process, while larger subgroups may be too sensitive to small, economically unimportant changes. When using $\tilde{x}$ charts the subgroup size should be kept small, say 9 or less. Median charts are less efficient statistically than X charts, and the inefficiency increases as the subgroup size increases. Selection of subgroups should be planned to minimize possible variation, this is usually accomplished by selecting consecutive units. Sampling should be frequent enough to detect the effect of special causes while the special cause itself can still be identified. This varies a great deal from process to process, but as a rule of thumb you should average about 1 out of control point per typical control chart of 25 groups. If you have more points out-of-control than that, increase the sampling frequency. If you have fewer, reduce the sampling frequency.

2. If possible, collect data from 20-25 subgroups, at least 100 individual values are recommended. If you can't get that much data, use whatever you can get (see the section in chapter 15 entitled "Exact method of computing control limits for short and small runs" if you have less than 25 sub-

groups.) While the data is being collected, you should minimize distur-
bances to the process. If a process change is unavoidable, develop a system for recording changes so that their effect can be determined. Make
notes of all changes directly on the chart.

3. Compute the control limits. Perform the necessary calculations using the
flowchart in figure 14.1 (Griffin, 1986). Each arithmetic instruction in the
flowchart is accompanied by a rectangle divided into three segments: (1)
an identification number, (2) a description of the data element or instruction, and (3) a blank space for recording the resultant data. Numbers written beneath the description or instruction in segment (2) refer you back to
the rectangles corresponding. In the descriptive portion of rectangle number 5 for example, 4/1 means that you should divide the data element written in rectangle number 4 by the data element in rectangle 1. By stepping
through this simple flowchart you will calculate control limits for both $\tilde{x}$
and range charts. The equations being solved with the flowchart are:

$$average \; \tilde{x} = \frac{total \; of \; medians}{number \; of \; medians} = \tilde{\tilde{x}} \tag{14.1}$$

$$LCL_{\tilde{x}} = \tilde{\tilde{x}} - \tilde{A}_2\overline{R} \tag{14.2}$$

$$UCL_{\tilde{x}} = \tilde{\tilde{x}} + \tilde{A}_2\overline{R} \tag{14.3}$$

Even though the flowchart includes calculation of control limits for range charts,
range charts are not usually kept when using $\tilde{x}$ charts. Instead the range is controlled with a "range control card" using a procedure described later in this chapter.

Interpretation of $\tilde{x}$ charts

The interpretation of control charts for the $\tilde{x}$ and the range is the same as described for averages and ranges chart in volume one chapter 8 in the section enti-
tle "Interpretation of Control Charts." However, unlike averages, the distribution of medians may not be normal. Thus, you should plot a histogram of the
medians and assure that they appear normal before you apply the run tests from
volume one chapter 8. If the distribution of medians doesn't appear normal you
can use the run tests described in volume one chapter 7; the run tests described
in volume one chapter 7 are *non-parametric*, which means that they can be applied regardless of the underlying distribution of the data.

MEDIAN CONTROL CHARTS

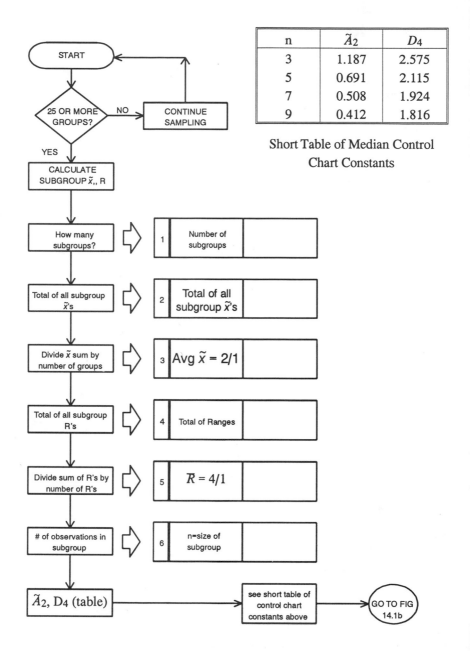

n	$\tilde{A}_2$	D_4
3	1.187	2.575
5	0.691	2.115
7	0.508	1.924
9	0.412	1.816

Short Table of Median Control
Chart Constants

START

25 OR MORE GROUPS? NO → CONTINUE SAMPLING

YES

CALCULATE SUBGROUP $\tilde{x}$,, R

How many subgroups? ⇨ 1 | Number of subgroups

Total of all subgroup $\tilde{x}$'s ⇨ 2 | Total of all subgroup $\tilde{x}$'s

Divide $\tilde{x}$ sum by number of groups ⇨ 3 | Avg $\tilde{x}$ = 2/1

Total of all subgroup R's ⇨ 4 | Total of Ranges

Divide sum of R's by number of R's ⇨ 5 | $\bar{R}$ = 4/1

# of observations in subgroup ⇨ 6 | n=size of subgroup

$\tilde{A}_2$, D$_4$ (table) → see short table of control chart constants above → GO TO FIG 14.1b

Figure 14.1a-Median Control Chart Calculation Flowchart

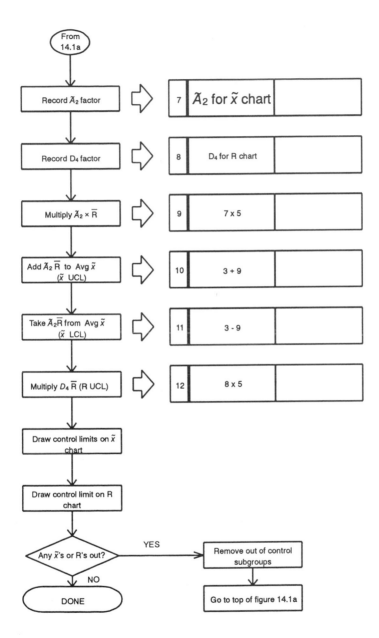

Figure 14.1b-Control Chart Calculation Flowchart (cont.)

Table 14.1-Raw Data for Median Control Chart

Row	No. 1	No. 2	No. 3	No. 4	No. 5	$\tilde{x}$	R
1	1.002	0.995	1.000	1.002	1.005	1.002	0.010
2	1.000	0.997	1.007	0.992	0.995	0.997	0.015
3	0.997	1.013	1.001	0.985	1.002	1.001	0.028
4	0.990	1.008	1.005	0.994	1.012	1.005	0.022
5	0.992	1.012	1.005	0.985	1.006	1.005	0.027
6	1.000	1.002	1.006	1.007	0.993	1.002	0.014
7	0.984	0.994	0.998	1.006	1.002	0.998	0.022
8	0.987	0.994	1.002	0.997	1.008	0.997	0.021
9	0.992	0.988	1.015	0.987	1.006	0.992	0.028
10	0.994	0.990	0.991	1.002	0.988	0.991	0.014
11	1.007	1.008	0.990	1.001	0.999	1.001	0.018
12	0.995	0.989	0.982	0.995	1.002	0.995	0.020
13	0.987	1.004	0.992	1.002	0.992	0.992	0.017
14	0.991	1.001	0.996	0.997	0.984	0.996	0.017
15	1.004	0.993	1.003	0.992	1.010	1.003	0.018
16	1.004	1.010	0.984	0.997	1.008	1.004	0.026
17	0.990	1.021	0.995	0.987	0.989	0.990	0.034
18	1.003	0.992	0.992	0.990	1.014	0.992	0.024
19	1.000	0.985	1.019	1.002	0.986	1.000	0.034
20	0.996	0.984	1.005	1.016	1.012	1.005	0.032

Example

In chapter 6 of volume one we prepared a histogram of data from measurements on the size of a shaft. The data that was used for preparing our histogram was also analyzed using averages and ranges control charts in chapter 8 of volume one. The same data will now be analyzed using $\tilde{x}$ control charts. The data is shown in table 14.1. Since there are 5 observations in each subgroup, the subgroup $\tilde{x}$ is simply the middle, or 3rd largest (or 3rd smallest) value in the subgroup. Using this data, we complete the form from figure 14.1, the results are shown in figure 14.2.

Note that when completing the form for rectangles 10, 11 and 12 we carried one more decimal place than the raw data contain. This eliminates the ambiguity

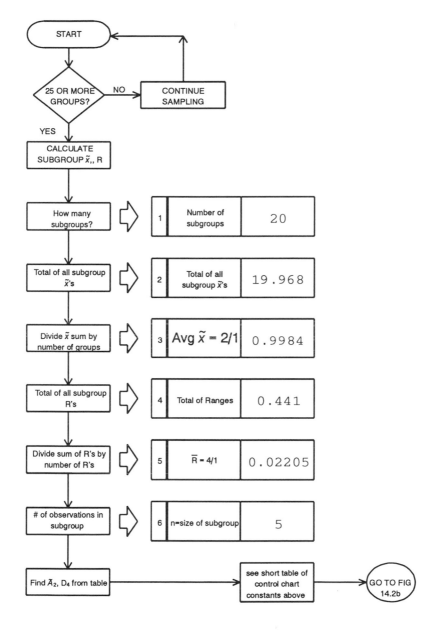

Figure 14.2a-Median Control Chart Calculation Flowchart

MEDIAN CONTROL CHARTS

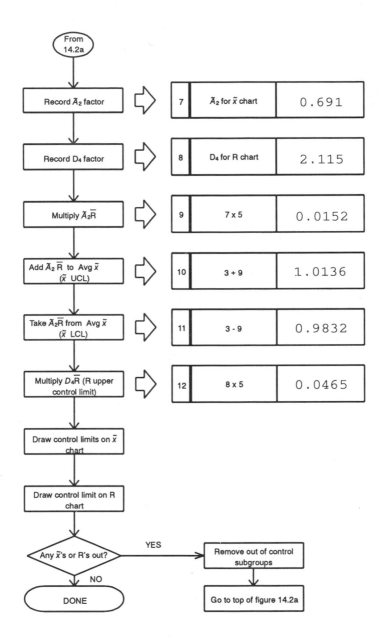

Figure 14.2b-Control Chart Calculation Flowchart (cont.)

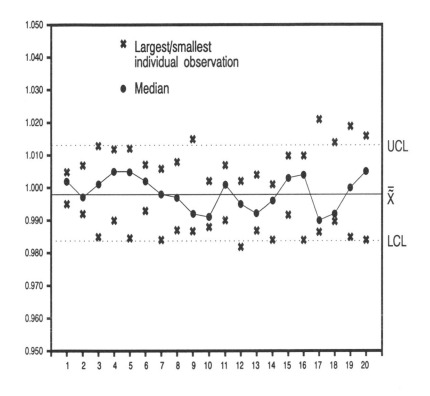

Figure 14.3-Control Chart for Medians

that might result if a sample $\tilde{x}$ or range fell exactly on the control limit. The completed control chart is shown in figure 14.3. On $\tilde{x}$ charts the smallest and largest points are plotted. The $\tilde{x}$ value of each subgroup is identified clearly on the chart. The $\tilde{x}$ values are joined with a line. We show only the $\tilde{x}$ chart because, typically, only the $\tilde{x}$ chart is placed on the operation. However, keep in mind that the range chart must be used during the initial capability study to determine if the process dispersion is in control. The $\overline{R}$ value from the range chart is also used to find the control limits for the $\tilde{x}$ chart. A procedure for dispersion control using a range control card is given later in this chapter.

In addition to the control limits we can also analyze the patterns on the median control chart. Patterns are analyzed using exactly the same procedures as described for averages and ranges charts in volume one chapter 8.

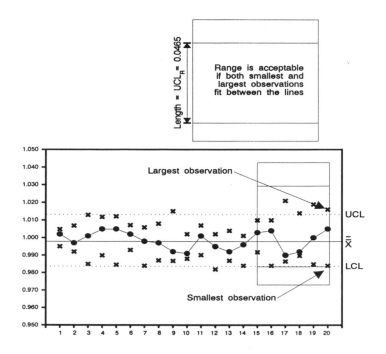

Figure 14.4-Using a Range Control Card

Related techniques

$\tilde{x}$ charts are charts of continuous variables. At times it may be appropriate to substitute run charts, individuals charts, averages charts, cumulative sum charts, moving average charts, exponentially weighted moving average charts or group control charts. Each of these procedures is discussed elsewhere in this *Guide*, consult the index for information.

Range control cards

As mentioned above, use of $\tilde{x}$ charts is usually motivated by a need to keep things as simple as possible. Because of this, the use of range charts is often undesirable. However, range control is necessary to control process dispersion. A solution to this problem involves making a transparent overlay or card marked with lines representing the upper and lower control limits for the range. An easy way to do this is to draw the card on paper, then run the drawing on transparency film through a copier. The resulting range control card is transparent, and nearly impervious to dirt and oil on the shop floor. This card is then placed over the $\tilde{x}$ chart to determine that the distance between the smallest and the largest value is no greater than the maximum allowable range. While this method doesn't allow the analysis of patterns as the range chart does, it is a reasonable compromise in most situations. The use of a "range control card" is illustrated in figure 14.4. In the example shown in figure 14.4, subgroup #20's range is being checked, the subgroup range is acceptable because the smallest and largest values fit between the lines on the range control card.

Pointers for using $\tilde{x}$ charts

- Be Timely! These charts are *tools* to assist you with process improvement by highlighting the existence of special causes. It does very little good to know that a special cause was present yesterday - you must know that it is happening **now**. Unless you are timely you will never be able to identify the special cause, it will be a "ghost." To assist you in finding ghosts, frequent small samples are generally better than occasional large samples.

- When performing the initial study using a range chart, evaluate the range chart before looking at the $\tilde{x}$ chart. The control limits for the $\tilde{x}$ chart are based on R thus the $\tilde{x}$ chart's control limits are meaningless unless the range chart shows control.

- When using the chart for operational process control, evaluate the subgroup range with the range control card before investigating an out of control subgroup $\tilde{x}$ value.

- Log in as much background information as possible. The background data will be very helpful in analyzing patterns that would otherwise seem random. For example, one operator of a lathe noticed that cold air blasted in a door every time a new load of material came in and he noted this fact on his control chart. After a few days it was clear that this caused variation in the size of the parts being made on the lathe. However, this discovery would never have been made without the operator's diligence.

- Write comments on the chart form itself. The most useful control charts are usually not the cleanest ones, they're the ones that have been used!

- Be an "active investigator." Using control charts to "study history" will only get you half of their potential benefit. If you deliberately try different things, and note these things on the charts, you will greatly accelerate the learning process. For example, if you have materials from 2 different sources, why not group one vendor's material together for several subgroups and the other vendor's material for several more, making a note of this on the control charts. If there is a difference, you've uncovered a cause of variation and you can make an immediate improvement!

- When a point is out of control, check the easiest things first, e.g., assure that the math was done correctly and that the point is plotted where it should be plotted. There should be a written procedure or flow chart describing the steps to be taken when a range or $\tilde{x}$ falls beyond a control limit. The procedure should also describe the action to be taken if the special cause can't be found.

References

Griffin, B. (1986), ASQC Statistics Division Newsletter, June.

CHAPTER 15

PROCESS CONTROL FOR SHORT AND SMALL RUNS

OBJECTIVES:

After completing this section you will:

- Understand basic strategies for controlling short and small run processes.
- Be able to correctly apply several methods for analyzing variables data from short and small production runs.
- Be able to analyze attribute data from short and small production runs.
- Understand that SPC is only one tool in the overall quality program for short and small run processes.

Introduction

A starting place for understanding SPC for short and small runs is to define our terms. The question "what *is* a short run?" will be answered for our purposes as an environment that has a large number of jobs per operator in a production cycle, each job involving different product. A production cycle is typically a week or a month. A *small run* is a situation where only a very few products of the same type are to be produced. An extreme case of a small run is the one-of-a-kind product, such as the Hubble Space Telescope. Short runs need not be small runs; a can manufacturing line can produce over 100,000 cans in an hour or two. Likewise small runs are not necessarily short runs, the Hubble Space Telescope took over 15 years to get into orbit (and even longer to get into orbit and working properly!) However, it is possible to have runs that are both short *and* small. Programs such as Just-In-Time inventory control (JIT) are making this situation more common all of the time.

Process control for either small or short runs involve similar strategies. Both situations involve markedly different approaches than those used in the classical mass-production environment. Thus, this chapter will treat both the small run and the short run situations simultaneously. You should, however, select the SPC tool that best fits your particular situation.

Strategies for Short and Small Runs

Juran's famous trilogy separates quality activities into three distinct phases: (Juran, 1988)

- Planning
- Control
- Improvement

Figure 15.1 provides a graphic portrayal of the Juran trilogy.

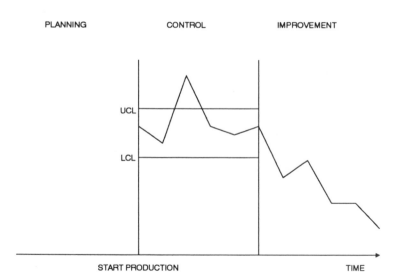

Figure 15-1-Juran's Trilogy

When faced with small or short runs the emphasis should be placed in the planning phase. As much as possible needs to be done *before* any product is made, because it simply isn't possible to waste time or materials "learning from mistakes" made during production. It is also helpful to realize that the Juran trilogy is usually applied to *products,* while SPC applies to *processes.* It is quite possible that the element being monitored with SPC is a process element and not a product feature at all. In this case there really is no "short run."

A common problem with application of SPC to short/small runs is that people fail to realize the limitations of SPC in this application. Even the use of SPC to *long production runs* will benefit from a greater emphasis on pre-production planning. In the best of all worlds, SPC will merely confirm that the correct process has been selected and controlled in such a way that it consistently produces well-designed parts at very close to the desired target values for every dimension.

Preparing the Short Run Process Control Plan (PCP)

Plans for short runs require a great deal of up-front attention. The objective is to create a list of as many potential sources of variation as possible and to take action to deal with them *before* going into production. One of the first steps to be taken is to identify which processes may be used to produce a given part; this is called the "Approved Process List." Analogously, parts that can be produced by a given process should also be identified; this is called the "Approved Parts List." These determinations are made based on process capability studies.

Chapter 13 describes process capability studies. Because short runs usually involve less than the recommended number of pieces the acceptability criteria is usually modified. When less than 50 observations are used to determine the capability I recommend that the capability indices described in Chapter 13 be modified by using a $\pm 4\sigma$ acceptable process width (instead of $\pm 3\sigma$) and a minimum acceptable C_{pk} of 1.5 (instead of 1.33). Don't bother making formal capability estimates until you have at least 30 observations. (You will see below that these observations need not always be from 30 separate parts.)

When preparing for short runs it often happens that actual production parts are not available in sufficient quantity for process capability studies. One way of dealing with this situation is to study process elements separately and to then sum the variances from all of the known elements to obtain an estimate of the best overall variance a given process will be able to produce.

For example, in an aerospace firm that produced conventional guided missiles, each missile contained thousands of different parts. In any given month only a small number of missiles were produced. Thus, the CNC machine shop (and the rest of the plant) was faced with a small/short run situation. However it was not possible to do separate pre-production capability studies of each part separately. The approach used instead was to design a special test part that would provide estimates of the machine's ability to produce every basic type of characteristic (flatness, straightness, angularity, location, etc.). Each CNC machine produced a number of these test parts under controlled conditions and the results were plotted on a Short Run $\overline{X}$ and R chart using the exact method (described later in this chapter). The studies were repeated periodically for each machine.

These studies provided pre-production estimates of the machine's ability to produce different characteristics. However, these estimates were always **better** than the process would be able to do with actual production parts. Actual production would involve different operators, tooling, fixtures, materials, and other common and special causes not evaluated by the *machine capability study*. Preliminary Approved Parts Lists and Preliminary Approved Process Lists were created from the capability analysis using the more stringent acceptability criteria described above (C_{pk} at least 1.5 based on a $\pm 4\sigma$ process spread). When production commenced the actual results of the production runs were used instead of the estimates based on special runs. Once sufficient data were available, the parts were removed from the preliminary lists and placed on the appropriate permanent lists.

When creating Approved Parts and Approved Process lists always use the most stringent product requirements to determine the process requirement. For example, if a process will be used to drill holes in 100 different parts with hole location tolerances ranging from 0.001 inches to 0.030 inches, the **process requirement** is 0.001 inches. The process capability estimate is based on its ability to hold the 0.001 inch tolerance.

The approach used is summarized as follows:

1. Get the process into statistical control.
2. Set the control limits **without regard to the requirement.**
3. Based on the calculated process capability, determine if the most stringent product requirement can be met.

Process Audit

The requirements for all processes should be documented. A process audit checklist should be prepared and used to determine the condition of the process prior to production. The audit can be performed by the operator himself, but the results should be documented. The audit should cover known or suspected sources of variation. These include such things as the production plan, condition of fixtures, gage calibration, the resolution of the gaging being used, obvious problems with materials or equipment, operator changes, and so on.

SPC can be used to monitor the results of the process audits over time. For example, an audit score can be computed and tracked using an individuals control chart or a demerit control chart (see below.)

Selecting Process Control Elements

Many short run SPC programs bog down because the number of control charts being used grows like Topsy. Before anyone knows what is happening they find the walls plastered with charts that few understand and nobody uses. The operators and inspectors wind up spending more time filling out paperwork than they spend on true value-added work. Eventually the entire SPC program collapses under its own weight.

One reason for this is that people tend to focus their attention on the *product* rather than on the *process*. Control elements are erroneously selected because they are functionally important. A great fear is that an important product feature will be produced out of specification and that it will slip by unnoticed. This is a misunderstanding of the purpose of SPC, which is to provide a means of *process* control; SPC is not intended to be a substitute for inspection or testing. The guiding rule of selecting control items for SPC is:

SPC control items should be selected to provide a maximum amount of information on the state of the process at a minimum cost.

Fortunately most process elements are correlated with one another. Because of this one process element may provide information not only about itself, but about several other process elements as well. This means that a small number of process control elements will often explain a large portion of the process variance.

Although sophisticated statistical methods exist to help determine which process components explain the most variance, common sense and knowledge of the process can often do as well, if not better. The key is to think about the process carefully.

- [ ] What are the "generic process elements" that affect all parts?
- [ ] How do the process elements combine to affect the product?
- [ ] Do several process elements affect a single product feature?
- [ ] Do changes in one process element automatically cause changes in some other process elements?
- [ ] What process elements or product features are most sensitive to unplanned changes?

Chapter 22 describes a rigorous approach to process control planning that helps SPC teams answer questions like these.

Example One

The CNC machines mentioned earlier were extremely complex. A typical machine had dozens of different tools and produced hundreds of different parts with thousands of characteristics. However, the SPC team reasoned that the machines themselves involved only a small number of "generic operations:" select a tool, position the tool, rotate the tool, move the part, remove metal. Further study revealed that nearly all of the problems encountered after the initial setup involved only the ability of the machine to position the tool precisely. A control plan was created that called for monitoring no more than one variable for each axis of movement. The features selected were those farthest from the machine's "home position" and involving the most difficult to control operations, not necessarily functionally important features. Often a single feature provided control of more than one axis of movement, for example the location of a single hole provides information on the location of the tool in both the X and Y directions. As a result of this system no part had more than four features monitored with control charts, even though many parts had thousands of features. Subsequent evaluation of the accumulated data by a statistician revealed that the choices made by the team explained over 90% of the process variance.

Example Two

A wave solder machine was used to solder printed circuit boards for a manufacturer of electronic test equipment. After several months of applying SPC the SPC team evaluated the data and decided that they needed only a single measure of product quality for SPC purposes: defects per 1,000 solder joints. A single control chart was used for dozens of different circuit boards. They also determined that most of the process variables being checked could be eliminated.

The only process variables monitored in the future would be flux density, solder chemistry (provided by the vendor), solder temperature, and final rinse contamination. Historic data showed that one of these variables was nearly always out-of-control when process problems were encountered. Other variables were monitored with periodic audits but not charted.

Notice that in both of these examples all of the variables being monitored were related to the *process,* even though some of them were product features. The terms "short run" and "small run" refer to the product variables only; the process is in continuous operation so its run size and duration is neither short nor small. It makes soldered joints continuously.

The Single Part Process

The ultimate small run is the single part. A great deal can be learned by studying single pieces, even if your situation involves more than one part.

The application of SPC to single pieces may seem incongruous. Yet when we consider that the "P" in SPC stands for *process* and not product, perhaps it is possible after all. Even the company producing one-of-a-kind product usually does so with the same equipment, employees, facilities, suppliers, etc.. In other words, they use the same *process* to produce different *products.* Also, they usually produce products that are similar, even though not identical. This is also to be expected. It would be odd indeed to find a company making microchips one day and baking bread the next. The processes are too dissimilar.

This discussion implies that the key to controlling the quality of single parts is to concentrate on the process elements rather than on the product features. This is the same rule we applied above to larger runs. In fact, it's a good rule to apply to all SPC applications, regardless of the number of parts being produced!

Consider a company manufacturing communications satellites. The company produces a satellite every year or two. The design and complexity of each satellite is quite different than any other. How can SPC be applied at this company? A close look at a satellite will reveal immense complexity. The satellite will have thousands of terminals, silicon solar cells, solder joints, fasteners, and so on. Hundreds, even thousands of people are involved in the design, fabrication, testing, and assembly. In other words, there are *processes* that involve massive amounts of repetition. The processes include engineering (errors per engineering drawing); terminal manufacture (size, defect rates); solar cell manufacture (yields, electrical properties); soldering (defects per 1,000 joints; strength); fastener installation quality (torque) and so on.

Another example of a single-piece run is software development. The "part" in this case is the working copy of the software delivered to the customer. Only a single unit of product is involved. How can we use SPC here?

Again, the answer comes when we direct our attention to the underlying process. Any marketable software product will consist of thousands, perhaps millions of bytes of finished machine code. This code will be compiled from thousands of lines of source code. The source code will be arranged in modules; the modules will contain procedures; the procedures will contain functions; and so on. Computer science has developed a number of ways of measuring the quality of computer code. The resulting numbers, called computer software metrics, can be analyzed using SPC tools just like any other numbers. The processes that produced the code can thus be measured, controlled and improved. If the process is in statistical control, the process elements, such as programmer selection and training, coding style, planning, procedures, etc. must be examined. If the process is not in statistical control, the special cause of the problem must be identified.

As discussed earlier, although the single part process is a small run, it isn't necessarily a short run. By examining the process rather than the part, improvement possibilities will begin to suggest themselves. The key is to find the process, to define its elements so they may be measured, controlled, and improved.

Other Elements of the PCP

In addition to the selection of process control elements, the PCP should also provide information on:

- ❑ the method of inspection
- ❑ dates and results of measurement error studies
- ❑ dates and results of process capability studies
- ❑ subgroup sizes and methods of selecting subgroups
- ❑ sampling frequency
- ❑ required operator certifications
- ❑ pre-production checklists
- ❑ setup approval procedures
- ❑ notes and suggestions regarding previous problems

In short, the PCP provides a complete, detailed roadmap that describes how process integrity will be measured and maintained. By preparing a PCP the *inputs* to the process are controlled ahead of time, thus assuring that the *outputs* from the process will be consistently acceptable.

Short Run SPC Techniques

Short production runs are a way of life with many manufacturing companies. In the future, this will be the case even more often. The trend in manufacturing has been toward smaller production runs with product tailored to the specific needs of individual customers. The days of "the customer can have any color, as long as it's black" have long since past.

Classical SPC methods, such as $\overline{X}$ and R charts, were developed in the era of mass production of identical parts. Production runs often lasted for weeks, months, or even years. Many of the "SPC rules of thumb" currently in use were created for this situation. For example, the rule that control limits not be calculated until data is available from at least 25 subgroups of 5. This may not have been a problem in 1930, but it certainly is today. In fact, many *entire production runs* involve fewer parts than required to start a standard control chart!

Many times the usual SPC methods can be modified slightly to work with short and small runs. For example, $\overline{X}$ and R control charts can be created using moving averages and moving ranges (See Volume One, chapter 8, page 100). However, there are special SPC methods that are particularly well suited to application on short or small runs.

VARIABLES DATA

Variables data involve measurements on a continuous scale such as size, weight, Ph, temperature, etc.. In theory data are variables data if no two values are exactly the same. In practice this is seldom the case. As a rough rule-of-thumb you can consider data to be variables data if at least ten different values occur and repeated values make up no more than 20% of the data set. If this is not the case, your data may be too discrete to use standard control charts. Consider trying an attribute procedure such as the demerit charts described later in this chapter. We will discuss the following approaches to SPC for short or small runs:

1. **Exact method:** Tables of special control chart constants are used to create X, $\overline{X}$ and R charts that compensate for the fact that a limited number of subgroups are available for computing control limits. The exact method is also used to compute control limits when using a code value chart or stabilized X or $\overline{X}$ and R charts (see below). The exact method allows the calculation of control limits that are correct when only a small amount of data is available. As more data becomes available the exact method updates control limits until, finally, no further updates are required and standard control chart factors can be used (see appendix table one.)

2. **Code Value Charts:** Control charts created by subtracting nominal or other target values from actual measurements. These charts are often stan-

dardized so that measurement units are converted to whole numbers. For example, if measurements are in thousandths of an inch a reading of 0.011 inches above nominal would be recorded simply as "11." Code value charts enable the user to plot several parts from a given process on a single chart, or to plot several features from a single part on the same control chart. The Exact Method can be used to adjust the control limits when code value charts are created with limited data.

3. **Stabilized Control Charts for Variables:** Statisticians have known about normalizing transformations for many years. This approach can be used to create control charts that are independent of the unit of measure and scaled in such a way that several different characteristics can be plotted on the same control chart. Since stabilized control charts are independent of the unit of measure, they can be thought of as true *process control charts*. The Exact Method adjusts the control limits for stabilized charts created with limited data.

Exact Method of Computing Control Limits for Short and Small Runs

This procedure applies to short runs or any situation where a small number of subgroups will be used to set up a control chart. It consists of three stages: (1) finding the process (establishing statistical control); (2) setting limits for the remainder of the initial run; and (3) setting limits for future runs. The procedure correctly compensates for the uncertainties involved when computing control limits with small amounts of data.

STAGE ONE: FIND THE PROCESS

1. Collect an initial sample of subgroups (g). The factors for the recommended minimum number of subgroups are shown in table five of the appendix enclosed in a dark box. If it is not possible to get the minimum number of subgroups, use the appropriate control chart constant for the number of subgroups you actually have.

2. Using table five in the appendix compute the Range chart control limits using the equation Upper Control Limit for Ranges $(UCL_R) = D_{4F} \times \bar{R}$. Compare the subgroup ranges to the UCL_R and drop any out-of-control groups after identifying and eliminating the special cause. Repeat the process until all remaining subgroup ranges are smaller than UCL_R.

3. Using the $\bar{R}$ value found in step #2, compute the control limits for the averages or individuals chart. The control limits are found by adding and subtracting $A_{2F} \times \bar{R}$ from the overall average. Drop any subgroups that have out-of-control averages and recompute. Continue until all remaining values are within the control limits. Go to stage two.

STAGE TWO: SET LIMITS FOR REMAINDER OF THE INITIAL RUN

1. Using table five in the appendix compute the control limits for the remainder of the run. Use the A_{2S} factors for the $\overline{X}$ chart and the D_{4S} factors for the R chart; g = the number of groups used to compute stage one control limits.

Stages one and two can be repeated periodically during the run, e.g., after the 5th, 10th, 15th etc. subgroup has been produced.

STAGE THREE: SET LIMITS FOR A FUTURE RUN

1. After the run is complete, combine the raw data from the entire run and perform the analysis as described in Stage One above. Use the results of this analysis to set limits for the next run, following the stage two procedure. If more than 25 groups are available, use a standard table of control chart constants, such as table one in the appendix.

NOTES ON THE EXACT METHOD

1. Stage Three assumes that there are no special causes of variation between runs. If there are, the process may go out of control when using the Stage Three control limits. In these cases, remove the special causes. If this isn't possible, apply this procedure to each run separately (i.e., start over each time).
2. This approach will lead to the use of standard control chart tables when enough data is accumulated.
3. The constants for subgroups of five is from Hillier (1969). The minimum number of subgroups recommended for groups of size two to five is from Proschan and Savage (1960) The control chart constants for the first stage are A_{2F} and D_{4F} (the "F" subscript stands for First-stage); for the second stage use A_{2S} and D_{4S} (the "S" stands for second stage.) These factors correspond to the A_2 and D_4 factors usually used, except that they are adjusted for the small number of subgroups actually available.

Setup Approval Procedure

The following procedure can be used to determine if a setup is acceptable using a relatively small number of sample units.

1. After the first-article approval, run n = 3 to 10 pieces *without adjusting the process.*
2. Compute the average and the range of the sample.
3. Compute $T = \left| \dfrac{average - target}{range} \right|$, use absolute values (i.e., ignore any minus signs.) The target value is usually the specification midpoint or nominal.
4. If T is less than the critical T in the table below, accept the setup. Otherwise adjust the setup to bring it closer to the target. NOTE: there is approximately 1 chance in 20 that an on-target process will fail this test.

n	3	4	5	6	7	8	9	10
Critical T	0.885	0.529	0.388	0.312	0.263	0.230	0.205	0.186

EXAMPLE

Assume we wish to use SPC for a process that involves producing a part in lots of 30 parts each. The parts are produced approximately once each month. The control feature on the part is the depth of a groove and we will be measuring every piece. We decide to use subgroups of size three and to compute the stage one control limits after the first five groups. The measurements obtained are shown in Table 15.1.

	Table 15-1 Raw Data for Example of Exact Method				
Subgroup	Sample Number			$\overline{X}$	R
Number	1	2	3		
1	0.0989	0.0986	0.1031	0.1002	0.0045
2	0.0986	0.0985	0.1059	0.1010	0.0074
3	0.1012	0.1004	0.1000	0.1005	0.0012
4	0.1023	0.1027	0.1000	0.1017	0.0027
5	0.0992	0.0997	0.0988	0.0992	0.0009

Using the data in table 15.1 we can compute the grand average and average range as

Grand average = 0.10053

Average range $(\overline{R})$ = 0.00334

From table five in the appendix we obtain the first stage constant for the range chart of $D_{4F} = 2.4$ in the row for g = 5 groups and a subgroup size of 3. Thus,

$$UCL_R = D_{4F} \times \overline{R} = 2.4 \times 0.00334 = 0.0080$$

All of the ranges are below this control limit, so we can proceed to the analysis of the averages chart. For the averages chart we get

$$LCL\overline{X} = \text{grand average} - A_{2F} \times \overline{R}$$
$$= 0.10053 - 1.20 \times 0.00334 = 0.09652$$

$$UCL\overline{X} = \text{grand average} + A_{2F} \times \overline{R}$$
$$= 0.10053 + 1.20 \times 0.00334 = 0.10454$$

All of the subgroup averages are between these limits. Now setting limits for the remainder of the run we use $D_4S = 3.4$ and $A_2S = 1.47$. This gives

$UCL_R = 0.01136$
$LCL_{\overline{X}} = 0.09562$
$UCL_{\overline{X}} = 0.10544$

If desired, this procedure can be repeated when a larger number of subgroups becomes available, say 10 groups. This would provide somewhat better estimates of the control limits, but it involves additional administrative overhead. When the entire run is finished you will have 10 subgroups of 3 per subgroup. The data from all of these subgroups should be used to compute stage one and stage two control limits. The resulting stage two control limits would then be applied to the *next run* of this part number.

By applying this method in conjunction with the code value charts or stabilized charts described below, the control limits can be applied to the next part(s) produced on this process (assuming the part-to-part difference can be made negligible). Note that if the standard control chart factors were used the limits for *both* stages would be

$UCL_R = 0.00860$
$LCL_{\overline{X}} = 0.09711$
$UCL_{\overline{X}} = 0.10395$

As the number of subgroups available for computing the control limits increases, the "short run" control limits approach the standard control limits. However, if the standard control limits are used when only small amounts of data are available there is a greater chance of erroneously rejecting a process that is actually in control.

Code Value Charts

This procedure allows the control of multiple features with a single control chart. It consists of making a simple transformation to the data, namely

$$\hat{x} = \frac{X - \textit{Target}}{\textit{unit of measure}} \tag{15.1}$$

The resulting $\hat{x}$ values are used to compute the control limits and as plotted points on the $\overline{X}$ and R charts. This makes the target dimension irrelevant for the purposes of SPC and makes it possible to use a single control chart for several different features or part numbers.

EXAMPLE

A lathe is used to produce several different sizes of gear blanks, as is indicated in figure 15.2.

Product engineering wants all of the gear blanks to be produced as near as possible to their nominal size. Process engineering believes that the process will have as little deviation for larger sizes as it does for smaller sizes. Quality engineering believes that the inspection system will produce approximately the same amount of measurement error for larger sizes as for smaller sizes. Process capa-

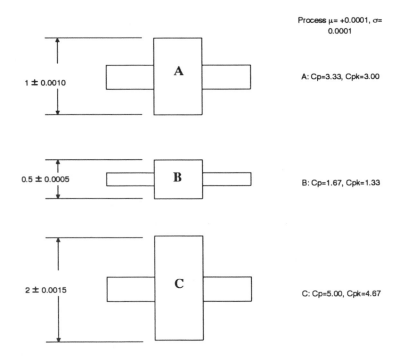

Figure 15-2-Some of the Gear Blanks to be Machined

bility studies and measurement error studies support these conclusions. I hope you are starting to get the idea that a number of assumptions are being made and that they must be valid before using code value charts.

Based on these conclusions, the code value chart is recommended. By using the code value chart the amount of paperwork will be reduced and more data will be available for setting control limits. Also, the process history will be easier to follow since the information won't be fragmented among several different charts. The data in table 15.2 show some of the early results.

Table 15-2 Deviation from Target in Hundred-Thousandths							
Part	Nominal	No.	Sample Number			X̄	R
			1	2	3		
A	1.0000	1	4	3	25	10.7	22
		2	3	3	39	15.0	36
		3	16	12	10	12.7	6
B	0.5000	4	21	24	10	18.3	14
		5	6	8	4	6.0	4
		6	19	7	21	15.7	14
C	2.0000	7	1	11	4	5.3	10
		8	1	25	8	11.3	24
		9	6	8	7	7.0	2

Note that the process must be able to produce the *tightest tolerance* of ±0.0005 inches (gear blank B.) The capability analysis should indicate its ability to do this; i.e., C_{pk} should be at least 1.33 based on the tightest tolerance. It will *not* be allowed to drift or deteriorate when the less stringently toleranced parts are produced. *Process control* is independent of the *product requirements*. Permitting the process to degrade to its worst acceptable (from the product perspective) level creates engineering nightmares when the more tightly toleranced parts come along again. It also confuses and demoralizes operators and others trying to maintain high levels of quality. Operators should be trained to control their own processes, which requires that they understand the relationship between product specifications and process control limits. They should also appreciate that *any* variation from the target value incurs some loss, even if the part is still within the specification limits.

The control chart of the data in table 15.2 is shown in figure 15.3. Since only nine groups were available, the exact method was used to compute the control limits. Note that the control chart shows the *deviations* on the $\overline{X}$ and R chart axes, not the actual measured dimensions, e.g., the value of Part A, subgroup #1, sample #1 was +0.00004" from the target value of 1.0000" and it is shown as a deviation of +4 hundred-thousandths; i.e., the part checked 1.00004". The stage one control chart shows that the process is in statistical control, but it is producing parts that are consistently too large - regardless of the nominal dimension. If the process were on target, the grand average would be very close to 0. The setup problem would have been detected by the second subgroup if the setup approval procedure described earlier in this chapter had been followed. This ability to see process performance across different part numbers is one of the advantages of Code Value Charts. It is good practice to actually identify the changes in part numbers on the charts, as is done in figure 15.3.

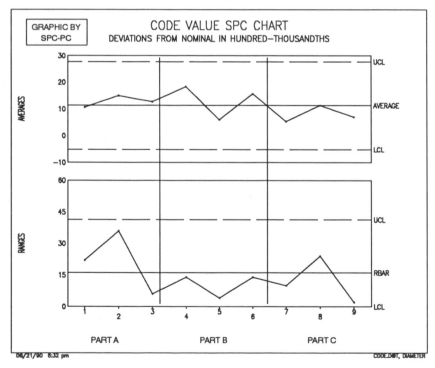

Figure 15-3-Code Value Chart of Table 15.2 Data

Stabilized Control Charts for Variables

All control limits, for standard sized runs or short and small runs, are based on methods that determine if a process statistic falls within limits that might be expected from chance variation alone. In most cases, the statistic is based on actual measurements from the process and it is in the same unit of measure as the process measurements. As we saw with code value charts, it is sometimes useful to transform the data in some way. With code value charts we used a simple transformation that removed the effect of changing nominal and target dimensions. While useful, this approach still requires that all measurements be in the same units of measurement, e.g., all inches, all grams, etc.. For example, all of the variables on the control chart for the different gear blanks had to be in units of hundred-thousandths of an inch. If we had wanted to plot, for example, the perpendicularity of two surfaces on the gear blank we would have needed a separate control chart because the units would be in degrees instead of inches. Stabilized control charts for variables overcome the units of measure problem by converting all measurements into standard, non-dimensional units. Such "standardizing transformations" are not new, they have been around for many years and they are commonly used in all types of statistical analyses. The two transformations we will be using here are shown in equations 15.2 and 15.3.

$$(\overline{X} \text{ - grand average}) / \overline{R} \qquad\qquad (15.2)$$

$$R / \overline{R} \qquad\qquad (15.3)$$

As you can see, equation 15.2 involves subtracting the grand average from each subgroup average (or from each individual measurement if the subgroup size is one) and dividing the result by $\overline{R}$. Equation 15.3 divides each subgroup range by the average range. Since the numerator and denominator of both equations are in the same unit of measurement, the unit of measurement cancels and we are left with a number that is in terms of the number of average ranges, $\overline{R}$'s. It turns out that control limits are also in the same units, i.e., to compute standard control limits we simply multiply $\overline{R}$ by the appropriate table constant to determine the width between the control limits.

Hillier (1969) noted that this is equivalent to using the transformations shown in equations 15.2 and 15.3 with control limits set at

$$-A_2 \leq (\overline{X} - \text{grand average}) / \overline{R} \leq A_2 \qquad (15.4)$$

for the individuals or averages chart. Control limits are

$$D_3 \leq R / \overline{R} \leq D_4 \qquad (15.5)$$

for the range chart. Duncan (1974) described a similar transformation for attribute charts, p charts in particular (see below) and called the resulting chart a "stabilized p chart." We will call charts of the transformed variables data stabilized charts as well.

Stabilized charts allow you to plot multiple units of measurement on the same control chart. The procedure described in this book for stabilized variables charts requires that all subgroups be of the same size[1]. When using stabilized charts the control limits are always fixed. The raw data are "transformed" to match the scale determined by the control limits. When only limited amounts of data are available, the constants in table five of the appendix should be used for computing control limits for stabilized variables charts. As more data become available, the table five constants approach the constants in standard tables of control chart factors. Table 15.3 summarizes the control limits for stabilized averages, stabilized ranges, and stabilized individuals control charts.

Table 15-3 Control Limits for Stabilized Charts						
Stage	Available groups		Chart			Appendix table
			$\overline{X}$	R	x	
One	25 or less	LCL	$-A_{2F}$	None	$-A_{2F}$	Five
		Average	0	1	0	
		UCL	$+A_{2F}$	D_{4F}	$+A_{2F}$	
Two	25 or less	LCL	$-A_{2S}$	None	$-A_{2S}$	Five
		Average	0	1	0	
		UCL	$+A_{2S}$	D_{4S}	$+A_{2S}$	
One or two	More than25	LCL	$-A_2$	D_3	-2.66	One
		Average	0	1	0	
		UCL	$+A_2$	D_4	+2.66	

The values for A_2, D_3 and D_4 can be found in table one in the appendix.

EXAMPLE

A circuit board is produced on an electroplating line. Three parameters are considered important for SPC purposes: lead concentration of the solder plating bath, plating thickness, and resistance. Process capability studies have been done using more than 25 groups; thus, from table 15.3, the control limits are

---

[1]   The procedure for stabilized attribute charts, described later in this chapter, allows varying subgroup sizes.

$-A_2 \le \overline{X} \le A_2$

for the averages control chart, and

$D_3 \le R \le D_4$

for the ranges control chart. The actual values of the constants A_2, D_3, and D_4 depend on the subgroup size, for subgroups of three $A_2=1.023$, $D_3=0$ and $D_4=2.574$.

The capabilities are given in table 15.4.

Table 15-4 Process Capabilities for Example			
Feature Code	Feature	Grand Average	Average Range
A	Lead %	10%	1%
B	Plating thickness	0.005"	0.0005"
C	Resistance	0.1Ω	0.0005Ω

A sample of three will be taken for each feature. The three lead concentration samples are taken at three different locations in the tank. The results of one such set of sample measurements is shown in table 15.5, along with their stabilized values.

Table 15-5 Sample Data for Example			
No.	Lead % (A)	Thickness (B)	Resistance (C)
1	11%	0.0050"	0.1000Ω
2	11%	0.0055"	0.1010Ω
3	8%	0.0060"	0.1020Ω
$\overline{X}$	10%	0.0055"	0.1010Ω
R	3%	0.0010"	0.0020Ω
$(x - \overline{x})/\overline{R}$	0	1	2
$R/\overline{R}$	3	2	4

On the control chart *only the extreme values are plotted*. This is a variation of the group control chart technique described in chapter 21. Figure 15.4 shows a stabilized control chart for several subgroups. Observe that the feature responsible for the plotted point is written on the control chart; features are identified by the feature code in table 15.4. If a long series of largest or smallest values come from the same feature it is an indication that the feature has changed. If the process is in statistical control for all features, the feature responsible for the extreme

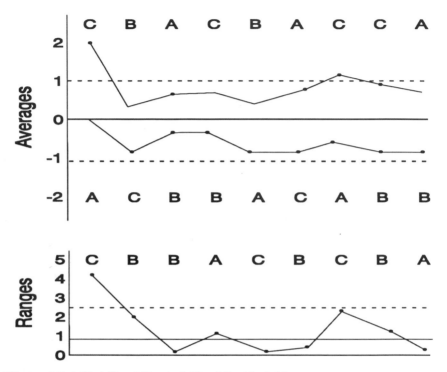

Figure 15-4-Stabilized Control Chart for Variables

values will vary randomly. Table six in the appendix can be used to determine if the same feature is showing up too often. See chapter 21 for a description of the run test procedure.

When using stabilized charts it is possible to have a single control chart accompany a particular part or lot of parts through the entire production sequence. For example, the circuit boards described above could have a control chart that shows the results of process and product measurement for characteristics at all stages of production. The chart would then show the "processing history" for the part or lot. The advantage would be a coherent log of the production of a given part. Table 15.6 illustrates a process control plan that could possibly use this approach.

Table 15-6 PWB Fab Process Capabilities & SPC Plan				
Operation	Feature	$\overline{X}$	$\overline{R}$	n
Clean	Bath Ph	7.5	0.1	3/hr
	Rinse contamination	100 ppm	5 ppm	3/hr
	Cleanliness quality rating	78	4	3pcs/hr
Laminate	Riston thickness	1.5mm	0.1mm	3pcs/hr
	Adhesion	7 in.-lbs.	0.2 in.-lbs.	3pcs/hr
Plating	Bath lead %	10%	1%	3/hr
	Thickness	0.005"	0.0005"	3pcs/hr
	Resistance	0.1Ω	0.0005Ω	3pcs/hr

A caution is in order if the processing history approach is used. When small and short runs are common, the history of a given process can be lost among the charts of many different parts. This can be avoided by keeping a separate chart for each distinct process; this involves additional paperwork, but it might be worth the effort. If the additional paperwork burden becomes large, computerized solutions may be worth investigating.

Attribute SPC for Small and Short Runs

When data is hard to come by, as it usually is when small or short runs are involved, you should use variables SPC if at all possible. A variables measurement on a continuous scale contains more information than a discrete attributes classification provides. For example, say a machine is cutting a piece of metal tubing to length. The specifications call for the length to be between 0.990" and 1.010" with the preferred length being 1.000" exactly. There are two methods available for checking the process. Method #1 involves measuring the length of the tube with a micrometer and recording the result to the nearest 0.001". Method #2 involves placing the finished part into a "go/not-go gage." With method #2 a part that is shorter than 0.990" will go into the "not-go" portion of the gage, while a part that is longer than 1.010" will fail to go into the "go" portion of the gage. With method #1 we can determine the size of the part to within 0.001" (assuming the measurement system was properly studied.) With method #2 we can only determine the size of the part to within 0.020"; i.e. either it is within the size tolerance, it's too short, or it's long. If the process could hold a tolerance of *less than 0.020"*, method #1 would provide the necessary information to hold the process to the variability it is capable of holding. Method #2 would not detect a process drift until out of tolerance parts were actually produced.

Another way of looking at the two different methods is to consider each part as belonging to a distinct category, determined by the part's length. We see that method #1 allows us to place any part that is within tolerance into one of twenty categories. When out of tolerance parts are considered, method #1 is able to place parts into even more than twenty different categories. Method #1 also tells us if the part is in the best category, namely within ±0.001" of 1.000"; if not, we know how far the part is from the best category. With method #2 we can place a given part into only three categories: too short, within tolerance, or too long. A part that is far too short will be placed in the same category as a part that is only slightly short. A part that is barely within tolerance will be placed in the same category as a part that is exactly on target.

SPC of Attributes Data from Short Runs

Special methods must be used for attributes data used to control short run processes. We will describe two such methods:

- Stabilized attribute control charts.
- Demerit control charts.

Stabilized Attribute Control Charts

When plotting attribute data statistics from short run processes we encounter two difficulties:

1. Varying subgroup sizes.
2. A small number of subgroups per production runs.

Item #1 results in messy charts with different control limits for each subgroup, distorted chart scales that mask significant variations, and chart patterns that are difficult to interpret because they are affected by both sample size changes and true process changes. Item #2 makes it difficult to track long-term process trends because the trends are broken up among many different control charts for individual parts. Because of these things, many people believe that SPC is not practical unless large and long runs are involved. This is not the case. In most cases stabilized attribute charts can be used to eliminate these problems. Although somewhat more complicated than classical control charts, stabilized attribute control charts offer a way of realizing the benefits of SPC with processes that are difficult to control any other way.

Stabilized attribute charts may be used if a process is producing part features that are essentially the same from one part number to the next. Production lot sizes and sample sizes can vary without visibly affecting the chart.

EXAMPLE ONE:

A lathe is being used to machine terminals of different sizes. Samples (of different sizes) are taken periodically and inspected for burrs, nicks, tool marks and other visual defects.

EXAMPLE TWO:

A printed circuit board hand assembly operation involves placing electrical components into a large number of different circuit boards. Although the boards differ markedly from one another, the hand assembly operation is similar for all of the different boards.

EXAMPLE THREE:

A job-shop welding operation produces small quantities of "one order only" items. However, the operation always involves joining parts of similar material and similar size. The process control statistic is weld imperfections per 100 inches of weld.

The techniques used to create stabilized attribute control charts are all based on corresponding classical attribute control chart methods. There are four basic types of control charts involved:

1. Stabilized p charts for proportion of defective units per sample.
2. Stabilized np charts for the number of defective units per sample.
3. Stabilized c charts for the number of defects per unit.
4. Stabilized u charts for the average number of defects per unit.

All of these charts are based on the transformation

$$Z = \frac{sample\ statistic - process\ average}{process\ standard\ deviation} \qquad (15.6)$$

In other words, stabilized charts are plots of the number of standard deviations (plus or minus) between the sample statistic and the long-term process average. Since control limits are conventionally set at ±3 standard deviations, stabilized control charts always have the lower control limit at -3 and the upper control limit at +3. Table 15.7 summarizes the control limit equations for stabilized control charts for attributes.

Table 15-7 Stabilized Attribute Chart Statistics					
Attribute	Chart	Sample statistic	Process average	Process σ	Z
Proportion defective units	p chart	p	$\bar{p}$	$\sqrt{\bar{p}(1-\bar{p})}$	$(p-\bar{p})/\sigma$
number of defective units	np chart	np	$\overline{np}$	$\sqrt{\overline{np}(1-\bar{p})}$	$(np-\overline{np})/\sigma$
defects per unit	c chart	c	$\bar{c}$	$\sqrt{\bar{c}}$	$(c-\bar{c})/\sigma$
average defects per unit	u chart	u	$\bar{u}$	$\sqrt{\bar{u}/n}$	$(u-\bar{u})/\sigma$

When applied to long runs, stabilized attribute charts are used to compensate for varying sample sizes; process averages are assumed to be constant. However, stabilized attribute charts can be created even if the process average varies. This is often done when applying this technique to short runs of parts that vary a great deal in average quality. For example, a wave soldering process used for several missiles had boards that varied in complexity from less than 100 solder joints to over 1,500 solder joints. Tables 15.8 and 15.9 show how the situation is handled to create a stabilized u chart. The unit size is 1,000 leads, set arbitrarily. It doesn't matter what the unit size is set to, the calculations will still produce the correct result since the actual number of leads is divided by the unit size selected. However, the unit size must be the same for all boards, e.g., if the unit is 1,000 leads, a board with 100 leads is $\frac{1}{10}$ unit, one with 2,000 leads is 2 units. $\bar{u}$ is the average number of defects per 1,000 leads.

Table 15-8 Data from a Wave Solder Process				
Missile	**Board**	**Leads**	**Units/board**	$\bar{u}$
Phoenix	A	1,650	1.65	16
	B	800	0.80	9
	C	1,200	1.20	9
TOW	D	80	0.08	4
	E	50	0.05	2
	F	100	0.10	1

EXAMPLE ONE

From the process described in Table 15.8 a sample of 10 TOW missile boards of type E are sampled. Three defects were observed in the sample. Using Tables 15.7 and 15.8 we compute Z for the subgroup as follows:

$\sigma = \sqrt{\bar{u}/n}$, We get $\bar{u} = 2$ from Table 15.8.

$$n = \frac{50 \times 10}{1000} = 0.5 units$$

$$\sigma = \sqrt{2/0.5} = \sqrt{4} = 2$$

$$u = \frac{number\ of\ defects}{number\ of\ units} = \frac{3}{0.5} = 6\ defects\ per\ unit$$

$$Z = \frac{u - \bar{u}}{\sigma} = \frac{6 - 2}{2} = \frac{4}{2} = 2$$

Since Z is between -3 and +3 we conclude that the process has not gone out of control, i.e., it is not being influenced by a special cause of variation.

Table 15.9 shows the data for several samples from this process. The resulting control chart is shown in figure 15.5. Note that the control chart indicates that the process was better than average when it produced subgroups 2 and 3 and perhaps 4. Negative Z values mean that the defect rate is below (better than) the long-term process average. Groups 7 - 8 show an apparent deterioration in the process with group 7 being out of control. Positive Z values indicate a defect rate above (worse than) the long term process average.

No.	Board	$\bar{u}$	units	# sampled	n	σ	de-fects	u	Z
1	E	2	0.05	10	0.50	2.00	3	6.00	2.00
2	A	16	1.65	1	1.65	3.11	8	4.85	-3.58
3	A	16	1.65	1	1.65	3.11	11	6.67	-3.00
4	B	9	0.80	1	0.80	3.35	0	0.00	-2.68
5	F	1	0.10	2	0.20	2.24	1	5.00	1.79
6	E	2	0.05	5	0.25	2.83	2	8.00	2.12
7	C	9	1.20	1	1.20	2.74	25	20.83	4.32
8	D	4	0.08	5	0.40	3.16	5	12.50	2.69
9	B	9	0.80	1	0.80	3.35	7	8.75	-0.07
10	B	9	0.80	1	0.80	3.35	7	8.75	-0.07

Table 15-9 Stabilized u Chart Data for Wave Solder

The ability to easily see process trends and changes like these in spite of changing part numbers and sample sizes, is the big advantage of stabilized control charts. The disadvantages of stabilized control charts are:

1. They convert a number that is easy to understand, the number of defects or defectives, into a confusing statistic with no intuitive meaning to operating personnel.

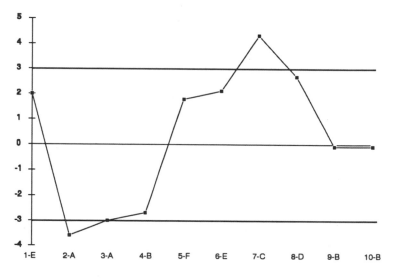

Figure 15-5 Control Chart of Z Values from Table 15.9

116

2. They involve tedious calculation.

Item #1 can only be corrected by training and experience applying the technique. Item #2 can be handled with computers; the calculations are simple to perform with a spreadsheet. Table 15.9 can be used as a guide to setting up the spreadsheet. Inexpensive programmable calculators can be used to perform the calculations right at the process, thus making the results available immediately.

Demerit Control Charts

As described above, there are two kinds of data commonly used to perform SPC: variables data and attributes data. When short runs are involved we can seldom afford the information loss that results from using attribute data. However, there are ways of extracting additional information from attribute data, they involve:

1. Making the attribute data "less discrete" by adding more classification categories.
2. Assigning weights to the categories to accentuate different levels of quality.

Consider a process that involves fabricating a substrate for a hybrid microcircuit. The surface characteristics of the substrate are extremely important. The "ideal part" will have a smooth surface, completely free of any visible flaws or blemishes. However, parts are sometimes produced with stains, pits, voids, cracks and other surface defects. Although imperfect, most of the less than ideal parts are still acceptable to the customer.

If we were to apply conventional attribute SPC methods to this process the results would probably be disappointing. Since very few parts are actually rejected as unacceptable, a standard p chart or stabilized p chart would probably show a flat line at "zero defects" most of the time, even though the quality level might be less than the ideal. Variables SPC methods can't be used because attributes data such as "stains" are not easily measured on a variables scale. Demerit control charts offer an effective method of applying SPC in this situation. To use demerit control charts we must determine how many imperfections of each type are found in the parts. Weights are assigned to the different categories. The quality score for a given sample is the sum of the weights times the frequencies of each category. Table 15.10 illustrates this approach for the substrate example.

Table 15-10 Demerit Scores for Substrates						
Subgroup No. →		1		2		3
Attribute	Weight	Freq.	Score	Freq.	Score	Freq.	Score
light stain	1	3	3				
dark stain	5			1	5	1	5
small blister	1			2	2	1	1
medium blister	5	1	5				
pit: 0.01-0.05mm	1					3	3
pit: 0.06-0.10	5			2	10		
pit: larger than 0.10 mm	10	1	10				
Total demerits →		18		17		9	

If the subgroup size is kept constant, the average for the demerit control chart is computed as follows (Burr, 1976),

$$\text{Average} = \overline{D} = \frac{sum\ of\ subgroup\ demerits}{number\ of\ subgroups} \tag{15.7}$$

Control limits are computed in two steps. First compute the average defect rate for each category. For example, we might have the following categories and weights

Category	Weight
Major	10
Minor	5
Incidental	1

We could compute three average defect rates, one each for major, minor and incidental. Let's designate these as

$\overline{c}_1$ = *Average number of major defects per subgroup*

$\overline{c}_2$ = *Average number of minor defects per subgroup*

$\overline{c}_3$ = *Average number of incidental defects per subgroup*

The corresponding weights are $W_1 = 10$, $W_2 = 5$, $W_3 = 1$. Using this notation we compute the demerit standard deviation for this three category example as

$$\sigma_D = \sqrt{W_1^2\,\overline{c}_1 + W_2^2\,\overline{c}_2 + W_3^2\,\overline{c}_3} \tag{15.8}$$

For the general case the standard deviation is

$$\sigma_D = \sqrt{\sum_{i=1}^{k} W_i^2\,\overline{c}_i} \tag{15.9}$$

The control limits are

$$LCL = \overline{D} - 3\sigma_D \qquad (15.10)$$

$$UCL = \overline{D} + 3\sigma_D \qquad (15.11)$$

If LCL is negative, it is set to zero.

Simplified Quality Score Charts

The above procedure, while correct, may sometimes be too burdensome to implement effectively. When this is the case a simplified approach may be used. The simplified approach is summarized as follows:

1. Classify each part in the subgroup the following classes (points are arbitrary)

Class	Description	Points
A	Preferred quality. All product features at or very near targets.	10
B	Acceptable quality. Some product features have departed significantly from target quality levels, but they are a safe distance from the reject limits.	5
C	Marginal quality. One or more product features are in imminent danger of exceeding reject limits.	1
D	Reject quality. One or more product features fail to meet minimum acceptability requirements.	0

2. Plot the total scores for each subgroup, keeping the subgroup sizes constant.
3. Treat the total scores as if they were variables data and prepare an individuals and moving range control chart or an $\overline{X}$ and R chart. These charts are described in Volume One, chapter 9 and in most texts on SPC.

Conclusion

Small runs and short runs are common in modern business environments. Different strategies are needed to deal with these situations. Advance planning is essential. Special variables techniques were introduced which compensate for small sample sizes and short runs by using special tables or mathematically transforming the statistics and charts. Attribute short run SPC methods were introduced that make process patterns more evident when small runs are produced. Demerit and scoring systems were introduced that extract more information from attribute data.

References

Burr, I.W. (1976), *Statistical Quality Control Methods,* Statistics: textbooks and monographs, Vol. 16. New York: Marcel-Dekker, Inc., pp. 140-142.

Duncan, A.J. (1974), *Quality Control and Industrial Statistics*, 4th ed., Homewood, IL: Irwin.

Foster, G. (1988), "Implementing SPC in low volume manufacturing," ASQC Quality Congress Transactions, pp 261-267, Milwaukee, WI: ASQC.

Hillier, F. S. (1969), "$\overline{X}$ and R-chart control limits based on a small number of subgroups," *Journal of Quality Technology,* Vol. 1, No. 1, January 1969, pp. 17-26.

Juran, J.M. (1988), *Juran's Quality Control Handbook, 4th Edition,* New York: McGraw-Hill.

Kane, V.E. (1988), *Defect Prevention,* Quality and Reliability, Vol. 17, New York: Marcel Dekker, Inc.

Proschan, F., and Savage, I.R., (1960), "Starting a control chart," *Industrial Quality Control,* Vol. 17, No. 3, Sept., 1960, pp. 12-13.

Seder, L. (1988), "Job shop industries," *Juran's Quality Control Handbook, 4th Edition,* Section 32, New York: McGraw-Hill.

CHAPTER 16

CUMULATIVE SUM (CUSUM) CHARTS

OBJECTIVES:
After completing this section you will:

- Understand when to use cusum process control schemes for variables, and when not to

- Learn how to use cusum process control schemes

Introduction

In SPC work the Shewhart control chart reigns supreme. Its simplicity, ease of use, and power makes it the preferred tool for most applications. However, there are times when a different tool is better. Cusum charts are such a tool. Cusum charts can be used to pick up small-to-medium sized process changes much faster than Shewhart charts, or to save sampling costs to detect changes of the same magnitude as a Shewhart chart.

Traditional Shewhart control charts use the most recent subgroup as an indicator of process control. The average and range are computed and plotted on a chart with control limits. A point exceeding the control limits indicates a process under the influence of special causes of variation. The use of Shewhart charts is recommended if:

- the process tends to go far out of control when special causes are present, say 2σ or more.

- small process changes are of little economic importance.

- simplicity in the process control procedure is extremely important.

- sampling costs are relatively small.

Cusum charts are recommended if:

- you need a faster indication of smaller changes. A "smaller change" is one in the range of 0.5σ - 2.0σ and "faster indication" means two to four times faster than a Shewhart chart with the same sample size.

- sampling costs are high and less sampling is important. A cusum chart will provide lower sampling costs for the same level of protection as a Shewhart chart.

- you need an indication of *when* the change occurred. Cusum charts provide reliable, objective estimates of when the process actually changed, something Shewhart charts are often unable to do.

- the process involves long runs. The methods described in chapter 15 for short runs are, generally, variations on the Shewhart charts. It is possible to use special cusum schemes, such as "fast initial response" (FIR) and exponentially weighted moving cusum schemes (Lucas, 1988), but these will not be discussed here in the interest of simplicity.

- the process variance is stable. The cusum charts described in this chapter assume that the process dispersion is stable.

- the process mean changes abruptly and infrequently and the change persists for several sampling intervals. Cusum charts do a poor job of detecting dramatic process changes that come and go quickly; Shewhart charts aren't much better. Large, sporadic effects from unknown causes are difficult to detect with anything other than massive inspection or sorting operations. Fortunately, this situation is not common in the real world. We usually know when something has been done which can have a big effect (e.g., an adjustment has been made) and the process can then be checked to verify it.

- the process can be set to run at a specified target value.

Combined plan

Most of the above "pros and cons" can be easily dealt with simply by using a combination of Shewhart control charts and cusum charts (Lucas, 1982). With this approach you would react to an out-of-control indication on *either chart*. Although this approach involves additional work, it is relatively minor since much of what is done can be used for both charts, for example, the subgroup average must be computed for both. If a combined plan is implemented, use the same subgroup size for both charts to avoid confusion.

When using a combined plan the Shewhart chart for averages will tend detect outliers which the cusum chart often misses. The cusum chart will pick up small changes in the process mean much sooner than the Shewhart chart. You should not use the run tests with the Shewhart charts, the cusum chart makes the run tests unnecessary. The range chart will detect changes in the process variance. There are two disadvantages to the combined plan approach. First, the added complexity and administrative burden associated with two different sets of charts. This will be kept to a minimum by maintaining the same sampling interval and subgroup size and by using the results of one calculation for both charts. A second problem is a slight increase in the number of "false alarms." Because both Shewhart charts and cusum charts have a small chance of indicating a problem when no problem exists, using both simultaneously increases the chance that one or the other will produce a false alarm. However, the false alarm probability of the cusum plans provided in this chapter is even less than the Shewhart charts' three chances per thousand, and the combined false alarm probability is less than five per thousand. Keeping false alarms down is another reason why run tests are not recommended when using the combined plan.

Procedure

Cusum plans have been discussed in the quality literature for at least three decades, but their use has always been limited. I believe that this is due in large part to the complexity involved in their design and use. I hope to avoid this by presenting an approach to designing cusum plans that is as simple as possible. Thus, all of the plans here are designed to have essentially the same statistical properties (probabilities are approximately matched to Shewhart charts). All are designed to use the same graph paper, which produces similar chart patterns for similar process behavior. Chart scales are forced into a relatively narrow range so that a limited number of V-masks are required. In other words, I have opted for an approach that is somewhat restrictive, but easy to apply. This approach to the design of cusum charts is modelled after the recommendations in Ewan (1962.) If you want to design a cusum plan customized to your particular application, consult the other references given at the end of this chapter.

The Shewhart control chart procedure has been discussed extensively in previous chapters and it will not be repeated here.

The cusum chart procedure described in this book is very simple. It is based on the use of a "v-mask," which is placed over a chart of plotted points. All of the plans presented here provide similar sensitivity to process changes, which is approximately the same as a Shewhart chart. However, these plans provide a much faster response to small or medium-sized process changes than their Shewhart brethren. The plans all assume a fixed physical chart scale, the english plans use graph paper with ten divisions per inch, metric plans use graph paper with 2mm divisions. Ten-by-ten and 2mm chart papers are widely available. The plans here will all provide cusum charts that look similar for processes that behave in a similar manner. In other words, a change of, say, 1σ will produce about the same pattern on all of the charts. This will make it easier for people using the charts to develop a "feel" for the interpretation of the charts. Figure 16.1 provides a worksheet for designing cusum charts.

1. The first step is a process capability analysis (PCA) using the approach described in chapter 13 of this book. Cusum charts require that you know what the process standard deviation is, at least approximately. This can only be determined if the process is in statistical control, which in turn requires a PCA. The PCA will also help you understand the process, which will be useful in investigating process changes signalled by the cusum chart. Since cusum charts flag smaller changes than Shew-hart charts, the special cause may sometimes be difficult to locate.

2. Cusum charts are based on economic considerations. The idea is that, as the process mean moves off the optimal target, losses increase. At some point the loss per unit time is large enough to justify investigating the cause. Specify the process change which justifies the investigation.

3. Divide the undesirable process change by the process standard deviation. This "standardizes" the change by restating it in standard deviation units instead of measurement units.

4. Determine the sample size by looking it up in table 16.2. As with all statistical procedures, larger sample sizes are required to obtain greater sensitivity. Table 16.2 provides sample sizes for process changes of 0.47σ to 1.50 or more sigma. It is my experience that finding special causes becomes difficult if the changes are much smaller than 1σ, but economics may justify the effort.

5. Determine the frequency of sampling. This is done by studying the results of the PCA. Observe the length of time that passes between out-of-control indications, find the minimum length of time T_{min}, and divide this by six. This is the recommended sampling interval. Modify this number if economic, engineering or administrative considerations make it necessary.

6. Find the standard error of the mean, Se.

7. Use Se to scale the vertical axis of the cusum chart. The plans presented here can be used if one vertical unit is between 1.30Se and 3.20Se.

8. Cusum charts are completely dependent on the way the chart is scaled. Since different chart scales will result in different patterns, even if the same data is plotted, there are twelve different V-masks for the different scale factors. The statistical properties are essentially the same for all plans, and the physical appearance of the charts are similar for similar processes. Using table 16.1 select the plan based on the scale factor k.

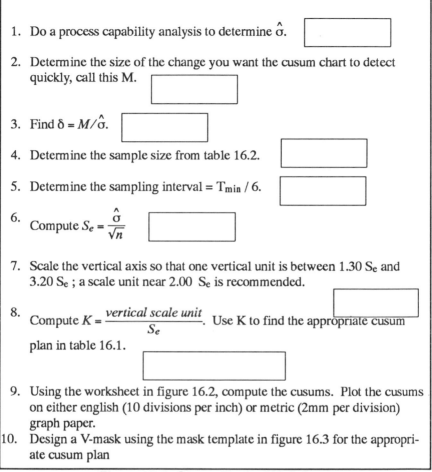

1. Do a process capability analysis to determine $\hat{\sigma}$.

2. Determine the size of the change you want the cusum chart to detect quickly, call this M.

3. Find $\delta = M/\hat{\sigma}$.

4. Determine the sample size from table 16.2.

5. Determine the sampling interval $= T_{min} / 6$.

6. Compute $S_e = \dfrac{\hat{\sigma}}{\sqrt{n}}$

7. Scale the vertical axis so that one vertical unit is between 1.30 S_e and 3.20 S_e ; a scale unit near 2.00 S_e is recommended.

8. Compute $K = \dfrac{vertical\ scale\ unit}{S_e}$. Use K to find the appropriate cusum plan in table 16.1.

9. Using the worksheet in figure 16.2, compute the cusums. Plot the cusums on either english (10 divisions per inch) or metric (2mm per division) graph paper.

10. Design a V-mask using the mask template in figure 16.3 for the appropriate cusum plan

Figure 16-1- Cusum Design Worksheet

9. Plot the cusums. Figure 16.2 contains a worksheet to be used for computing the cumulative sums for plotting. You must plot the cusums on plotting paper with 10 squares to the inch, or with 2mm divisions. None of the horizontal plot intervals should be skipped, i.e., there should be 10 plotted points to the inch on english graph paper or a plotted point every 2mm on metric graph paper.

10. There are two sets of v-masks provided in figure 16.3. The English plans in figure 16.3A are designed for use with plotting paper that has ten squares to the inch, both vertically and horizontally. The metric plans in

Table 16.1-Cusum Plan Selection Guide

K	Plan Number
Less than 1.30	No plan
1.30 - 1.39	1
1.40 - 1.49	2
1.50 - 1.59	3
1.60 - 1.69	4
1.70 - 1.79	5
1.80 - 1.89	6
1.90 - 2.09 (recommended)	7
2.10 - 2.19	8
2.20 - 2.39	9
2.40 - 2.59	10
2.60 - 2.89	11
2.90 - 3.20	12
Greater than 3.20	No plan

figure 16.3B are designed for use with plotting paper which has plotting intervals of 2mm. Ten-by-ten and 2mm graph paper is widely available in office and art supply stores.

How to use the cusum chart

With the approach described in this book it's easy to create and use cusum charts. You don't need to solve complex formulas or keep track of data with intricate tables. All you need to do is follow these steps.

1. Scale the cusum chart and select a plan as described above.
2. Trace the V-mask for the selected plan on a sheet of plain white paper, such as copy paper or graph paper with non-reproducing lines. Use a black pen which produces sharp, thin lines. Extend the two outside lines of the "V" until the width of the V-mask is at least twice as great as the vertical size of your cusum chart. Identify the plan number of the V-mask on the paper.
3. Copy the paper V-mask onto a clear transparency. This can be done on most copiers. DO NOT REDUCE OR ENLARGE THE V-MASK WHEN COPYING! Compare the copy to the master to verify that they are the same size. The paper V-mask can be used as a master to create as many V-mask transparencies as needed.

Table 16.2-Sample Size Selection Guide

δ	Sample Size (n)
1.50 or larger	1
1.06 - 1.49	2
0.87 - 1.05	3
0.75 - 0.86	4
0.67 - 0.74	5
0.61 - 0.67	6
0.57 - 0.60	7
0.53 - 0.56	8
0.50 - 0.52	9
0.47 - 0.49	10

4. Collect subgroups and compute the averages and cumulative sums, using the worksheet in figure 16.2. Cusums are the sum of the deviations of the subgroup $\overline{X}$s from the target value. For example, if the target is 10 and groups 1 and 2 have averages of 12 and 13 respectively, the first cusum is $12 - 10 = 2$ and the second cusum is $(2) + (13 - 10) = 5$.
5. Plot the cumulative sums on the chart. Place the V-mask over the most recently plotted point such that the "crosshair" symbol is centered over the plotted point. The line leading up to the crosshair should be parallel to the bottom axis. If all of the previously plotted points lie within the V-mask, the process is acceptable, otherwise, process mean has changed. The first point which lies outside of the mask indicates about when the process mean changed. If the cusum line has been increasing, then the process mean has shifted upward from the target; if the cusum line has been decreasing, then the process mean has shifted downward.
6. To estimate the new process mean, compute the grand average using only the data from the time the process mean changed as indicated by the cusum chart. Adjust the process so that the process average is brought back on target.

Cusum charts contain many more points than Shewhart charts. This is because cusum plans don't evaluate only the most recently plotted point, they evaluate the *pattern* of the plotted points. Thus, I recommend that when starting subsequent cusum charts you begin the new charts with at least the last ten cusums from the existing chart.

Example

This is example is based on an actual application.

No.	$\overline{X}$	Cusum	No.	$\overline{X}$	Cusum	No.	$\overline{X}$	Cusum
1			31			61		
2			32			62		
3			33			63		
4			34			64		
5			35			65		
6			36			66		
7			37			67		
8			38			68		
9			39			69		
10			40			70		
11			41			71		
12			42			72		
13			43			73		
14			44			74		
15			45			75		
16			46			76		
17			47			77		
18			48			78		
19			49			79		
20			50			80		
21			51			81		
22			52			82		
23			53			83		
24			54			84		
25			55			85		
26			56			86		
27			57			87		
28			58			88		
29			59			89		
30			60			90		

Part No.:

Part Name:

Dimension:

Target:

Notes

Figure 16.2-Cusum Plotting Worksheet

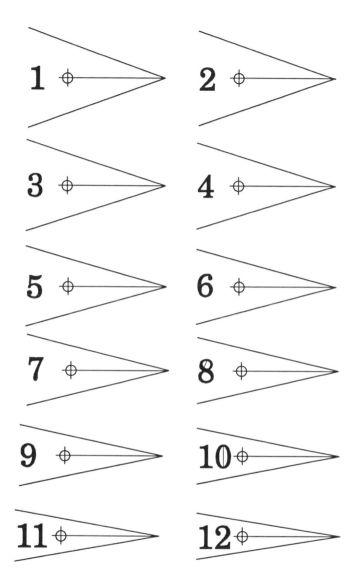

Figure 16.3A-Cusum Plans, English Version (10 div/inch)

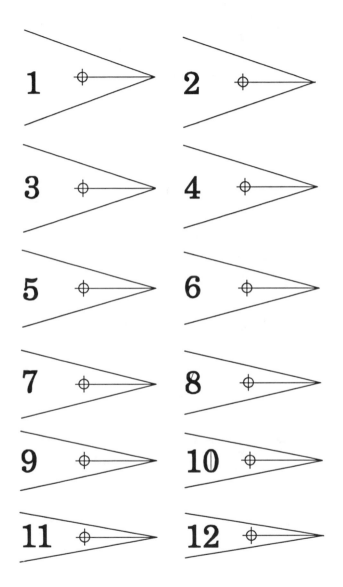

Figure 16.3B-Cusum Plans, Metric Version (2mm grid)

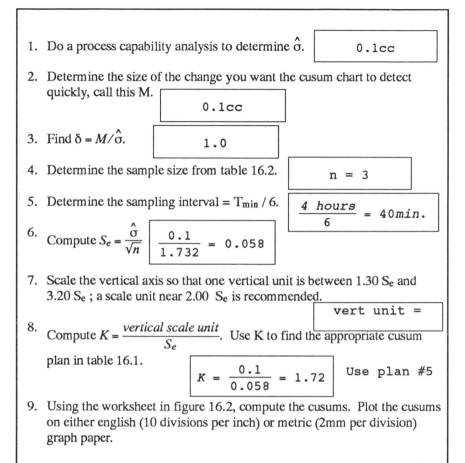

1. Do a process capability analysis to determine $\hat{\sigma}$.   `0.1cc`

2. Determine the size of the change you want the cusum chart to detect quickly, call this M.   `0.1cc`

3. Find $\delta = M/\hat{\sigma}$.   `1.0`

4. Determine the sample size from table 16.2.   `n = 3`

5. Determine the sampling interval $= T_{min} / 6$. $\dfrac{4\ hours}{6} = 40min.$

6. Compute $S_e = \dfrac{\hat{\sigma}}{\sqrt{n}}$ $\dfrac{0.1}{1.732} = 0.058$

7. Scale the vertical axis so that one vertical unit is between $1.30\ S_e$ and $3.20\ S_e$; a scale unit near $2.00\ S_e$ is recommended.   `vert unit =`

8. Compute $K = \dfrac{vertical\ scale\ unit}{S_e}$. Use K to find the appropriate cusum plan in table 16.1. $K = \dfrac{0.1}{0.058} = 1.72$ `Use plan #5`

9. Using the worksheet in figure 16.2, compute the cusums. Plot the cusums on either english (10 divisions per inch) or metric (2mm per division) graph paper.

10. Design a V-mask using the mask template in figure 16.3 A or B for the selected cusum plan. Use the V-mask to check the process.

Figure 16-4- Completed Design Worksheet for Example

A process involves filling bottles with nail enamel. The requirements call for putting 17cc to 19cc of nail enamel into each bottle. A process capability analysis provided the following information:

Grand average = 18.5cc

$\hat{\sigma} = 0.10cc$

The PCA indicated that the process usually ran at least four hours at one level before it changed. When it did change, it tended to run at its new level for several hours.

The first question to answer is: Is this a good cusum chart candidate? This is an economic question. To find the answer we must determine if the savings justify the added complexity and expense associated with cusum charts. We see immediately that the process mean is 1.5cc above the low specification. This represents $15\hat{\sigma}$! The people in charge of setting up the process felt that management's major concern was underfilling the bottle. Underfilled bottles might be a matter of concern to the FDA as well as the customer. Thus, the tendency was to run the process "to the high side." With a $15\hat{\sigma}$ "safety factor," underfilled bottles were certainly no concern, but what was the cost of this hyper-safe policy? And could cusum charts provide an economical alternative?

A cusum plan was setup where the process mean was set to $4\hat{\sigma}$ above the low specification, or 17.4cc. This would allow a process change of more than 1.5σ before violating FDA requirements which allowed a small percentage below the low specification. The size of the change we wanted the cusum procedure to detect was set at $1\hat{\sigma}$, which still provided a margin of safety. A shift of $1\hat{\sigma}$ would result in only about 1 bottle-per-thousand below the low specification, and then only until it was detected and corrected. The actual expected number of underfilled bottles in the delivered product was in the "parts-per-million" range, far better than FDA fill requirements specified.

A cost study showed the nail enamel cost to be about $15 per liter. Approximately 55 million bottles had been filled in the previous year. The material savings was 1.1cc per bottle. The dollar savings was estimated as

$$\$saved = \frac{1.1cc \times 55 \text{ million bottles} \times \$15/liter}{1,000 \text{ cc per liter}} = \$907,500 / year$$

The savings certainly justify the small increase in complexity added by using a cusum chart. The risk of underfilling is extremely small with this procedure. The design worksheet of this cusum plan is shown in figure 16.4. The data is shown in figure 16.5 (data recorded are the deviations from the target value of 17.4cc). Note that the cusum is restarted if an adjustment is made.

The cusum chart of the data in figure 16.5 is shown in figure 16.6. The V-mask is shown detecting the change at subgroup #67; when the V-mask is placed on

No.	$\overline{X}$	Cusum	No.	$\overline{X}$	Cusum	No.	$\overline{X}$	Cusum
1	0.009	0.009	31	-0.033	0.100	61	-0.007	0.263
2	0.046	0.055	32	-0.018	0.082	62	0.020	0.283
3	-0.135	-0.080	33	0.063	0.145	63	0.001	0.284
4	-0.162	-0.242	34	-0.009	0.136	64	-0.128	0.156
5	0.055	-0.187	35	-0.007	0.129	65	-0.144	0.012
6	-0.014	-0.201	36	-0.032	0.097	66	-0.121	-0.109
7	-0.022	-0.223	37	0.053	0.150	67	-0.073	-0.182[b]
8	-0.019	-0.242	38	0.059	0.209	68		
9	0.036	-0.206	39	0	0.209	69		
10	-0.107	-0.313	40	0.061	0.270	70		
11	-0.053	-0.366	41	0.054	0.324	71		
12	0.001	-0.365	42	0.070	0.394	72		
13	0.048	-0.317	43	-0.032	0.362	73		
14	-0.043	-0.360	44	-0.021	0.341	74		
15	0.068	-0.292	45	0.044	0.385	75		
16	0.102	-0.190	46	0.033	0.418	76		
17	0.033	-0.157	47	-0.016	0.402	77		
18	0.046	-0.111	48	-0.076	0.326	78		
19	0.030	-0.081	49	-0.047	0.279	79		
20	-0.015	-0.096	50	-0.099	0.180	80		
21	0.024	-0.072	51	0.091	0.271	81		
22	0.145	0.073	52	-0.076	0.195	82		
23	0.198	0.271[a]	53	-0.040	0.155	83		
24	0.041	0.041	54	0.014	0.169	84		
25	0.034	0.075	55	-0.032	0.137	85		
26	0.056	0.131	56	0.078	0.215	86		
27	0.026	0.157	57	0.073	0.288	87		
28	0.066	0.223	58	-0.002	0.286	88		
29	-0.063	0.160	59	0.027	0.313	89		
30	-0.027	0.133	60	-0.043	0.270	90		

Part No.: LC-2A122

Part Name: Dazzle

Dimension: Fill

Target: 17.4cc

Notes:

Using Plan #5, English scale.

(a) Adjusted @ #23, restarted cusum.

(b) Adjusted @ #67, restarted cusum.

Figure 16.5-Cusum Plotting Worksheet for Example

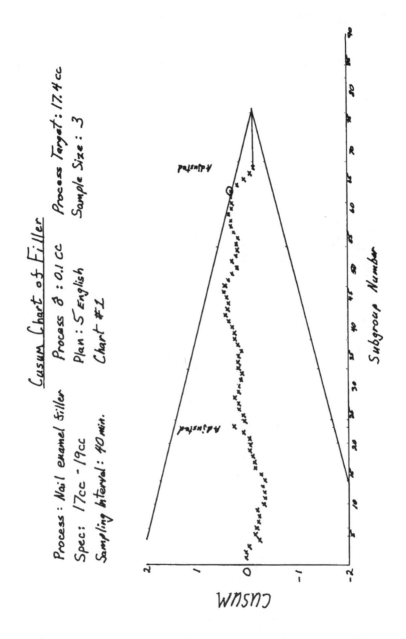

Figure 16.6-Cusum Chart for Example (English scale)

this point, point #63 falls outside of the V-mask. This indicates that the process mean changed at point #63. *This doesn't mean that you should reject everything that has been produced since that time!* Cusum charts are process control devices, **not** product sorting schemes. Because the cusum target was set $4\hat{\sigma}$ above the low specification and the cusum plan will detect $1\hat{\sigma}$ process changes very quickly, in all likelihood there was no product produced below the low specification.

Guidelines

Cusum charts can be made much more practical if a few common sense rules are used. The system described here will lead to the use of one of twelve plans; all have the same statistical properties. Since each plan is tied to a particular chart scale, the plan being used should be clearly marked on the chart itself (see figure 16.6). If this is not done someone may use the wrong V-mask and obtain an erroneous result.

To implement the cusum plan, produce several V-masks for each plan in advance. To produce the V-mask, use tracing paper and trace over the V-mask using figure 16.3. Mark the plan number clearly on the V-mask trace. The paper V-masks can be used as masters to create V-masks on transparency film using a copier.

References

Ewan, W.D. (1962), "When and how to use cusum charts," *Technometrics,* Vol. 5, No. 1, pp 1-22.

Johnson, N.L. and Leone, F.C. (1962), "Cumulative sum control charts - mathematical principles applied to their construction and use," *Industrial Quality Control,* Vol. 18, No. 12 and Vol. 19, Nos. 1-2, pp 15-21, 29-36, 22-28.

Lucas, J.M. (1976), "The design and use of v-mask control schemes," *Journal of Quality Technology,* Vol. 8, No. 1, pp 1-12.

Lucas, J.M. (1982), "Combined Shewhart-cusum quality control schemes," *Journal of Quality Technology,* Vol. 14, No. 2, pp 51-59.

Lucas, J.M. (1988), "Exponentially weighted moving average control," ASQC Annual Quality Congress Transactions, pp. 414-422.

Chapter 17

SPC FOR CONTINUOUS AND BATCH PROCESSES

OBJECTIVES
After completing this section you will

- Understand the distinction between continuous, batch and discrete processes
- Understand the reason traditional $\overline{X}$ and R charts often fail when applied to continuous and batch processes
- Know how to use one control chart to control two sources of variation simultaneously

Introduction

The "traditional" SPC tools were designed and developed in industries that produced discrete piece parts. It is not surprising that they don't work quite as well when applied to processes that don't produce discrete parts. The output from many continuous or batch processes comes in a variety of forms, for example

- continuous sheets of steel, paper, gypsum or some other material
- continuous extruded forms such as metal pipe or plastic tubing
- a flow of chemicals such as petroleum or solvents
- a stream of loose dry matter such as a ceramic powder, sugar or flour
- a slurry of solid matter in solution such as paint or syrup
- a coating applied to a base, such as coated paper, adhesive tape or audio magnetic tape
- a stream of a gaseous substance such as industrial gasses

The list can be extended indefinitely. Such processes are common. Fortunately, the fundamental principles of SPC can be applied just as successfully to these continuous or batch processes as they are to discrete processes. In fact, as we will see, many of the SPC techniques used for discrete processes can be used with continuous processes too, if it is done properly.

Continuous or batch versus discrete processes

There are a number of differences between continuous or batch and discrete processes. The differences have made it difficult for many to successfully use SPC with continuous or batch processes. It will be easier to understand the application of SPC to continuous or batch processes if we can see how traditional SPC actually implies a process that produces discrete parts.

Table 17.1 compares the characteristics of discrete and continuous or batch processes. After studying table 17.1, consider some of the words used in the instructions typically provided when most people or textbooks discuss the application of SPC.

- "select a rational subgroup"
- "draw a sample of consecutive items from the process"
- "always check the part in the same location"
- "the sensitivity of the $\overline{X}$ chart can be increased by using a larger subgroup size"
- "the range is computed by subtracting the smallest measurement in each subgroup from the largest"

When applying SPC to continuous or batch processes these instructions often sound like so much gibberish to the people in charge. If the process output is a pressurized industrial gas what is a "rational subgroup?" What are "consecutive units?" What is the "location on the part?" Can I really improve sensitivity by checking more samples?

To make it even more confusing, sometimes traditional SPC does work! Most continuous and batch processes have numerous discrete aspects to them. As the examples provided later in this chapter will show, when deciding whether the process is continuous, batch or discrete it is usually best to consider each variable within the process separately.

Table 17-1-Types of Processes Compared

Item	Discrete Process	Continuous/batch Process
Raw materials	Manufactured items; controllable.	Crude natural constituents; largely uncontrollable.
Process control	Manual or semi-automated; few in number; changing something produces an immediate result.	Often fully automated; many in number; changing something produces a delayed and gradual result.
Output	Piece parts or assemblies of piece parts; output can change instantaneously.	Flow of materials or bulk containers of materials; output changes gradually.

Statistical obstacles

The differences between continuous or batch and discrete processes create a number of statistical problems.

1. When sampling from processes that produce a continuous flow of output, such as a fluid or a gas, subgroups formed by taking samples at or near the same point in time will produce control limits for the X chart that are too close together. The process will appear to be out of control when it really isn't.

2. When sampling from processes that produce output in well-mixed batches, such as tank cars or truckloads of bulk material, subgroups formed by taking multiple samples from the batch will produce control limits for the X chart that are too close together. The process will appear to be out of control when it really isn't.

3. Some processes produce an output whose characteristics are determined by mixing inputs, as shown in figure 17.1. The output from the entire process cannot change instantaneously, it is "buffered" by the material already in the system. For example, if the input of ingredient A were to suddenly change drastically the output of ingredient A would change only gradually. The output from the entire process would change even more slowly. If X and R charts or X and moving range charts were used to monitor this process they would show the process to be out of control even if it was in perfect control. This would happen because these traditional SPC tools assume that each observation is completely independent of every other observation, which means the process must be capable of instantaneous change; this is known as the assumption of statistical independence. This clearly is-

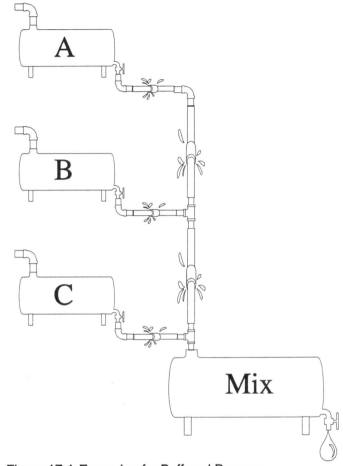

Figure 17-1-Example of a Buffered Process

n't the case with many continuous and batch processes. Although some quality experts maintain that statistical independence isn't all that important, my experience suggests otherwise where continuous processes are concerned.

Observe that this buffering effect would also apply to the tanks for the separate ingredients. We could not apply traditional SPC to the output of ingredient A, B or C any more than we can apply it to the output of the mixture of A, B and C. It may not be possible to measure each ingredient at the inlet into the tank either since the inlet pipe itself is a buffer.

4. Since we can't improve the sensitivity of the control chart simply by taking more samples, what can we do if we need to detect small changes in the process?
5. Continuous processes often involve the measurement of many similar characteristics, for example we may check the coating thickness of facsimile paper at several locations across the roll. If we created a separate control chart for each measurement we would have dozens, perhaps hundreds of control charts. This situation is intolerable from an administrative point of view.

Can anything be done? Yes. The remainder of this chapter describes alternative to traditional SPC.

Statistical alternatives for continuous or batch processes

Many of the problems experienced when applying traditional SPC to continuous or batch processes are caused by violating the assumption of statistical independence. It is quite simple to check the assumption of statistical independence with a scatter diagram, see volume one chapter 6 for a description of scatter diagrams. Table 17.2 contains the first three observations on the temperature of a solder flux bath. The first column shows the time the temperature reading was taken, the second column contains the temperature as recorded every five minutes, the third column has the same data as the first, except the readings are each shifted upward by one time interval. The scatter diagram will show the data in the second column on the horizontal (X) axis and the data in the third column on the vertical axis (Y). If the temperatures are truly independent, the scatter diagram will show a pattern with random scatter.

As the scatter diagram in figure 17.2 shows, the data with a lag of five minutes are not independent. As would be expected, there is a definite correlation between what the temperature is "now" and what the temperature was five minutes before. If the solder flux bath temperature is 165 degrees and we turned up the

Table 17-2-Testing for Statistical Independence

Time	Temperature (X)	Temperature Lagged (Y)
8:00 am	165.7	165.9
8:05 am	165.9	165.4
8:10 am	165.4	163.1

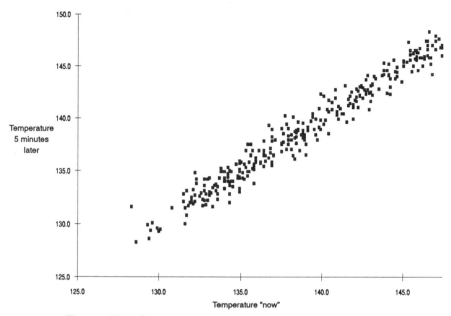

Figure 17-2-Scatter Diagram for Five Minute Time Lag

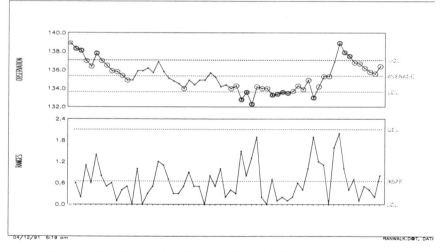

Figure 17-3-X, Moving Range Chart of Flux Temperature

heat source to the solder flux bath to 170 degrees, the temperature of the bath cannot change to 170 degrees instantly; it will change gradually. The solder flux process, like the process shown in figure 17.1, is buffered. If the temperature at the source is in statistical control, changes in the bath temperature will still gradually occur; we say such a process is on a "random walk." A traditional $\overline{X}$ and R chart or X and moving range chart will not work with data like that shown in table

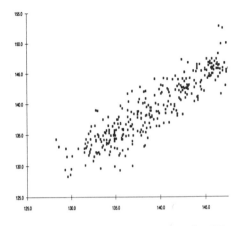

Figure 17-4A-Scatter Diagram for 25 Minute Time Lag

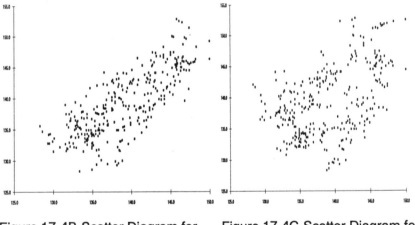

Figure 17-4B-Scatter Diagram for 50 Minute Time Lag

Figure 17-4C-Scatter Diagram for 100 Minute Time Lag

17.2. Figure 17.3 shows the X and moving range chart of the temperature data. Note that the moving range chart shows statistical control while the X chart is out of control. That is because the temperature *changes* are statistically independent, although the magnitude of the change is determined by how often the process is checked. In other words, the amount the temperature can change in five minutes is smaller than the amount of change that can appear in an hour. Of course, the information in the moving range chart is of limited value since it

142

doesn't tell us what the solder flux bath temperature actually is, only how much it has changed since the last time it was checked. A gradual increase or decrease in the temperature would not be detected by the moving range chart by itself, even though the final result might be a big change in the temperature of the solder flux bath.

Let me emphasize that the process shown in figure 17.3 is actually in statistical control! No special causes are affecting this process. The apparent out-of-control condition is caused by using the wrong SPC tool for this batch process. There are many ways to deal with this situation. One way is to use a different control chart; in chapter 18 we describe one such control chart, the exponentially weighted moving average (EWMA) chart, cusum charts can also be used (see chapter 16.) In this chapter we will discuss a simpler method that can be used for a large percentage of the cases encountered in practice.

We can use the fact that the process cannot change instantaneously to our advantage. Since it takes time for changes to appear, why not check the process less frequently? After all, the purpose of SPC is to detect important changes and if important changes can't happen in a short time interval it makes no sense to check the process frequently.

The question arises: how long should the time interval between samples be? The answer, from a purely statistical perspective, is as long as necessary to obtain approximate statistical independence between consecutive samples.

Again, scatter diagrams can help provide the answer. Figures 17.2 and 17.4A, 17.4B and 17.4C show scatter plots for different time lags for the solder flux bath temperature. On each figure, the bottom axis shows the temperature at a given point in time, while the vertical axis shows the temperature at a later point in time. If the time interval is short, the two temperatures are highly correlated. As the time between samples is extended, the correlation becomes weaker and weaker; when the time interval is 100 minutes, the correlation is negligible (figure 17.4C).

This implies that the process can be checked about once every two hours, the results could then be plotted on a traditional control chart, such as the X and moving range chart. This reduces our sampling costs by a factor of 24! With the longer time interval, a controlled process will show statistical control on both the X and moving range control charts.

This solution has an advantage over the use of the EWMA or cusum charts in that most people who have had SPC training already understand these charts.

However, it has the disadvantage of leaving a two-hour gap between process samples. The fact that the observations are statistically independent means that the process can change quite dramatically in the elapsed time, although a large change may be unlikely. If this presents a serious problem, as determined by SPC team discussions, the process must be checked more often. Since checking the process more often will produce data that are not statistically independent, the X chart cannot be used. In these situations, another SPC tool, such as the EWMA chart or cusum chart, should be considered.

Two-way Control Charts

One problem commonly encountered when trying to apply SPC to continuous and batch processes is enormous number of charts that result. The operators are so overwhelmed by the massive display of paperwork that they can't see the forest for the trees. One solution to this problem is the group control chart described in chapter 21 In this section we will present an example of a continuous process that would benefit from the application of a group control chart. Consider the process shown in figure 17.5. The process output is a continuous sheet of coated paper, which is cut into discrete rolls. A sample is taken from the front of each roll and measurements of the coating thickness are taken in three places across the sheet. The variation among the three readings provides a measure of the process consistency across the sheet. The average coating weight of the three readings for each roll provide a measure of the consistency along the sheet. Since the variation across the sheet is likely to be much smaller than the variation along the sheet, traditional $\overline{X}$ and R charts using the three readings as a subgroup are not advised.

How should SPC be applied to such a process? The brute-force answer is to create three separate control charts, one for each sample location on the sheet. This would be statistically correct, but in a real-world operation the result would be too many control charts. What is needed is a single control chart that shows the process state both across and along the sheet simultaneously.

The group control chart described in chapter 21 can be applied to this situation. This special control chart was designed for discrete processes, so it may be difficult to see the application to this continuous process. The key is to think of the three positions across the sheet as representing three different process streams. The output from each of the three streams is hypothetically identical. With this in mind, the methods described in chapter 21 can be applied to create one control chart to control this process. In fact, a single control chart would result even

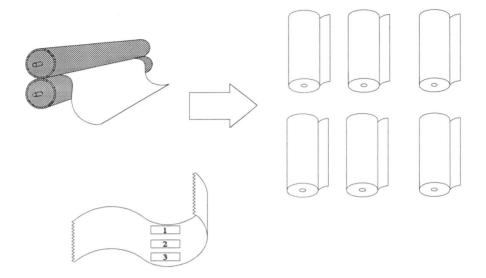

Figure 17-5-A Paper Coating Process

if more than three specimens were taken. You could also take multiple readings at a given position to create a group $\overline{X}$ and R chart. In real-world applications you would likely have several rolls cut across a single large sheet, and multiple coaters producing the sheets. By using the group control chart you could monitor everything with a single control chart. However, although it is possible to have only one chart, you would probably want separate control charts for each coater. The objective isn't to mindlessly minimize the number of charts, it is to minimize the number of charts while providing good information regarding process quality.

Examples

Bottling

Figure 17.6 shows a bottling process. The operation consists of filling small containers, the bottles, with the contents of larger containers, the drums. This simple process is representative of many similar processes encountered in practice. For example, the drums are themselves small containers filled from even larger containers, e.g., a tank car. The tank car is in turn filled at a centralized storage tank. The storage tank is filled from the refinery, a continuous process and therefore conceptually infinite. All of these processes have a great deal in common when thinking about them for SPC purposes.

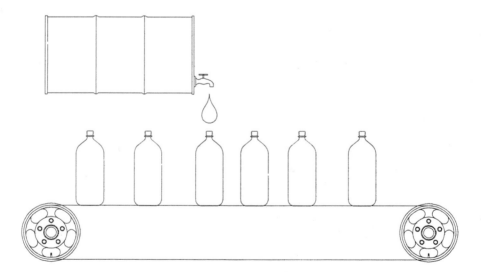

Figure 17-6-A Bottling Process

The bottling process has both discrete and continuous elements. The discrete elements include variables dependent on the bottles themselves and the filler. For example, the amount of material in each bottle can be handled as a discrete variable. In the real world filling processes usually involve fillers with multiple heads. A group control chart (see chapter 21) can be used to track all of the heads with one chart.

Other elements of the process are continuous in nature. Any variable associated with the drum of material is inherently continuous. For example, if the material being bottled was nail polish, the viscosity of the nail polish would change very little for a given drum and a control chart showing the viscosity of the nail polish would probably show very little change until the drum was changed. The drum's contents flow into the bottles continuously. Also, the filler will have a certain amount of material that will gradually change when the drum runs empty and is replaced with another drum. The control chart would show a gradual change to the new level. A traditional control chart might work if the viscosity were tracked drum-to-drum, but it would fail if applied to the viscosity bottle-to-bottle. I say it "might work drum-to-drum" because, remember, that the drums themselves may be small containers created from a larger batch of homogenous material in, say, a tank car or a storage tank.

Extrusion and coating

Figure 17.7 shows the output of a simple wire-coating process. A spool of wire is placed on the process and an electrically insulating material is placed on the wire in a continuous operation. Variations of this type of process are common and they can become quite complex, a few examples are shown in figure 17.8. Again, we will have both continuous and discrete variables to deal with. Most of the variables associated with the coating itself are continuous. Plastic coatings are usually formed by the mechanical mixing of several constituents under controlled conditions of temperature and pressure. The constituents are usually stored in hoppers and the hoppers are in turn filled from bags or drums. The hoppers act as buffers, preventing instantaneous change in the properties of the final material. Therefore, traditional control charts should not be used for variables associated with the material properties.

Other variables may behave as though they were discrete. For example, mechanical properties of the coating, such as thickness, may be dominated by process elements that can and do change instantaneously. If the coating is placed on the wire as the wire is drawn past a nozzle or through a vat of material, the

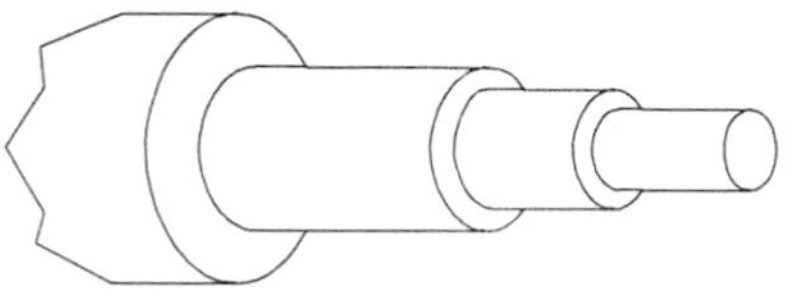

Figure 17-7-A Simple Coating & Extrusion Process

speed of the wire may be the dominant factor. If so, the coating thickness may be discrete, allowing the use of traditional control charts. However, if the temperature of the coating material is the dominant factor, coating thickness may act as if it were continuous. Unfortunately, there is no way of knowing which situation exists without studying the process and thinking carefully about what is actually happening.

The properties of the wire may also have an influence. The wire on a given spool is probably quite consistent, with spool-to-spool variation dominating. Thus, if control charts are to be used to track wire quality, you should probably use individuals and moving range charts to track variability spool-to-spool. Use of traditional $\overline{X}$ charts with subgroups of samples from one spool is not recommended because within-spool readings are probably highly correlated.

Distillation

Distillation occurs when a liquid is heated until some of its molecules escape as a gas. The molecules return to a liquid state when they encounter a colder medium and condense. Some substances evaporate more readily than others, some don't evaporate at all. Thus, distillation is used to separate evaporable from non-evaporable substances and to separate substances which evaporate at different rates.

Distillation processes are very common in modern industry. Distillation is one of the most important methods of purifying volatile substances. It is also used to extract substances with different properties from raw materials, for example, crude oil is distilled into such diverse materials as propane, gasoline and asphalt.

148

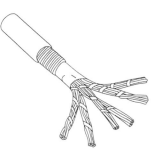

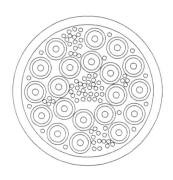

Figure 17-8-Coating, Extrusion and Assembly Processes

As with the previous examples, there are both discrete and continuous aspects in the distillation process. The discrete variables appear in the containerized output, such as tankers of gasoline. The continuous variables appear in the buffered portions of the process. In many distillation processes the material to be processed is in raw natural form, such as crude oil. The constituents of the raw material are vital to the output of the process, but difficult or impossible to control at the source. The process is modified to compensate for the variability in the input. The objective of the distillation process is, however, the same as it is for any process: consistent quality of output at the highest level possible. SPC is one tool used to accomplish this.

Often, the buffering in the distillation process is quite extensive. For example, before crude oil reaches the refinery it is pumped from several oil fields, loaded on to huge tankers, transported to storage tanks at a seaport, and then pumped into several storage tanks at the refinery through a pipeline. In some cases the storage tanks at the refinery contain oil from several pipelines. However, unlike other buffered processes, the consistency of the material in the buffer can't be assumed. With most standard operations, the buffered material is processed to a homogeneous state before being placed in the buffer. For example, every drop of the material in the barrel of nail polish was produced under essentially the same conditions. This is not the case with buffered raw materials, which may be quite different from location-to-location within the buffer. Thus, frequent sampling of materials coming from the buffers is important. However, any given sequence of samples may still exhibit the lack of independence which is characteristic of buffered processes. Thus, traditional control charts may not always work well. As is often the case, there is no single recipe for setting up SPC with this type of process.

In situations like this, the best course is to start SPC and to learn by carefully thinking about the results. The true purpose of SPC is to accelerate learning. By collecting valid data and presenting it in graphical form, you will see things that you would not otherwise see. You will have the opportunity to learn from what you see. You may see, for example, that the input material variation follows a pattern; perhaps there are a few levels that tend to repeat themselves over time. This new knowledge may help you develop a new strategy for changing your process settings to compensate, perhaps you will even invent a new process that is robust to these changes (i.e., a process insensitive to these changes.) The important thing is acquisition of the knowledge, nothing can occur until then.

Chapter 18

SPC FOR AUTOMATED MANUFACTURING

OBJECTIVES
After completing this section you will

- Understand the special aspects of automated manufacturing
- Understand the reason traditional $\overline{X}$ and R charts often fail when applied to automated manufacturing
- Know how to use SPC to monitor special and common causes of variation in automated manufacturing processes
- Understand the complementary relationship between SPC and Automated Process Control (APC)

Introduction

The "traditional" SPC tools were designed and developed in the era before automatic process control was possible. It is not surprising that they don't work quite as well when applied to fully automated processes. Compared to traditional manufacturing, automated manufacturing operations have several distinctive characteristics

- they operate with very little human intervention
- it is possible to sense some departures from target and make adjustments *before* the part is produced
- there is an abundance, perhaps an overabundance of process data, rather than a scarcity of data as with traditional manufacturing
- complex methods of analysis are possible because they are "transparent" to the human beings who operate the process
- special methods are sometimes required because the data are serially correlated, i.e., the observations are not statistically independent

151

- forecasting methods are useful in detecting and reacting to trends automatically
- automated processes often have inherent cycles and drift that make it impossible to use regular SPC techniques

All of these things impact the way in which SPC is applied. However, the basic principles of SPC remain unchanged. When dealing with automated manufacturing processes we are still trying to determine when special causes are affecting the process. However, in many cases we will need to use different tools to operationally define a special cause. The definition of control does not change, it is still as defined by Shewhart (1931, 1980)

> *A phenomenon will be said to be controlled when, through the use of past experience, we can predict, at least within limits, how the phenomenon may be expected to vary in the future.*

Like traditional methods, some of the methods described in this chapter are designed to provide an operational definition of a special cause. However, unlike traditional SPC techniques, we will describe other methods which deal with common causes exclusively. Traditional SPC methods require that common cause variation be left chance; we will see that, at times, common cause variation from automated manufacturing processes require active intervention to minimize economic loss.

SPC techniques for automated manufacturing

Many people erroneously believe that statistics are not needed when automated manufacturing processes are involved. Since we have measurements from every unit produced, they reason, sampling methods are inappropriate. We will simply correct the process when the characteristic is not on target.

This attitude reflects a fundamental misunderstanding of the relationship between a process and the output of a process. It also shows a lack of appreciation for the intrinsic variability of processes and of measurements. The fact is, even if you have a "complete" data record of every feature of every part produced, you still have only a sample of the output of the process. The process is future-oriented in time, while the record of measurements is past-oriented. Unless statistical control is attained, you will be unable to use the data from past production to predict the variability from the process in the future (refer to the definition of statistical control above.) And without statistical tools you have no sound basis for the belief that statistical control exists.

Another reason process control should be based on an understanding and correct use of statistical methods is the effect of making changes without this understanding. Consider, for example, the following process adjustment rule:

> *Measure the diameter of the gear shaft. If the diameter is above the nominal size, adjust the process to reduce the diameter. If the diameter is below the nominal size, adjust the process to increase the diameter.*

The problem with this approach is described by Deming's "funnel rules" (Deming, 1986, pp 327-334.) This approach to process control will *increase* the variability of a statistically controlled process by 141%, certainly not what the process control engineer had in mind. The root of the problem is a failure to realize that the part measurement is a sample from the process and, although it provides information about the state of the process, the information is incomplete. Only through by using proper statistical methods can the information be extracted, analyzed and understood.

Problems with traditional SPC techniques

A fundamental assumption underlying traditional SPC techniques is that the observed values are independent of one another. Although the SPC tools are quite insensitive to moderate violations of this assumption (Wheeler, 1991), automated manufacturing processes often breach the assumption by enough to make traditional methods fail (Alwan and Roberts, 1989.) By using scatter diagrams, as described in the previous chapter, you can determine if the assumption of independence is satisfied for your data. If not, you should consider using the methods described below instead of the traditional SPC methods.

A common complaint about non-standard SPC methods is that they are usually more complex than the traditional methods (Wheeler, 1991.) This is often true. However, when dealing with automated manufacturing processes the analysis is usually handled by a computer. Since the complexity of the analysis is totally invisible to the human operator, it makes little difference. Of course, if the operator will be required to act based on the results, he or she must understand how the results are to be used. The techniques described in this chapter which require human action are interpreted in much the same way as traditional SPC techniques.

Special and common cause charts

When using traditional SPC techniques the rules are always the same, namely

1. As long as the variation in the statistic being plotted remains within the control limits, leave the process alone.
2. If a plotted point exceeds a control limit, look for the cause.

This approach works fine as long as the process remains static. However, the mean of many automated manufacturing processes often drift because of inherent process factors. In other words, the drift is produced by *common causes*. In spite of this, there may be known ways of intervening in the process to compensate for the drift. Traditionalists would say that the intervention should be taken in such a way that the control chart exhibits only random variation. However, this may involve additional cost. Mindlessly applying arbitrary rules to achieve some abstract result, like a stable control chart, is poor practice. All of the options should be considered.

One alternative is to allow the drift to continue until the cost of intervention equals the cost of running off-target. This alternative can be implemented through the use of a "common cause chart." This approach, described in Alwan and Roberts (1989) and Abraham and Whitney (1990), involves creating a chart of the process mean. However, unlike traditional $\overline{X}$ charts, there are no control limits. Instead, *action limits* are placed on the chart. Action limits differ from control limits in two ways

- They are computed based on costs rather than on statistical theory.

- Since the chart shows variation from common causes, violating an action limit does not result in a search for a special cause. Instead, a prescribed action is taken to bring the process closer to the target value.

These charts are called "common cause charts" because the changing level of the process is due to built-in process characteristics. The process mean is tracked by using exponentially weighted moving averages (EWMA.) While somewhat more complicated than traditional $\overline{X}$ charts, EWMA charts have a number of advantages for automated manufacturing.

- they can be used when processes have inherent drift.

- EWMA charts provide a forecast of where the next process measurement will be. This allows feed-forward control.

- EWMA models can be used to develop procedures for dynamic process control, as described later in this section.

EWMA common cause charts

When dealing with a process that is essentially static, the predicted value of the average of the every sample is simply the grand average. EWMA charts, on the other hand, use the actual process data to determine the predicted process value for processes that may be drifting. If the process has trend or cyclical components, the EWMA will reflect the effect of these components. Also, the EWMA chart produces a forecast of what the *next* sample mean will be; the traditional $\overline{X}$ chart merely shows what the process was doing at the time the sample was taken. Thus, the EWMA chart can be used to take preemptive action to prevent a process from going too far from the target.

If the process has inherent non-random components, an EWMA common cause chart should be used. This is an EWMA chart with economic action limits instead of control limits. EWMA control charts, which are described in the next section, can be used to monitor processes that vary within the action limits.

The equation for computing the EWMA is

$$EWMA = \hat{y}_t + \lambda(y_t - \hat{y}_t) \tag{18.1}$$

In this equation $\hat{y}_t$ is the predicted value y at time period t, y_t is the actual value at time period t, and λ is a constant between 0 and 1. If λ is close to 1, equation 18.1 will give little weight to historic data; if λ is close to 0 then current observations will be given little weight. EWMA can also be thought of as the forecasted process value at time period t+1, in other words, $EWMA = \hat{y}_{t+1}$.

Since most people already understand the traditional $\overline{X}$ chart, thinking about the relationship between $\overline{X}$ charts and EWMA charts can help you understand the EWMA chart. It is interesting to note that traditional $\overline{X}$ charts give 100% of the weight to the current sample and 0% to past data. This is roughly equivalent to setting $\lambda = 1$ on an EWMA chart. In other words, the traditional $\overline{X}$ chart can be thought of as a special type of EWMA chart where past data is considered to be unimportant (assuming run tests are not applied to the Shewhart chart.) This is equivalent to saying that the data points are all independent of one another. In contrast, the EWMA chart uses the information from all previous samples. Although equation 18.1 may look as though it is only using the results of the most recent data point, in reality the EWMA weighting scheme applies progressively less weight to each sample result as time passes. Figure 18.1 compares the weighting schemes of EWMA and $\overline{X}$ charts.

In contrast, as lambda approaches 0 the EWMA chart begins to behave like a cusum chart (see chapter 16.) With a cusum chart all previous points are given

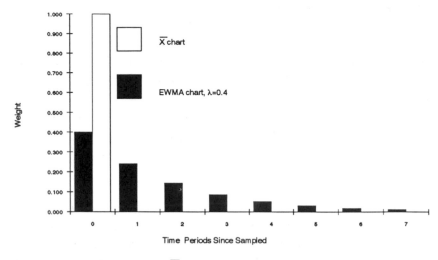

Figure 18-1-$\overline{X}$ versus EWMA Weighting

equal weight. Between the two extremes the EWMA chart weights historical in importance somewhere between the traditional Shewhart chart and the cusum chart. By changing the value of lambda the chart's behavior can be "adjusted" to the process being monitored.

In addition to the weighting, there are other differences between the EWMA and the $\overline{X}$ chart. The "forecast" from the $\overline{X}$ chart is always the same: the next data point will be equal to the historical grand average. In other words, the $\overline{X}$ chart treats all data points as coming from a process that doesn't change its central tendency (implied when the forecast is always the grand average.)[1]

When using an $\overline{X}$ chart it is not essential that the sampling interval be kept constant. After all, the process is supposed to behave as if it were static. However, the EWMA chart is designed to account for process drift and, therefore, the sampling interval should be kept constant when using EWMA charts. This is usually not a problem with automated manufacturing.

Example

Krishnamoorthi (1991) describes a mold line that produces green sand molds at the rate of about one per minute. The molds are used to pour cylinder blocks for

---

[1]   We aren't saying this situation actually exists, we are just saying that the $\overline{X}$ chart treats the process *as if* this were true. Studying the patterns of variation will often reveal clues to making the process more consistent, even if the process variation remains within the control limits.

large size engines. Application of SPC to the process revealed that the process had an assignable cause that could not be eliminated from the process. The mold sand, which was partly recycled, tended to increase and decrease in temperature based on the size of the block being produced and the number of blocks in the order. Sand temperature is important because it affects the compactability percentage, an important parameter. The sand temperature could not be better controlled without adding an automatic sand cooler, which was not deemed economical. However, the effect of the sand temperature on the compactability percent could be made negligible by modifying the amount of water added to the sand so feed-forward control was feasible.

Although the author doesn't indicate that EWMA charts were used for this process, it is an excellent application for EWMA common cause charts. The level of the sand temperature doesn't really matter, as long as it is known. The sand temperature tends to drift in cycles because the amount of heated sand depends on the size of the casting and how many are being produced. A traditional control chart for the temperature would indicate that sand temperature is out-of-control, which we already know. What is really needed is a method to predict what the sand temperature will be the next time it is checked, then the operator can add the correct amount of water so the effect on the sand compactability percent can be minimized. This will produce an in-control control chart for compactability percent, which is what really matters.

The data in table 18.1 show the EWMA calculations for the sand temperature data. Using a spreadsheet program, Microsoft Excel for Windows, the optimal value of λ, that is the value which provided the "best fit" in the sense that it produced the smallest sum of the squared errors, was found to be close to 0.9. Figure 18.2 shows the EWMA common cause chart for this data, and the raw temperature data as well. The EWMA is a *forecast* of what the sand temperature will be the next time it is checked. The operator can adjust the rate of water addition based on this forecast.

EWMA control charts

Although it is not always necessary to put control limits on the EWMA chart, as shown by the above example, it is possible to do so when the situation calls for it. Three sigma control limits for the EWMA chart are computed based on

$$\sigma_{EWMA}^2 = \sigma^2 [\lambda/(2-\lambda)] \tag{18.2}$$

Table 18-1-Data for EWMA chart of sand temperature

Sand Temp	EWMA	Error
125	125.00*	0.00
123	125.00	-2.00**
118	123.20***	-5.20
116	118.52	-2.52
108	116.25	-8.25
112	108.83	3.17
101	111.68	-10.68
100	102.07	-2.07
98	100.21	-2.21
102	98.22	3.78
111	101.62	9.38
107	110.6	-3.06
112	107.31	4.69
112	111.53	0.47
122	111.95	10.05
140	121.00	19.00
125	138.10	-13.10
130	126.31	3.69
136	129.63	6.37
130	135.36	-5.36
112	130.54	-18.54
115	113.85	1.15
100	114.89	-14.89
113	101.49	11.51
111	111.85	-0.85
128	111.08	16.92
122	126.31	-4.31
142	122.43	19.57
134	140.64	-6.04
130	134.60	-4.60
131	130.46	0.54
104	130.95	-26.95
84	106.69	-22.69
86	86.27	-0.27
99	86.03	12.97
90	97.70	-7.70
91	90.77	0.23
90	90.98	-0.98
101	90.10	10.90

Table 18-1 continued

---

*   The starting EWMA is either the target or, if there is no target, the first observation.

**   Error = Actual observation - EWMA. e.g., -2 = 123 - 125.

***   Other than the first sample, all EWMAs are computed as EWMA = last EWMA + λ error. e.g., 123.2 = 125 + 0.9 * (-2).

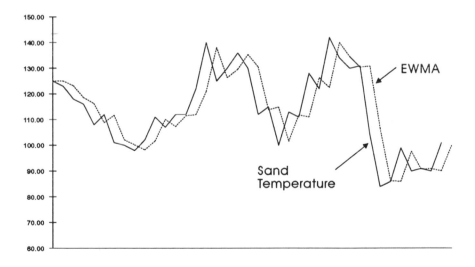

Figure 18-2-EWMA chart of sand temperature

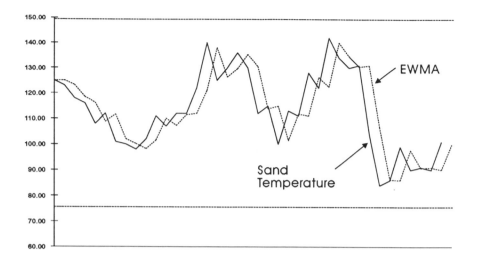

Figure 18-3-EWMA control chart of sand temperature

For the sand temperature example above, $\lambda = 0.9$ which gives

$$\sigma^2_{EWMA} = \sigma^2 \times \frac{0.9}{2 - 0.9} = 0.82\sigma^2.$$ σ^2 is estimated using all of the data. For the

sand temperature data $\sigma = 15.37$ so $\sigma_{EWMA} = 15.37 \times \sqrt{0.82} = 13.92$. The 3σ control limits for the EWMA chart are placed at the grand average plus and minus 41.75. Figure 18.3 shows the control chart for this data. The EWMA line must remain within the control limits. Since the EWMA accounts for "normal drift" in the process centerline, deviations beyond the control limits imply assignable causes other than those accounted for by normal drift. Again, since the effects of changes in temperature can be ameliorated by adjusting the rate of water input, the EWMA control chart may not be necessary.

Choosing the value of λ

The choice of λ is the subject of much literature. A value of λ near 0 provides more "smoothing" by giving greater weight to historic data, while a λ value near 1 gives greater weight to current data. Most authors recommend a value in the range of 0.2 to 0.3. The justification for this range of λ values is probably based on applications of the EWMA technique in the field of economics, where EWMA methods are in widespread use. Industrial applications are less common, although the use of EWMA techniques is growing rapidly.

Hunter (1989) proposes a EWMA control chart scheme where $\lambda = 0.4$. This value of λ provides a control chart with approximately the same statistical properties as a traditional $\overline{X}$ chart combined with the run tests described in the *AT&T Statistical Quality Control Handbook* (commonly called the Western Electric Rules.) It also has the advantage of providing control limits that are exactly half as wide as the control limits on a traditional $\overline{X}$ chart. Thus, to compute the control limits for an EWMA chart when λ is 0.4 you simply compute the traditional $\overline{X}$ chart (or X chart) control limits and divide the distance between the upper and lower control limit by two. The EWMA should remain within these limits.

As mentioned above, the optimal value of λ can be found using some spreadsheet programs. The sum of the squared errors is minimized by changing the value of λ. If your spreadsheet doesn't automatically find the minimum, it can be approximated manually by changing the cell containing λ or by setting up a range of λ values and watching what happens to the cell containing the sum of the squared errors. A graph of the error sum of the squares versus different λ values can indicate where the optimum λ lies.

Special cause charts

Whether using a EWMA common cause chart without control limits or an EWMA control chart, it is a good idea to keep track of the forecast errors using a control chart. The special cause chart is a traditional X chart, created using the difference between the EWMA forecast and the actual observed values. Figure 18.4 shows the special cause chart of the sand temperature data analyzed above.

SPC and automatic process control

As SPC has grown in popularity its use has been mandated with more and more processes. When this trend reached automated manufacturing processes there was resistance from process control engineers who were applying a different approach with considerable success (Palm, 1990.) Advocates of SPC attempted to force the use of traditional SPC techniques as feedback mechanisms for process control. This inappropriate application of SPC was correctly denounced by process control engineers. SPC is designed to serve a purpose fundamentally different than automatic process control (APC.) SPC advocates correctly pointed out that APC was not a cure-all and that many process controllers added variation by making adjustments based on data analysis that was statistically invalid.

Both SPC and APC have their rightful place in quality improvement. APC attempts to dynamically control a process to minimize variation around a target value. This requires valid statistical analysis, which is the domain of the statisti-

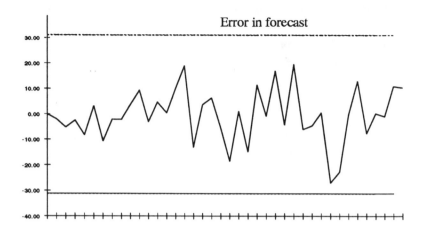

Figure 18-4-Special cause control chart of EWMA errors

cal sciences. SPC makes a distinction between special causes and common causes of variation. If APC responds to all variation as if it were the same it will result in missed opportunities to reduce variation by attacking it at the source. A process that operates closer to the target without correction will produce less variation overall than a process that is frequently returned to the target via APC. However, at times APC must respond to *common cause variation that can't be economically eliminated*, e.g., the mold process described above. Properly used, APC can greatly reduce variability in the output.

Hunter (1986) shows that there is a statistical equivalent to the PID control equation commonly used. The PID equation is

$$u(t) = Ke(t) + \frac{K}{T_I} \int_0^t e(s)\, ds + KT_D \left(\frac{de}{dt}\right) \qquad (18.3)$$

The "PID" label comes from the fact that the first term is a proportional term, the second an integral term and the third a derivative term. Hunter modified the basic EWMA equation by adding two additional terms. The result is the *empirical control equation*

$$\hat{y}_{t+1} = \hat{y}_t + \lambda_1 e_t + \lambda_2 \sum e_t + \lambda_3 \nabla e_t \tag{18.4}$$

The term ∇e_t means the first difference of the errors e_t i.e., $\nabla e_t = e_t - e_{t-1}$.

Like the PID equation, the empirical control equation has a proportional, an integral and a differential term. It can be used by APC or the results can be plotted on a common cause chart and reacted to by human operators, as described above. A special cause chart can be created to track the errors in the forecast from the empirical control equation. Such an approach may help to bring SPC and APC together to work on process improvement.

References

Abraham, B. and Whitney, J.B. (1990), "Applications of EWMA charts to data from continuous processes," Annual Quality Congress Transactions, ASQC, Milwaukee, Wisconsin.

Alwan, L. C. and Roberts, H. V. (1989), "Time series modeling for statistical process control," in *Statistical Process Control in Automated Manufacturing*, Keats, J. B. and Hubele, N. F. eds., Marcel Dekker, New York.

Deming, W.E. (1986), *Out of the Crisis*, MIT Center for Advanced Engineering Study, Cambridge, Mass..

Hunter, J. S. (1986), "The exponentially weighted moving average," Journal of Quality Technology 18, pp 203-210.

Hunter, J. S. (1989), "A one-point plot equivalent to the Shewhart chart with Western Electric rules," Quality Engineering 2, pp. 13-19.

Krishnamoorthi, K.S. (1991), "On assignable causes that cannot be eliminated -- An example from a foundry," Quality Engineering 3, pp. 41-47.

Palm, A. C. (1990), "SPC versus automatic process control," Annual Quality Congress Transactions, ASQC, Milwaukee, Wisconsin.

Shewhart, W. A. (1930, 1980), *Economic Control of Quality of Manufactured Product*, ASQC Quality Press, Milwaukee, Wisconsin.

Wheeler, D. J. (1991), "Shewhart's Charts: Myths, Facts, and Competitors," Annual Quality Congress Transactions, ASQC, Milwaukee, Wisconsin.

Chapter 19

SPC FOR SERVICES AND ADMINISTRATIVE PROCESSES

OBJECTIVES

After completing this section you will

- Understand the importance of the service sector to the economy
- Understand the unique aspects of quality in the service sector
- Know when the methods used to improve quality in manufacturing can be adapted to services, and when they can't be
- Know how to measure the quality of services
- Know how to use SPC to monitor service quality

Introduction

The "quality issue" didn't become an issue until American manufacturing businesses began loosing market share in critical industries to foreign competitors who did a better job. Quality became a matter of economic survival for many businesses. Over a decade has passed since the quality revolution started, and there are a number of stars in the world of American manufacturing. Companies that have stopped the outflow of business (and jobs) and shown that market share can be regained by a focus on the customer.

But manufacturing accounts for only 14% of gross national product, an that number is shrinking fast. The quality of life, as measured by economic criteria, will not improve if the service sector, which represents the vast bulk of all economic activity, doesn't make dramatic improvements in quality. Productivity increases drive improvements in the standard of living, and quality improvements are one proven source of productivity improvements.

165

The quality problems of the service sector are well documented. In the first three years of the Malcolm Baldrige National Quality Award all six large manufacturing awards were bestowed. However, only one of the six service awards was granted. Of course, not everyone is convinced that there is really a problem. However, there doesn't appear to be much confusion from the customers. Zemke and Schaaf (1989) reports one survey that showed 42% of the respondents rated services as fair or poor. Fully $\frac{1}{3}$ of the respondents believed that service quality was getting worse. Another study reported by Zemke and Schaaf indicated that 40% of those who complain about the service they received were unhappy with the response to their complaint. Only 5% even bothered to complain. The effect of poor service is at best mildly annoying. At worst it can lead to tragedy, as the following examples illustrate.

- A report in the Archives of Surgery reported that the incidence of sponges being left inside of surgery patients was "grossly underestimated."
- A study of 1,293 people denied payments by the Social Security Administration showed that 1,091 had been "incorrectly" suspended from the rolls. For many of the recipients, the payments constituted their sole source of income and their removal resulted in "extreme hardship."

In spite of the evidence, expect a fight to improve quality in the services. The resistance will be at least as great as it was (and still is, to a considerable degree) in the manufacturing sector. The popular press quotes executives in many service companies as stating that the Baldrige criteria "doesn't relate to what service companies do." As in manufacturing, there are a number of people who are what I term "poor quality's constituency." The legacy of decades of poor quality service is an entrenched industry whose very existence depends on the continuance of quality trouble. Employees in complaint departments, government agencies dedicated to looking into complaints, repair shops, customer service departments, etc. may not welcome the elimination of the quality problems their jobs depend on. Ultimately, as the manufacturing experience demonstrates, quality and productivity must be improved if we are to improve the quality of life for everyone.

Unique service industry characteristics

The manufacturing model fails the service sector in many ways. Service businesses, and service-oriented operations within manufacturing companies, are different in fundamental ways from manufacturing. Many attempts to apply the approach that worked so well in manufacturing have ended in failure when applied to service operations.

There are many differences between manufacturing and service operations. Sometimes the fundamental purpose of the entity is completely different than the manufacturing model presumes. For example, the manufacturing model assumes that maximizing efficiency over the long term is desirable. But if the operation is a government service, efficiency is secondary to providing equity. Healthcare operations are often "optimized" when they are operating at less than maximum efficiency as measured by resource utilization.

Quality standards are different in service businesses. There is no objective reality with most services. Unlike the manufacturing sector, it is entirely possible for two people to give different quality ratings the exact same service. When this happens in manufacturing something is wrong, the two inspectors are "calibrated" by training or by returning to an established standard. In service industries two people provide different responses to the same event and *both of them are correct*. My father can be extremely upset over a small oil leak that my wife would completely dismiss; both are correct in their assessment of the quality of the automobile.

The perspective of the different customers is another source of variation. In a hospital there are "customers" who are patients, families of patients, professional staff, administrators, physicians, insurers, and so on. The quality of the hospital's service is evaluated much differently by each group. The term "quality of service" has no single meaning.

The expectations of the customer have a tremendous influence on the perceived quality of the service experience. Expectations are influenced by many factors that have little to do with the service per se. A bank advertising that its people are "always ready to meet you with a smile" creates a more demanding customer than one that advertises high rates. The customer's expectations are partly determined by your competitor. Chances are the customer at the first bank just mentioned wants the high rates the second bank advertised, in addition to the smile! Because quality depends so much upon the customer's expectations, you don't have complete control over quality, a situation that doesn't exist in the manufacturing environment.

Zemke and Schaaf (1989) list several other important differences between products and services:

- products are tangible, services are intangible

- products can be inventoried, services don't exist until they are delivered
- quality of product can be determined using physical means, service quality cannot
- products can be sampled prior to purchase, services generally cannot
- the service customer's interaction is more important in service quality ("a little more off of the top, please")
- sale, production and consumption of services are often simultaneous

The traditional manufacturing-based definitions of quality also transfer poorly to service businesses. Defining quality as "conformance to requirements" or "fitness for use" beg the questions of *whose requirements?* and *whose definitions of fitness?* Many service businesses have wrestled with the problem of applying these product-oriented definitions of quality to their operations, to no avail.

In services, the customer's own actions may affect quality. If a customer gives the wrong information it will not be possible to provide the correct medical treatment, ship the product to the correct address, or provide accurate billings. In services, quality is the result of a joint effort by the customer and service provider. For example, Quality Publishing, Inc. obtains the names of prospective customers from postcards in card decks. Since postcards are small only a limited amount of descriptive information can be provided. Many people return the card to obtain additional information, and we try to respond to each request within one business day. Figure 19.1 shows a card that is typical of many re-

Figure 19-1-Information Request From ???

ceived. Observe that the customer dutifully placed the appropriate postage on the card before mailing it. However, *there is no return address*! If this person places an order in the future he or she will receive a quality rating form with the order. The quality rating we receive may comment on how long they waited for their information.

Lessons from manufacturing

Because of the differences just described, many managers of service businesses and administrative operations have concluded that there is nothing to learn from manufacturing's experience with quality improvement. Such is simply not the case. While there are obviously differences in the two sectors, there are many quality improvement lessons that can be transferred from manufacturing to service processes with no modification whatever. Other lessons can be transferred with appropriate consideration of the differences involved. True, the services sector will still have to develop some new approaches tailored specifically to the services, but that doesn't justify ignoring the seventy years of learning that took place in manufacturing.

The standard of living of a nation is largely determined by the productivity of that nation's people. Figure 19.2 compares the change in productivity for the United States manufacturing and service sectors between 1973 and 1991. Since

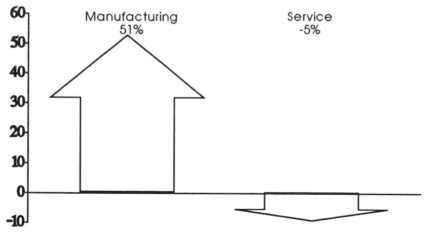

Figure 19-2-Productivity (Investor's Daily 4-26-91)

the bulk of the US economy consists of services, the message in figure 19.2 is not a good one. Other studies show that the rate of increase in productivity for the manufacturing sector has also been increasing in the 1980s. Most manufacturing executives attribute the bulk of the increase to quality improvement. Quality of service has been a subject of considerable controversy. As mentioned earlier, between 1988 and 1990 the Malcolm Baldrige National Quality Award program has bestowed the honor on six large manufacturers. However, only one of the six service awards was presented during the period because there were no other service business applicants who met the stringent quality standards of the award. Some service executives cried foul, but the award administrators insist that the criteria is fair. There is simply a shortage of service sector applicants who meet the world-class standards of the award.

Evidence that the some of the same methods applied to manufacturing can be applied to service businesses can be found in actual cases. Rosander (1990) reports that these methods have been applied to service processes for at least fifty years. During the 1940 census Dr. W. Edwards Deming worked with the Bureau of the Census to successfully apply statistical methods of quality improvement. Berwick (1990) reports on the National Demonstration Project which was a national program designed to demonstrate how industrial quality improvement methods can be used to improve quality in the healthcare industry. The popular and trade press report case-after-case of service improvements brought about by applying the same tools and methods used in manufacturing.

In short, many of the concepts used in manufacturing can also be applied to services. The remainder of this chapter will discuss those concepts specifically related to applying SPC to service processes. The key to success is not to invent totally different tools, it is to understand how the tools can be used in the service context -- and how they should not be used.

Measuring service quality

In my opinion, one of the major factors limiting the application of SPC to services has been the commonly used definitions of quality. In manufacturing quality has been traditionally defined as either conformance to requirements or fitness for use. Both of these definitions allow product quality to be measured by comparing engineering requirements to actual product characteristics. They are inherently oriented to physical products. They have been "adapted" to service processes with varying degrees of success. By and large, the definitions have not transferred well to services. In fact, even manufacturing companies are moving away from these limiting definitions of quality.

I believe that this is one example of an area where service businesses would do well to invent their own new approach. Here is a possible alternative definition of quality:

> *Quality is delivering a total experience to the customer that consistently exceeds the customer's expectations.*

This definition encompasses the entire customer experience. Quality can be measured using one or more of the approaches described later in this chapter. It focuses attention on the customer, who can be either an internal customer or an external customer. By defining quality in terms of expectations, the impact of such things as advertising and competitors must be considered.

Deciding where to measure

Zemke and Schaaf (1989) describe a concept that is helpful in evaluating service quality. They call this the "moment of truth". A moment of truth occurs any time the customer comes in contact with some aspect of the organization and uses that opportunity to judge the quality of service the organization is providing. Moments of truth can be initially identified by creating a process flow chart (see volume one, pp 31-34) and evaluating the points of direct contact with the customer. However, to be sure you have correctly identified the moments of truth you must contact the customer.

Deciding what to measure

Some service SPC teams have found another approach to be helpful. They brainstorm to get every possible answer to the question "how can we do a *lousy job*". For example, a catering department in a hotel might come up with items like

❑ deliver the coffee late

❑ serve stale rolls

❑ deliver the ham sandwiches to the Bar Mitzvah

Each of these service failures indicate potential measurement items. Often, teams are able to be more creative when a bit of humor is injected into the process.

Davidow and Uttal (1989) suggest that service quality metrics be divided into three different categories: process metrics, product metrics and satisfaction metrics. Process control metrics focus on the process of creating the service and would include such things as how long it takes to answer the phone. Product metrics focus on the outcomes of the service that can be measured without involving the customer, for example the percentage of claims settled without dispute.

Both process and product metrics suffer because they measure quality indirectly. The definition of quality provided earlier makes it clear that the customer is the ultimate judge. Thus, the satisfaction metric is the most important. Although it is difficult to obtain accurate data, it must be done. Without metrics to determine customer satisfaction your quality improvement program is flying blind. It is important to keep your metrics simple and understandable. The success of SPC methods over the years is due largely to their simplicity. Zemke and Schaaf (1989, p 55) provides several pointers for setting up a service quality measurement system.

DO's

- ❑ DO begin with your service strategy
- ❑ DO measure frequently
- ❑ DO ask customer-based questions
- ❑ DO ask fair questions
- ❑ DO collect data useful to both individuals and work groups
- ❑ DO get information about competitors for benchmarking
- ❑ DO collect both qualitative and quantitative data
- ❑ DO make the results visible
- ❑ DO make the results easy to use for employees
- ❑ DO be sure the results are believed by the employees
- ❑ DO make sure the results are used

There are a number of things to avoid as well.

DON'Ts

- ❑ DON'T use the information to punish people.
- ❑ DON'T provide people with information that is not relevant to them, extract the meaningful information and report only that which is needed.
- ❑ DON'T delay in getting the information to those who need it. Service information becomes dated quickly.

❑ DON'T tell the employee about things that they are powerless to change (e.g., customer X said you were too short.)

❑ DON'T make the system too complex. Be sure the information is as easy as possible to collect and record.

Zeithaml, Parasuraman and Berry (1990) define service quality in terms of "gaps." Briefly, there are four primary service gaps:

Gap 1: not knowing what customers expect	The difference between what a customer actually expects and what management perceives that they expect.
Gap 2: The wrong ser- vice-quality standard	The discrepancy between managers' perceptions of customers' expectations and the actual specifications they establish for service delivery. This presumes that gap 1 has been rendered negligible.
Gap 3: The service per- formance gap	The difference between service specifications and the actual service delivery.
Gap 4: When prom- ises do not match deliv- ery	The difference between what the firm promised to the custo- mer and what the firm actually delivered.

In the appendix of their book, Zeithaml, Parasuraman and Berry provide ques-tionnaires, forms and worksheets for quantifying the four service quality gaps and their causes. SPC can be applied to the results.

Most organizations have existing systems for collecting business-related infor-mation. Often this same information can be used by SPC teams. Berwick, God-frey and Roessner (1990) point out "...data for useful quality improvement abound in healthcare." Berwick, Godfrey and Roessner's entire book is dedi-cated to applications of the industrial model of quality improvement to healthcare. Much of what they describe applies to other service industries as well. Many detailed SPC applications are shown.

If the data doesn't already exist, you may need to establish your own service quality measures. Deming (1986, chapter 7) presents examples of quality im-provement in the following industries: motor freight, administrative areas of manufacturing, government services, medical services, airlines, Bureau of the Census, Bureau of Customs, payroll departments, hotels, railroads, the Postal Service, copy machine service, restaurants, public transit, telephone service, department stores, banking (in great detail) and electric utilities.

Many service quality measures are inspired by the desire to document quality costs. ASQC provides four standard quality cost accounting categories that are useful in locating sources of service quality costs. The four categories are

1. Prevention costs.
2. Appraisal costs.
3. Internal failure costs.
4. External failure costs.

When using these categories, or when setting up a quality cost accounting system, to-the-penny accuracy is not usually required. The objective of such a system is to obtain information to guide management decision making, which can be done with moderately accurate accounting information.

Davidow and Uttal (1989, p 191) describe a service category used by American Express. Called "avoidable input," this category is roughly equivalent to scrap or rework in manufacturing. Avoidable input is caused when some aspect of the operation confuses or displeases customers and results in a customer inquiry. Avoidable input, in SPC terms, is a common cause that needs to be addressed by taking action on the system.

When implementing a quality measurement system in a service organization it is important that the measurements be constantly "recalibrated" to the final objective of customer-perceived quality. For example, American Express conducts 12,000 customer interviews each year to verify that the data in their Service Tracking Report accurately reflects the customers' perception of their experience with the company.

How to measure service quality

Many service companies believe that they are tracking quality if they keep track of how many customer complaints they receive. Of course, this is an important quality indicator. However, it is simply not enough. As stated previously, studies show that only 5% of those who are dissatisfied with a service actually complain. Most customers who are unhappy simply take their business elsewhere.

Surveys and sampling

Service quality must be measured pro-actively. The customer must be found and contacted. In most cases, this implies sampling. Even if every customer is given an opportunity to respond, many will choose to not respond, so the data still represents a sample of the entire population of customers. Furthermore, some people become unhappy before receiving the service and never become customers. This group of people represents an opportunity to increase business and their impressions are also important.

The subject of conducting a proper survey is quite involved. Historical records are filled with stories of surveys gone wrong because of improperly conducted sampling. The only thing worse than a poorly done survey is the survey that is not done at all. In the service industries the survey is the primary tool for measuring quality. It is the best way to get to the voice of the customer. Although many of the survey results can be tracked using traditional SPC tools, great care must be taken to get accurate results. I will provide a brief overview of a number of important issues involved in conducting surveys, you are advised to consult the references given for additional information

The frame   Sampling implies a statistical approach. Deming (1960) describes sampling for business research in detail. While much of Deming's work is technically beyond the layman (suggesting the need for the services of a statistician), the discussion of the frame (Deming, 1960, chapter 3) should be read by anyone contemplating a customer survey. "The frame is an aggregate of identifiable tangible physical units of some kind, any or all of which may be selected and investigated. The frame may be lists of people, areas, establishments, materials, or of other identifiable units that would yield useful results if the whole content were investigated." (Deming, 1975)

Enumerative versus analytic statistical studies   An enumerative study has for its aim an estimate of the number of units of a frame that belongs to a specified class. An analytic study has for its aim a basis for action on the cause-system or the process, in order to improve product in the future. In other words, enumerative studies attempt to provide descriptions of frames which are *static*. Enumerative studies don't try to answer "why are things the way they are?" In an enumerative study action will be taken on the units in the frame studied.

Analytic studies are efforts to understand *why* things are the way they are. Statistical methods, to the extent that they are used, provide clues to understanding the underlying process. Analytic studies provide help in formulating theories of cause and effect. In an analytic study action will be taken on the cause system that produced the frame rather than on the frame itself. The vast majority of quality improvement studies are analytic in nature.

A simple way of deciding which type of study you are contemplating is to answer the question "if I had 100% information about 100% of the units in the frame, do I have *complete information* or are there still unanswered questions?" If the information is complete, the study is enumerative, otherwise it is analytic. For example, if I was interested in the quality of a shipping operation and surveyed every customer and every customer responded I would not have complete information. The information I obtained would be applied to the *shipping process* which would impact *future customers*. In other words, the action is taken on the cause system that produced the frame, not the frame itself.

Non-sampling errors

Errors are sometimes classified into two basic categories: random errors and systematic errors. Random errors include sampling variation. Random error can be reduced by increasing the sample size. Systematic errors are those caused by the way the survey is designed and conducted. Systematic errors include procedures, interviewer technique, design of questions, and other factors that cannot be impacted by increasing the sample size. The total error is the sum or the sampling and non-sampling errors; if non-sampling errors dominate, it is often more economical to invest in a well-designed and executed survey of a smaller sample. Non-sampling errors are discussed in Rossi, Wright and Anderson (1983, pp. 289-328) and Deming (1960, pp 102-109.)

Non-response

Non-responses occur when a person selected as part of the sample cannot be contacted or refuses to participate in the survey. Non-responses are usually ignored, which is tantamount to assuming that they would respond in the same way as those who did respond. This assumption is risky. Deming (1960, pp 102-109) describes a rigorous method of handling non-responses.

Self-administered survey

A survey completed without the services of an interviewer. The comment cards handed out in hotels are examples of a self-administered survey. Self-administered surveys are potentially the most cost-effective way of obtaining customer input, and they are by far the most commonly used survey method in business. However, they have a number of shortcomings and

176

potential traps and pitfalls that often keep them from meeting their potential. Low response rates and respondent bias are two especially difficult problems.

A self-administered survey method that works

Dillman (1983) describes an approach self-administered surveys called the Total Design Method (TDM). Dillman claims that by using the TDM approach self-administered surveys have produced response rates averaging 77% for surveys with an average of 10 pages. No survey using TDM reported less than a 60% response rate.

Although doubtful, I decided to try the TDM in a survey of the customers for my own business. Our previous survey had consisted of two pages and it had been repeated many times and the average response rate was about 20%, without using TDM. Our TDM survey was ten pages long and the response rate was 95%!

TDM is demanding. Its procedure must be followed in every detail. No short-cuts are allowed. But TDM works and the results make the effort worth it. The procedure is as follows:

Questionnaire design

1. The questionnaire is designed as a booklet, the normal dimensions being $6\frac{1}{2} \times 8\frac{1}{4}$ inches.

2. The questionnaire is typed on regular sized ($8\frac{1}{2} \times 11$ in. pages and these are photo-reduced to fit into the booklet, thus providing a less imposing image.

3. Resemblance to advertising brochures is strenuously avoided; thus, the booklets are printed on white paper. Slightly lighter than normal paper (16# versus 20#) can be used to lower mailing costs.

4. No questions are printed on the first page (cover page); it is used for an interest-getting title, a neutral but eye-catching illustration, and any necessary instructions to the respondent.

5. Similarly, no questions are allowed on the last page (back cover); it is used to invite additional comments and express appreciation to the respondent.

6. Questions are ordered so that the most interesting and topic-related questions (as explained in the accompanying cover letter) come first; potentially objectionable questions are placed later and those requesting demographic information last.

7. Special attention is given to the first question; it should apply to everyone, be interesting, and be easy to answer.

8. Each page is formulated with great care in accordance with principles such as these: lowercase letters are used for questions and uppercase letters for answers; to prevent skipping items each page is designed so that whenever possible respondents can answer in a straight vertical line instead of moving back and forth across the page; overlap of individual questions from one page to the next is avoided, especially on back-to-back pages; transitions are used to guide the respondent much as a face-to-face interviewer would warn of changes in topic to prevent disconcerting surprises; only one question is asked at a time; and visual cues (arrows, indentations, spacing) are used to provide direction.

The design procedure is quite demanding. You will probably go through multiple drafts before you get it right.

Survey implementation

The respondent should be told in a cover letter that the survey is being done to help improve quality, which will help him or her. They should also be offered something tangible for their participation, such as a small amount of money or a copy of the survey results. We included a crisp new $2 bill with our survey, obtained from a local bank. The details for implementing TDM are as demanding as those for designing the TDM questionnaire:

1. A one-page cover letter (on $10\frac{7}{8} \times 7\frac{1}{8}$ inch stationery) is prepared. It explains *(a)* that a socially useful study is being conducted; *(b)* why each respondent is important; and *(c)* who should complete the questionnaire. It also promises confidentiality in conjunction with an identification system used to facilitate follow-up mailings.

2. The exact mailing date is added onto the letter, which is then printed on the sponsoring company's letterhead stationery.

3. Individual names and addresses are typed onto the printed letters in matching type and the researcher's name is individually signed with a blue ballpoint pen using sufficient pressure to produce slight indentations.

4. Questionnaires are stamped with an identification number, the presence of which is explained in the cover letter.

5. The mailout packet, consisting of a cover letter, questionnaire, and business reply envelope $(6\frac{3}{8} \times 3\frac{1}{2}$ inches) is placed into a monarch-sized envelope $(7\frac{3}{8} \times 3\frac{3}{4}$ inches) on which the recipient's name and address has been individually typed (address labels are *never* used) and first-class postage is affixed.

6. Exactly 1 week after the first mailout, a postcard follow-up reminder is sent to all recipients of the questionnaire.

7. Exactly 3 weeks after the first mailout, a second cover letter and question-naire is sent to everyone who has not responded.
8. Exactly seven weeks after the first mailout, a second cover letter complete with another original of the first cover letter and a replacement question-naire is sent by certified mail.

I know this all seems incredibly tedious, but it works splendidly. I strongly advise against cutting corners; I have seen many easier approaches to surveys, but none better.

ASQC survey of service quality

In 1985 and again in 1988 ASQC commissioned the Gallup Organization to conduct a national survey of consumers' perceptions concerning the quality of American products and services. The survey was conducted by telephone and it included 1,005 respondents. A portion of the survey was devoted to questions relating to the quality of service. Of particular interest to service companies trying to use SPC to analyze service quality data is a question that reads

> *We have been talking about the quality of products. Now, I would like to ask you about services, that is, airlines, banks, hotels and other organizations that provide a service rather than a product. How do you determine the quality of services rather than products?*

As you would expect, the consumers mentioned a long list of considerations. Figure 19.3 indicates the percentage of respondents who mentioned the item. The categories shown in figure 19.3 include the following factors:

People	Courteous/polite treatment; attitude of personnel; helpful; friendliness; personal attention.
The service itself	satisfies my needs; price; availability of services; variety of services.
Efficiency	Promptness; cleanliness; efficiency of staff; convenience of using service.
Experience	past experience/trial & error; recommendations/word of mouth.
The Company	dependability, somebody to depend on and trust; company name; reputation; length of time in business.
Reliability	trouble-free, no mistakes; accuracy.

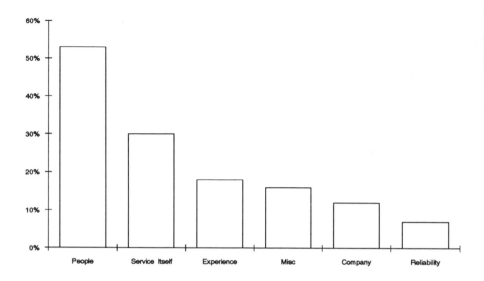

Figure 19-3-How do you determine service quality?

| Miscella-
neous | advertising; don't know; other response. |

When should we measure service quality?

In manufacturing SPC is usually applied to samples from processes. Every hour, say, a sample of some size is taken from the process and measured. The statistics that result are plotted on some sort of SPC chart, e.g., an $\overline{X}$ chart. It's all very simple.

But how do we do this with a service process? Surprisingly, in many cases the approach is nearly identical. Let's say the process involves accounts receivable and the SPC team determines that the average time between billing and receipt of payment is an appropriate performance statistic. A sample of five invoices could be selected from those invoices paid on a given day, the average time computed, and the result recorded on an $\overline{X}$ chart.

In other cases, the process performance measure can't be determined from any tangible item like an invoice. For example, a banking SPC team might determine that an important measure is the number of cars in line awaiting drive-through service. This can be determined in a variety of ways. One way would be to have the drive-through teller count the number of cars every hour. Another method would be to use random work sampling. Devices are available that signal at random intervals throughout a day; you can select the number of times you want to sample the process in a day, but the times actually chosen will be determined at random. Both approaches have positive and negative aspects. The periodic sample may produce a biased average because of some systematic pattern; e.g., the length of the line may be longer at opening time, lunch time and near the close of business. If these were selected as the sampling times the average length of the line would be overstated by the periodic approach, while the random sample would be less likely to show a bias. On the other hand, it may be that the "process" the bank is trying to improve is the length of the line at these critical times. If so, the periodic sample would be superior.

The "moments of truth" described earlier are potential sampling points. A moment of truth occurs any time the customer comes in contact with some aspect of the organization and uses that opportunity to judge the quality of service the organization is providing. As a rule, collect data before, during and after the moment of truth.

Collection of data for SPC purposes should be done repeatedly. Process patterns and trends cannot be determined from a single sample. It is generally better to collect small samples frequently than large samples infrequently.

Analyzing service quality data

By and large, the traditional SPC tools described in volume one of this series work for service process data as well as for manufacturing data. There are three classes of SPC tools, each with a different purpose. The table below lists the basic SPC tools and their uses.

Category	SPC Tools	Purpose
Descriptive	Pareto analysis, histogram, checksheets, location diagrams	Provide basic factual information in an organized, visual format

Category	SPC Tools	Purpose
Problem analysis tools	Brainstorming, cause and effect diagrams, scatter diagrams	Analyze the reasons why certain events occur; discover root causes; prevent future problems
Control charts	$\overline{X}$, R, p, np, c, u, time-based control charts, other special control charts	Determine if a special cause is affecting the service process; estimate the common cause variability; decide when to intervene in the service process

Basic business graphics are also useful in analyzing data from service processes. Due care should be taken when using standard business graphs. Simple line charts and bar charts are good choices. Pie charts, while very common, are notoriously difficult for people to interpret properly. Modern computers have made it possible to fill bars on bar charts with all sorts of patterns. "Area charts", line charts which show several categories and fill the space between the lines with patterns, are also possible. Studies have shown that charts with complex fill patterns are hard for people to interpret and they should be avoided. Computers have made 3-D charts popular; 3-D charts are nearly impossible for people to properly read. Remember, the purpose of the chart is to improve the understanding of the data. If your charts fail to do this, they should be redesigned. KISS.

Control charts of time-based performance measures

Service quality depends on efficiency. In ASQC's survey over 28% of the respondents mentioned efficiency as an important criterion for them. In SPC of service processes efficiency is even more important because it is one of the easier things to measure in a process. Efficiency can be described in a variety of ways, such as "sales clerks are available when I need them," quick claim processing, promptly answers the phone, 911 calls are responded to quickly, short lines at the checkout, short waits in the emergency room, etc.. One thing all of these efficiency measures have in common is that they involve measuring time. Time-based measures can usually be placed into one of three categories: time between events, waiting times and service times. Time between events may measure, for example, how much time passes between customers arriving for service. Waiting time might be obvious, such as how long a customer waits in the doctor's office; or it might be less obvious, such as how long it takes the 911 operator to answer the phone. Service times measure the duration between the time the customer service begins and the time it ends. Examples of service times are the time it takes to process an insurance claim and the time it takes an agent to process an airline passenger.

Unlike most service quality measures, time-based performance measures cannot be monitored with only traditional SPC tools. In particular, these performance measures give erroneous signals when plotted on control charts with subgroup sizes smaller than 5. The reason is that time measurements are extremely non-normally distributed even when the process is in statistical control. The result is a large number of false alarms and attempts to find special causes of variation when none exist. The effect is often unnecessary process tampering, which increases costs and decreases the quality of service.

It is easy to compute control limits for time-based performance measures to provide the same probability of a false alarm as a traditional control chart with normal data. If the control chart shows individual times, compute the control limits using equations 19.1 and 19.2 instead of the usual control limit equations.

$$LCL = 0.00135\overline{X} \qquad (19.1)$$

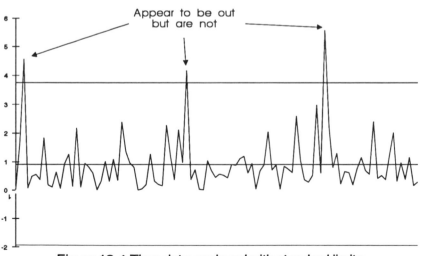

Figure 19-4-Time data analyzed with standard limits

$$UCL = 6.6\overline{X} \qquad (19.2)$$

The value of $\overline{X}$ is computed as usual, namely $\overline{X} = \dfrac{sum\ of\ observations}{number\ of\ observations}$. Assuming the distribution of the observations is exponential (which is common for
inter-arrival times) the probability of observing a value beyond these limits is approximately 0.0027%, the same as with a traditional $\overline{X}$ chart with normal data.
Also, using these control limit equations you will never produce a lower control
limit below zero. Negative control limits are confusing when the performance
measure is time. Figures 19.4 and 19.5 show time data analyzed using traditional and time-based control limit equations. Notice that the control limits
based on traditional equations (figure 19.4) indicate that the process was out-of-
control several times, while the time-based equations (figure 19.5) show that the
process was actually in statistical control.

A case study in non-manufacturing SPC

Quality America, Inc. was founded by the author of this series. Consistent with
its mission, Quality America, Inc. has been experimenting in the use of advanced methods of quality improvement, including SPC, throughout all of their

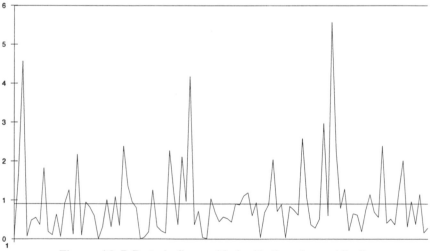

Figure 19-5-Data in figure 19-4 with time-based limits

operations since 1983. Although SPC is only a small part of the total quality management picture, it is also a very important part. The following describes some of the applications of SPC to non-manufacturing areas within Quality America, Inc. (Keller, 1990)[1].

SPC control charting in the service industries

Introduction

Quality America is a company which produces SPC software as well as publishing books and training materials on general quality issues, and more specifically SPC. The company's mission statement is

> ...to help customers in the private and public sectors find ways to improve the quality of their products and services ... to lead by example by continually seeking better ways to accomplish its mission.

Obviously, the focus of the company's mission statement (and by extension, the company) is on customer satisfaction and continuous improvement. Each employee is given training on SPC, various topic in the quality field and customer relations before any contact with a customer is allowed. The question arises: How can the effectiveness of this focus be measured?

Applications

Volume one, p. 55 describes Pareto analysis as "*the process of ranking opportunities to determine which of many potential opportunities should be pursued first.*" Pareto charts are used at Quality America for three purposes:

- to determine repeated problems customers may have.
- to determine customer needs.
- to determine the most effective use of the company's resources.

At Quality America we have incorporated Pareto analysis in our technical support function. When software users call the toll free number for tech support, a log entry is made to classify the reason for the call. These entries are tabulated at the end of each month and a Pareto chart is constructed. By collecting and analyzing this data we are able to quickly discover trends. For instance, Pareto

---

1   the following material is copyright © 1990 by David M. Keller, reprinted with permission.

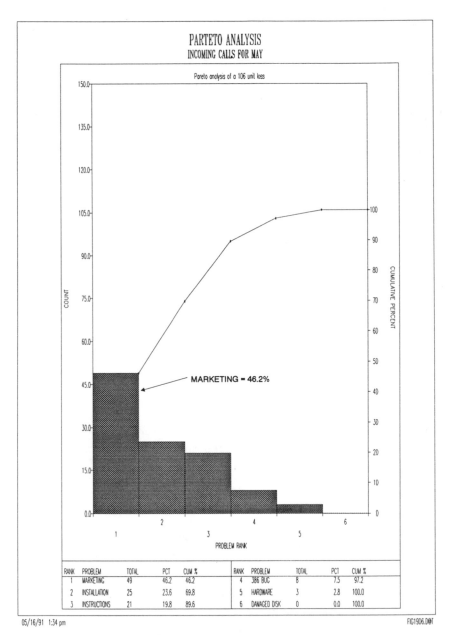

PARTETO ANALYSIS
INCOMING CALLS FOR MAY

Pareto analysis of a 106 unit loss

MARKETING = 46.2%

RANK	PROBLEM	TOTAL	PCT	CUM %	RANK	PROBLEM	TOTAL	PCT	CUM %
1	MARKETING	49	46.2	46.2	4	386 BUG	8	7.5	97.2
2	INSTALLATION	25	23.6	69.8	5	HARDWARE	3	2.8	100.0
3	INSTRUCTIONS	21	19.8	89.6	6	DAMAGED DISK	0	0.0	100.0

05/16/91 1:34 pm

FIG1906.DØT

Figure 19-6-Pareto chart of tech support calls

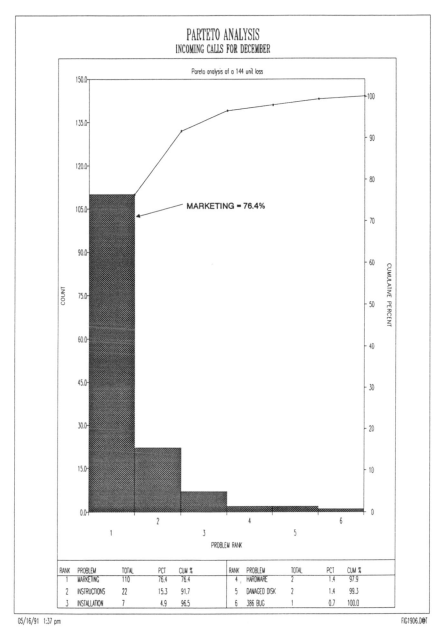

PARTETO ANALYSIS
INCOMING CALLS FOR DECEMBER

Pareto analysis of a 144 unit loss

MARKETING = 76.4%

RANK	PROBLEM	TOTAL	PCT	CUM %	RANK	PROBLEM	TOTAL	PCT	CUM %
1	MARKETING	110	76.4	76.4	4	HARDWARE	2	1.4	97.9
2	INSTRUCTIONS	22	15.3	91.7	5	DAMAGED DISK	2	1.4	99.3
3	INSTALLATION	7	4.9	96.5	6	386 BUG	1	0.7	100.0

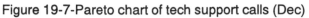

05/16/91 1:37 pm   FIG1906.D0T

Figure 19-7-Pareto chart of tech support calls (Dec)

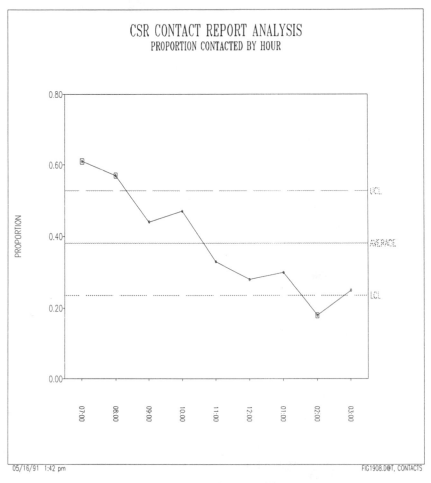

Figure 19-8-P chart of proportion of contacts per hour

charts allowed us to identify a problem an earlier version of our software had
with the then newly released 80386 computer. Our product development team
used this information to address the defect before it became a costly problem for
the company.

Another use of the Pareto chart at Quality America was in determining critical
customer support requirements. A tabulation of responses from customer inquir-
ies resulted in the editing of our manual to make it more user friendly. Pareto
analysis indicated repeated problems with installations, prompting us to rewrite

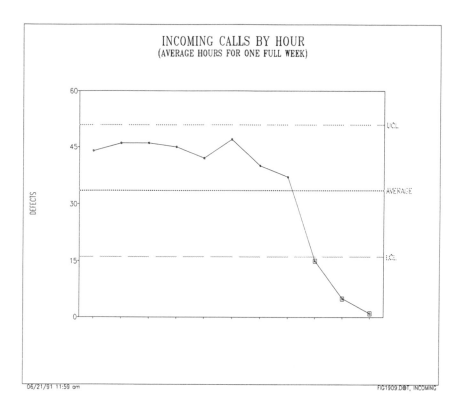

Figure 19-9-c chart of incoming calls per hour

that section of the manual for easier comprehension by those unfamiliar with computers. This resulted in fewer tech support calls.

We have also used Pareto charts to more effectively allocate human resources. For example, it was found that fewer calls were received for tech support at the same time marketing related calls increased. This was not mere coincidence, but rather a result of the changes outlined above. The data became justification for moving resources from tech support into the marketing function.

Figures 19.6 and 19.7 illustrate the effect of the changes. These charts were not the only ones used, but they do indicate the changes made over a 7 month period. In addition to Pareto charts, Quality America has successfully applied control charts to several service processes. Our Customer Service Representatives (CSRs) are responsible for calling prospects who have recently requested product information as well as answering questions and taking orders from incoming

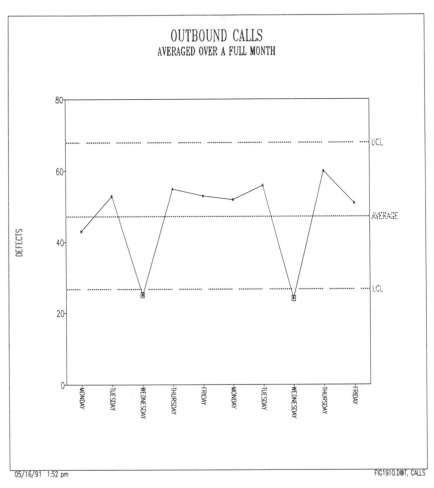

Figure 19-10-c chart of outbound calls per day

phone calls. Each CSR maintains a call log which tallies the number of incoming marketing phone calls or orders, number of outgoing contact attempts and number of actual contacts.

To determine personnel scheduling, p charts and c charts were used. A p chart is a chart which measures the proportion of an attribute where the sample size can vary. In this application, the number of contact attempts are tabulated against actual contacts for each hour of any particular day. From figure 19.8, we

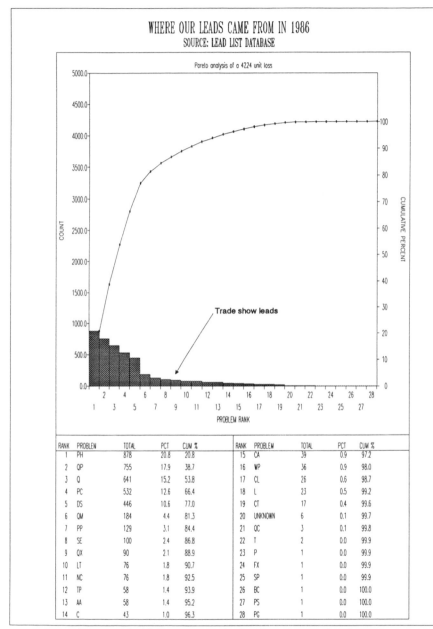

Figure 19-11-Pareto analysis of customer leads

The table portion of the figure:

RANK	PROBLEM	TOTAL	PCT	CUM %	RANK	PROBLEM	TOTAL	PCT	CUM %
1	PH	878	20.8	20.8	15	CA	39	0.9	97.2
2	QP	755	17.9	38.7	16	WP	36	0.9	98.0
3	Q	641	15.2	53.8	17	CL	26	0.6	98.7
4	PC	532	12.6	66.4	18	L	23	0.5	99.2
5	DS	446	10.6	77.0	19	CT	17	0.4	99.6
6	QM	184	4.4	81.3	20	UNKNOWN	6	0.1	99.7
7	PP	129	3.1	84.4	21	QC	3	0.1	99.8
8	SE	100	2.4	86.8	22	T	2	0.0	99.9
9	QX	90	2.1	88.9	23	P	1	0.0	99.9
10	LT	76	1.8	90.7	24	FX	1	0.0	99.9
11	NC	76	1.8	92.5	25	SP	1	0.0	99.9
12	TP	58	1.4	93.9	26	BC	1	0.0	100.0
13	AA	58	1.4	95.2	27	PS	1	0.0	100.0
14	C	43	1.0	96.3	28	PG	1	0.0	100.0

were able to determine the best time of day to call customers. This resulted in more efficient scheduling of CSR's work hours.

The number of incoming phone calls per hour were also taken from the CSR call log and analyzed with a c chart. A c chart maintains *"control of performance that involves occurrence per unit counts. The unit can be a fixed number of items, a time period, or any opportunity for the occurrence to appear."* (volume one, p. 130). C charts answer the question *"has a special cause of variation caused this process to produce an abnormally large or small number of occurrences over the time period observed?"* In this application, the number of incoming calls are entered for each hour. The "unit" is one hour and the "occurrence" is an incoming call. The results in figure 19.9 show the time periods with the greatest number of incoming calls and, hence, the greatest need for CSRs. Again, our CSR scheduling was based upon the results shown.

The c chart can also be used to analyze total calls (incoming and outgoing) on a daily basis. Each week, the CSR and his/her supervisor analyze the chart to explain any point above or below the statistical control limits. For instance, in fig-

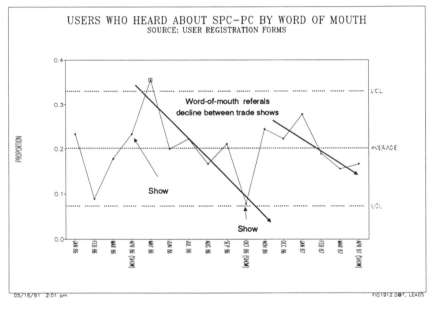

Figure 19-12-Proportion of word-of-mouth leads

ure 19.10, one CSR's outbound phone calls were consistently falling below the lower control limits every Wednesday. It was discovered that he was preparing information brochures for mailing because not enough were being prepared at the beginning of the week. This discovery allowed more efficient use of a highly trained CSR.

Control charts have also been used at Quality America to track the efficiency of order processing. For instance, problems were discovered from customer quality cards sent with each order. These indicated that our order processing dropped from "excellent" to somewhere between "better than most" and "average." To determine the cause, a team of employees from the Shipping and CSR departments was formed. Team meetings resulted in little consensus of problem areas. The Shipping area blamed the CSR's for incomplete or misspelled order forms and the CSRs blamed the shipping department for incorrect data entry.

In order to resolve the controversy, an audit system was put in place. A supervisor from a neutral area would check order forms before they reached data entry and construct a u chart showing errors per 100 orders. If any order form was incomplete or incorrect, it would be returned to the CSR responsible for correction after it had been tabulated on the u chart. Likewise, the Shipping manager would independently check for order errors. The result of the study showed neither side could be completely vindicated, but rather brought the team together for brainstorming sessions to determine ways to improve their respective processes. In other words, the control chart showed that problems were caused by the system. New forms were designed and new procedures developed which dramatically improved the process.

SPC charts were also used to evaluate various marketing expenditures. For example, by analyzing where registered SPC-PC [software] users heard about the product, a better allocation of the marketing budget was determined. Using figure 19.11 it appeared that the number of leads generated from trade shows (ranked 9th) did not justify the cost of attending the shows. However, using figure 19.12 we were able to discover that although the number of direct sales from trade show leads was small, the word-of-mouth sales after a trade show increased dramatically. From this data it was determined that trade shows were a worthwhile investment after all.

Conclusion

It should be stressed that the control charts in an of themselves have limited use; the collection of valid data and adherence to Deming's 14 Points are critical for the control charts to have meaning. For example, in the above scenarios, if the parties involved had not collected data or had been afraid of management (to the point of falsely reporting data), no improvement in the processes could have occurred.

(the previous material was written by David M. Keller)

Quality improvement

With service industries, as with manufacturing, SPC is only one aspect of total quality management. The goal of quality improvement requires that the facts discovered using SPC techniques be *used*. At Quality America the quality improvement process involved an innovation called "Quality Hour." The last hour of each work day was reserved for activities that were specifically directed towards quality improvement.

The initial response of employees to quality hour was overwhelmingly negative. They protested that they would never get their "real work" finished if they "lost" $\frac{1}{8}$ of their work day. Management responded by allowing overtime to complete critical tasks, and by standing firm on quality hour.

During the first several weeks quality hour was devoted entirely to education and training. Actual quality improvement projects were integrated into the educational activities. Employees were educated in the philosophy of quality improvement, SPC techniques, group dynamics and problem solving skills. The new knowledge was immediately useful because management was already versed in the subject matter and they had a backlog of projects in need of some attention. After several months the employees were allowed a referendum on quality hour. The vote to keep quality hour was unanimous. In fact, the consensus was that the activities which began with quality hour had become the activities that everyone did throughout the day. Quality improvement had become the routine. Most executives would consider quality hour to be an extremely radical idea, but Quality America's experience suggests that, if anything, an hour a day dedicated to quality improvement isn't nearly enough.

A common pitfall

One big danger in measuring some aspect of service performance and focusing attention on improving the performance is *suboptimization*. Suboptimization occurs when people "manage the number." Instead of concentrating on the reason the measurement is being taken and taking appropriate action, people concentrate on improving the number itself.

For example, let's say that the SPC team is given the assignment of improving customer satisfaction in a banking operation. They do some research and find that customers are unhappy because it takes a long time for the bank to answer the phone when they call. The team decides to measure the time it takes to answer the phone. The computerized phone system keeps track of the time elapsed from the first ring until the receiver is picked up by the bank employee. Soon the people who are answering the phone learn that this aspect of their performance is being measured. Their response might be to answer the phone and immediately put the caller on hold so fast that the caller wonders if "pleasehold" is one word or two. The control chart may show a dramatic improvement, but the customer is probably no happier.

References

Berwick, D.M., Godfrey, A.B. and Roessner, J. (1990), *Curing Health Care*, Jossey-Bass Publishers, San Francisco, California.

Davidow, W.H. and Uttal, B. (1989), *Total Customer Service, The Ultimate Weapon*, Harper & Row, New York.

Deming, W.E. (1975), "On probability as a basis for action," *The American Statistician* 29, 146-152.

Deming, W.E. (1986), *Out of the Crisis*, MIT Center for Advanced Engineering Study, Cambridge, Mass..

Deming, W.E. (1960), *Sample Design in Business Research*, John Wiley & Sons, New York.

Dillman, D.A. (1983), "Mail and other self-administered questionnaires" in *Handbook of Survey Research*, Rossi, P.H., Wright, J.D. and Anderson, A.B. editors, Academic Press, Inc., New York.

Keller, D.M. (1990), "SPC in service industries," 17th Annual ASQC National Energy Division Conference Proceedings, pp. W1.1 - W1.8.

Rosander, A.C. (1990), *The Quest for Quality in Services*, copublished by Quality Press, Milwaukee, Wisconsin and Quality Resources, White Plains, New York.

Rossi, P.H., Wright, J.D. and Anderson, A.B. editors(1983), *Handbook of Survey Research,* Academic Press, Inc., New York.

Zeithaml, V.A., Parasuraman, A., and Berry, L.L. (1990), *Delivering Quality Service,* The Free Press, New York.

Zemke, R. and Schaaf, Dick (1989), *The Service Edge, 101 Companies That Profit From Customer Care,* NAL Books, New York.

Chapter 20

SPC FOR PROCESSES WITH LINEAR DRIFT

OBJECTIVES
After completing this section you will

- Know how to use SPC on processes with linear drift.

- Understand that process drift is an economic issue, not a philosophical issue

Introduction

A central maxim of SPC is that special causes must be eliminated. Special causes are those causes which have a large effect of economic significance. Although common causes of variation might have more impact overall, special causes are usually easier to fix economically. Any single common cause will have only a small effect, while a single special cause will have a noticeable effect.

While removing special causes is the rule in SPC work, there are exceptions. The well-known Western electric statistical quality control handbook states (page 150)

> "Not all assignable causes in a process are bad or need to be eliminated. For example, tool wear is an assignable cause, but it is accepted as an essential part of any process which involves tooling."

This chapter describes statistical methods of dealing with processes such as these. However, there are valid reasons to use these methods only as a last resort. Whenever possible, the linear drift should be eliminated. Any drift will increase total variability in the process, and quality suffers when variability increases. Figure 20.1 shows the effect of process drift on total variability. At times the increased variability is large. The cost of allowing this to occur can also be large. The true cost can be larger than the cost of the part. An American automobile company had a process which created parts for one of its automatic transmissions. The process used 70% of the tolerance, on average. A Japanese plant was producing the same part (for the American manufacturer) and using only 27% of the tolerance. The Japanese-built transmissions performed noticeably better than those built by the American company, they also had lower repair costs and they lasted longer in service. The total cost, including the ownership costs to the customer, were higher for the American built transmissions, even though the machines used by the American plant were less expensive than those used by the Japanese plant. These costs must be considered when deciding how to deal with process variation from any source, including drift. Before accepting that drift is something that must be tolerated the SPC team should give *serious* thought to finding ways of eliminating it.

Examples

By and large, the literature treats linear drift as if it were caused exclusively by tool wear. Actually, there are a number of other process that have the problem, here are a few examples:

- A plating process deposits solder on etched circuit boards through electro-deposition. The lead concentration of the plating bath is an important parameter. The process consumes the lead from the bath at a rate dependent on the surface area plated.

- The color in a printing process is determined in part by the solvent in which the pigments are suspended. As the process runs the solvent evaporates from the ink, causing the color to change.

- The number of pieces of mail processed at various post offices is dependent on the total number of hours of labor used by the post office.

- The viscosity of the metallic paste used in a screen printing process for hybrid micro-circuits is dependent upon the temperature of the paste. The paste heats up during the run due to the friction of the squeegee across the printing screen, and other sources.

There are many, many other processes where the level of a variable changes due to factors that are an intrinsic part of the process.

There are also cases where the hypothesis of linear drift doesn't prove to be accurate. That is, at first glance it appears that there should be a linear drift, but the data show otherwise. For example, a process produces ceramic micro-cir-

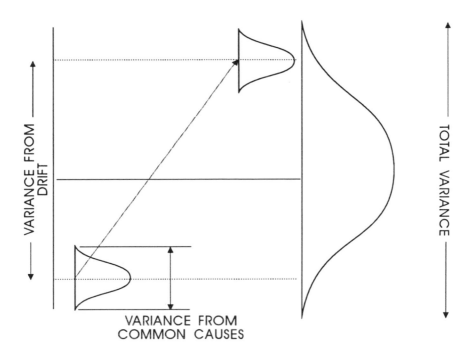

Figure 20-1-Why drift is undesireable

cuit substrates by compressing B_eO powder on a press. The powder is supplied in plastic bottles that are mounted on the press and gravity-fed into the press through a tube. As the bottle is used up the pressure from the weight of the powder is reduced. The theory was that the part size would be affected by this in an approximately linear fashion. Studies failed to show this. The SPC team learned that the powder fed from the middle of the bottle, like sand leaving an hourglass. The cone-shaped hole would eventually collapse in on itself, perhaps several times during the run. When the collapse occurred the part size would change dramatically, then stabilize. The increased knowledge of what was actually happening helped the SPC team improve the quality of the process, which is, after all, the primary purpose of SPC. You should always test your assumptions, including the assumption of linear drift.

SPC and linear drift

Traditional control charts won't work with processes that have persistent drift, linear or otherwise. Persistent, non-random drift will show up as an out-of-control condition. That is because the processes are out-of-control in the sense that special causes are present. If you want to use a control chart for with a process that has linear drift, you will need something other than the traditional control chart.

The first step is to confirm that the process does in fact behave as you think it behaves. Just because there is a general tendency for the process to drift doesn't mean that the drift is linear, or that it is consistent. A good place to start is to do a controlled study of the process and to create a scatter diagram of the results. Study the scatter diagram and ask the questions like these

❑ Is there a trend?

❑ Does the trend tend to follow a straight line?

❑ Does the rate of process drift tend to increase? Decrease?

❑ Does the slope of the trend line change with different materials? For different tools? From other factors?

❑ Is the trend consistent, or does it change drastically?

❑ Is the trend due to a known cause that can be controlled?

A few representative patterns are shown in figure 20.2. The SPC team should make their own list of questions. The team's answers should be arrived at by consensus. If the team concludes that there is a trend that follows a straight line, is consistent and is due to causes that cannot be eliminated (at least in the short term), then the methods described below may be appropriate. Some non-linear trends can be accommodated by the EWMA charts described in chapter 18.

Control charts for linear trends

The method described here will keep things simple by staying as close as possible to traditional SPC control charts. The controlled study, conducted as described in chapter 13, must indicate a very capable process based on the estimate of *process* σ. The estimate if σ should be based on the traditional R or s chart as described in volume one, chapter 8; do *not* calculate σ by grouping all of the data together. However, the $\overline{X}$ chart will show a linear trend, and some $\overline{X}$s will probably be outside of the control limits. Since the process has a linear drift, you won't be able to analyze the process central tendency using the traditional $\overline{X}$ chart. The true capability of the process must be determined using the method

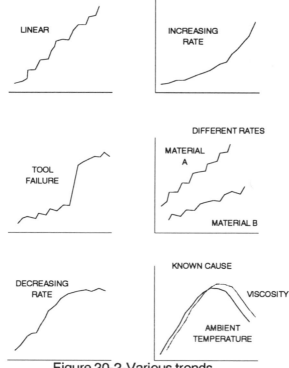

Figure 20-2-Various trends

described below. However, the process dispersion, measured with the R or s chart, must be in control before proceeding.

I don't recommend this approach unless $\dfrac{process\ specification}{\sigma} \geq 10$. If the process capability is less than this there is no room for drift. However, don't allow drift simply because the process specification is wide. This practice, once widespread, is based on the goalpost mentality described in volume one, chapter 5. This mentality assumes that no cost is incurred as long as parts meet the specification. As the transmission example described above shows, this assumption is often wrong. Later in this chapter we will describe an alternative method for setting limits on the drift based on Taguchi's cost model.

Essentially the linear-trend control chart is an ordinary $\overline{X}$ chart with a center line that is sloped rather than flat. The slope of the line can be determined by eye, but a study I conducted suggested that this approach is unreliable. I recommend that the slope be determined by least-squares regression analysis. Many calculators and spreadsheet programs (such as Lotus 123) have this ability built in. Remember that in the regression the independent variable, X, is the number of pieces and the dependent variable, Y, is the process average. For example, if the chart shows the outside diameter the X variable would be how many pieces were produced with the tool and the Y variable would be the average diameter. The slope can also be determined with equation 20.1

$$\frac{\sum XY - \frac{\sum X \sum Y}{N}}{\sum X^2 - \left(\frac{\sum X}{N}\right)^2} \tag{20.1}$$

Example:
The data in the table below will be used with equation 20.1

Piece No. (X)	Size (Y)	X^2	XY
1	25	1	25
2	17	4	34
3	16	9	48
4	23	16	92
5	15	25	75
6	12	36	72
7	12	49	84
8	23	64	184
9	15	81	135
10	17	100	170
11	19	121	209
12	17	144	204
13	18	169	234
14	17	196	238
15	16	225	240
16	15	256	240
17	23	289	391
18	17	324	306

Piece No. (X)	Size (Y)	X^2	XY
19	24	361	456
20	25	400	500
21	26	441	546
22	27	484	594
23	28	529	644
24	23	576	552
25	21	625	525
$\Sigma X = 325$	$\Sigma Y = 491$	$\Sigma X^2 = 5525$	$\Sigma XY = 6798$

Substituting these numbers into equation 20.1 gives

$$slope = \frac{6798 - \dfrac{325 \times 491}{25}}{5525 - \dfrac{(325)^2}{25}} = 0.319$$

The center line is drawn with a slope of 0.319, i.e., a change of 1 on the X axis = a change of 0.319 on the Y axis. Another way of looking at the slope is that it shows how much linear drift to expect per part. The starting size will be determined after computing how much drift will be allowed (see below).

How much drift should be allowed?

When discussing tool wear most books allow the process to drift until the production of out-of-specification parts is imminent. Such specification-based schemes tacitly assume that the only source of loss is scrap or rework of parts that fail to meet the requirements. It is now well established that any deviation from target (usually the nominal specification is the target) incurs additional loss. Taguchi suggests that the loss can be modelled using a quadratic loss function. The method of calculating the allowable drift that is offered here is based on Taguchi's suggestion.

The nominal-is-best total loss function is

$$L = k\,(\,x - nominal\,)^2 \tag{20.2}$$

where k is a constant, and x is the observed value. Usually x and nominal are known and k must be computed. A common way of calculating k is to use the loss value associated with producing an out of tolerance part. For example, if a process has a tolerance of ±0.005 inches and parts beyond this are scrapped for a loss of $10 per part, k is found as

$$k = \frac{\$10}{(0.005 - 0)^2} = \frac{\$10}{0.000025} = \$400,000 \, per \, in^2$$

The nominal-is-best average loss per part is

$$\$L = k \, S^2 \, (\overline{X} - nominal)^2 \qquad (20.3)$$

where S^2 is the variance around the mean, $\overline{X}$ and the term $(\overline{X} - nominal)$ measures the deviation of $\overline{X}$ from the target value. If the process is allowed to drift symmetrically across the nominal value, the overall average may equal the nominal value. However, there is a loss associated with the drift.

Consider figure 20.3. Costs are shown for a process with linear drift. It is possible to adjust the process to compensate for the drift. There is a cost associated with the drift of the process, and a cost associated with the adjustment of the process. What is desired is the minimum total cost which includes both the drift cost and the adjustment cost.

Ross (1988) has shown that if a process drifts in a linear fashion over a distance W the additional loss due to the drift is

$$L_A = k \frac{W^2}{12} \qquad (20.4)$$

As you can see, the drift cost is completely determined by the constant k and the amount of the drift. It is independent of the original process variance. The process should be adjusted when the amount of drift, W, is costing more than the cost of adjusting the process. The allowable drift is then

$$W = \sqrt{\frac{C_A \times 12}{k}} \qquad (20.5)$$

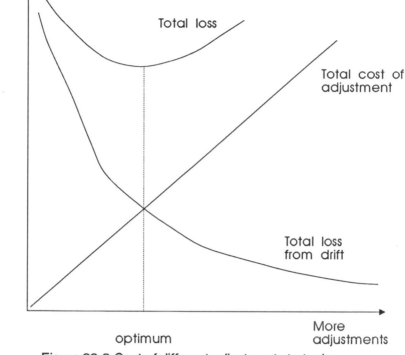

Figure 20-3-Cost of different adjustment strategies

where CA is the cost of making an adjustment.

Example of computing allowable drift

A printing process measures the color using a color index. The specification calls for keeping the color index between ± 0.02 of the target. Using a range chart control chart with subgroups of five gave $\overline{R}$ = 0.0045, the process standard deviation was estimated from $\overline{R}/d2$ as s = 0.002. Since $\frac{spec}{\sigma} = \frac{0.04}{0.002} = 20$ is greater than 10, we can tolerate some drift from this process. As the process runs the solvent evaporates slowly from the ink, causing the color index to drift in a linear fashion from higher to lower. The rate of drift is approximately 0.00004 per sheet printed, computed from equation 20.1.

It costs approximately $50 per hour to adjust the solvent level. If the process is allowed to drift beyond the 0.02 limit it produces scrap at the rate of $5,000 per hour. Find the allowable drift, if any.

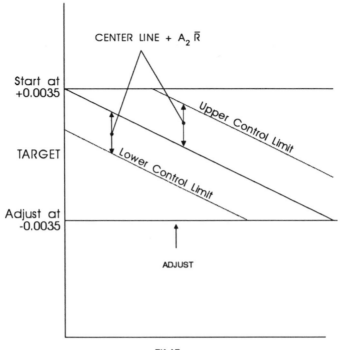

TIME

Figure 20-4-Printer process control chart

First we will find the constant K using equation 20.2.

$$k = \frac{\$5,000}{(0 - 0.02)^2} = \$12,500,000 = \$12.5M$$

The cost of adjusting the process is fixed at \$50 per hour. Using equation 20.5 we find W as

$$W = \sqrt{\frac{\$50 \times 12}{\$12.5M}} = 0.007$$

Thus the initial process setup will be $\frac{0.007}{2} = 0.0035$ above the target color index and the process mean will be allowed to drift until it is 0.0035 below the target color index. The control limits around this slanting center line will be the usual $\overline{X}$ control limits of $\pm A_2\overline{R}$ measured vertically. For this example we have $\overline{R} = 0.0045$ and for subgroups of 5 $A_2 = 0.577$, so the control limits are placed at a distance of 0.0026 on either side of the slanting center line, measured vertically. Figure 20.4 shows the control chart for this process.

Using the older method of modified control limits the process would be allowed a much greater drift. The additional drift allowed by the older method would result in greater color variation and less value to the customer, i.e., greater loss. In fact, the printer would do well to determine if the estimated cost of running off of the target is accurately estimated by the Taguchi cost equation.

References

Kane, V.E. (1989), *Defect prevention*, Marcel Dekker, Inc., New York, pp. 136-138.

Mandel, B.J. (1969), "The regression control chart," Journal of Quality Technology, 1(1), pp. 1-9.

Ross, P.J. (1988), *Taguchi techniques for quality engineering*, McGraw-Hill, New York, pp. 7-16.

Chapter 21

SPC FOR MULTIPLE STREAM PROCESSES

OBJECTIVES

After completing this section you will

- be able to identify "multiple-stream processes"

- know why traditional SPC tools are difficult to use with multiple-stream processes

- know how to use alternative SPC tools for multiple-stream processes

Introduction

The traditional SPC control chart is designed to be used with processes that produce a single steady "stream of output." Usually the process measurement involves measuring a very small number of variables, perhaps even a single variable. Under these circumstances the process owner has a fairly straightforward task to determine if the process is in control or out of control. If the process is out of control, the action needed to bring it back into control is usually known or relatively easy to ascertain.

Such is not the case with many processes commonly encountered in practice. Many processes generate not a single stream of output, but many. Here are a few examples.

- A machine shop in an automobile plant has ten spot-facing machines with eight spindles on each machine.

- A cosmetic manufacturer has four lines producing nail polish. Each line has a filler with twenty-four heads.

- An aerospace manufacturer has a numerically controlled machine which places dozens of similar features on each part using one tool. It has a magazine with forty different tools.

- A plastics manufacturer has six molds producing electrical box covers for use in housing construction. Each mold has twenty cavities.

Applying traditional SPC methods to one of these processes would require up to 120 separate control charts. In addition to the sheer volume of paperwork (and the associated expense), a large number of charts are very difficult to interpret simultaneously. Displaying the charts at the process is an exercise in futility. Tracking the historical trends and filing the charts is nearly impossible. This situation leads many to conclude that applying SPC is more trouble than it is worth. This chapter describes two alternatives that make the application of SPC to this type of process much more practical.

Analyzing multiple-stream processes

Ideally the multiple streams should be the same. If this were the case there would be no measurable difference between the output of one stream and that of any other stream. This is the goal of SPC, to minimize the total variation in the output. You should begin your analysis of any multiple-stream process by attempting to identify and eliminate significant differences between streams. Ott and Snee (1973) describe an approach to the analysis of a particular type of multiple-stream process, a multiple-head machine. However, the approach they describe can be easily applied to other types of multiple-stream processes. See the section below entitled "implementing group control charts" for a method of analyzing multiple stream processes using control charts.

When differences are found the SPC team should make a *serious* effort to identify the causes and take action to eliminate the differences. If the differences cannot be completely eliminated, perhaps they can be minimized. The action necessary to eliminate or reduce variation is not a statistical question, it requires insight into the process. The group control chart described below requires that the differences between streams be negligible.

A modification is described later that allows the use of group control charts when there are differences between streams. However, it is a serious blunder to simply apply a statistical technique that will accommodate the difference between streams. The customer could care less that the charts show the process to be in control. Improving quality by reducing variation is always preferable to statistical smoke and mirrors. Allowing significant differences to exist between streams should always be viewed as a temporary situation that will be remedied as soon as it is practical to do so.

The group control chart

The basic idea behind the group control chart is quite simple: plot only the extreme cases, if they are okay everything else is okay too. This approach still requires that all of the streams be checked, it's the only way to identify which streams are the extremes. However, the result is a single control chart for $\overline{X}$ and R, regardless of the number of streams being monitored. If the group control chart shows that statistical control exists you know the entire operation is in statistical control. Boyd (1950) describes the basic group control chart.

The basic idea of the group control chart is shown in figure 21.1. Figure 21.1 shows a filling process with three heads connected to a common supply source (fill station.) The filler line moves forward three bottles at a time. Each filling head is a separate stream or subprocess. Every hour a sample of six bottles is taken from the process. The sample consists of two consecutive bottles from head #1, head #2 and head #3. The bottles are weighed to determine their fill level and the deviation from the nominal fill weight is recorded in grams. The results for each head are recorded so that the head which produced the result is identified. The subgroup $\overline{X}$ and R is calculated for each head and recorded on the control chart form. The smallest and largest $\overline{X}$s and the largest R is plotted on the chart. The head which produced the plotted point is identified on the control chart, if more than one head had the same $\overline{X}$ or R, both heads are identified. Traditional control charts are designed to determine if the process has changed due to a special cause of variation. The group control chart has two objectives: determine if one of the streams (heads) is more extreme than the others, and determine if all heads have shifted away from the common target value. The extreme high or low individual stream can be determined by looking at the numbers recorded on the group control chart. For example, if the process shown in figure 21.1 always had the largest $\overline{X}$ as coming from head #2 we would suspect that head #2 was set higher than heads #1 or #3. An overall process shift would show on the control chart as points outside of the control limits, with no single head showing up as an extreme value too often.

Nelson (1986) describes a procedure for detecting a significantly long series of extreme values from the same stream. Table six in the appendix can be used to implement the approach described by Nelson. Table six shows the number of consecutive extreme values from a single stream that signals a problem. For example, a problem would be indicated for the three stream process in figure 21.1

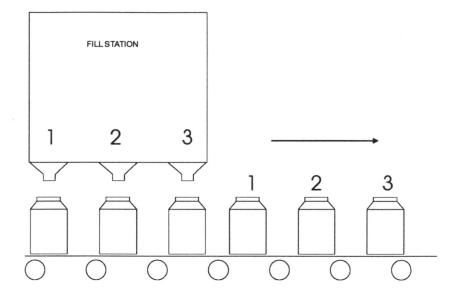

Time		8:00			9:00			10:00		
Stream		1	2	3	1	2	3	1	2	3
Sample	1	8	6	7	5	7	10	8	5	5
	2	7	9	5	7	7	9	8	5	9
$\bar{X}$		7.5	7.5	6.0	6.0	7.0	8.0	8.0	5.0	7.0
R		1	3	2	2	0	1	0	0	4

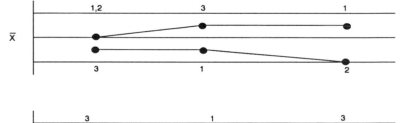

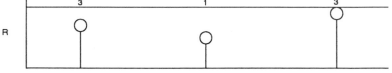

Figure 21-1-Group control chart layout

if the same head appeared as the highest (or lowest) value five times in a row. The approach can be used for both the $\overline{X}$ chart and the R chart.

Implementing group control charts

As with all other control charts, implementing the group control chart should begin with a process capability analysis (PCA). The procedure for performing PCA is described in chapter 13. When applying the PCA procedure to multiple stream processes, each process stream should be studied separately, i.e, conduct a complete PCA for each separate stream.

Once each stream has been brought into a state of statistical control on its own separate control chart, the differences *between streams* should be considered. Some questions that must be answered are:

❑ Are there statistically or economically important differences between the averages or ranges of the different streams?

❑ What might cause the differences?

❑ Can the differences be economically eliminated?

When performing the PCA, try to use the same subgroup size for each stream. This will make it easier to compare one stream to another. If the PCA shows the different streams to be essentially the same and each stream shows statistical control, arrange the different streams using the layout shown in figure 21.1 and plot the group control charts. The control limits for the group control chart are computed using traditional control chart constants. The subgroup size is the number of pieces taken from each stream, *not* the number of streams. For example, the subgroup size for the process in figure 21.1 is two, not three. The control limits for the group control chart are based on the data from all of the streams combined, e.g., if your PCA involved taking 20 subgroups of 5 from a process with three streams, the group control chart limits would be based on $20 \times 3 = 60$ subgroups of 5. The subgroup $\overline{X}$s and Rs will be based on units from the same stream, *not* on the differences between streams. The group control chart for the process would only have 20 sets of extreme values plotted, not 60.

After plotting the group control chart, analyze the number of times a particular stream produces the point plotted on the control chart. Use table six in the appendix to determine if one stream is responsible for too many plotted values. If it is, you should determine the reason and take corrective action (which is often easier said than done.)

Using the group control chart when all streams are not the same

As discussed above, every effort should be made to make the process streams consistent. The purpose of SPC is to improve quality by reducing variation from both common causes and special causes. Still, it will sometimes happen that the different streams produce inconsistent results that must be tolerated. When this happens the group control chart procedure described above will fail. The extreme stream will always be plotted, concealing changes in the other streams.

If the averages vary from stream to stream, but the ranges are consistent from stream to stream, a simple transformation will make it possible to use the group control chart despite the differences. The procedure is

1. Perform the PCA for each stream as described in the previous section.
2. Find the grand average for each stream.
3. For each stream, subtract the stream grand average from the observations obtained from the stream.
4. Construct a group control chart using the *differences* found in step 3.

For example, if a PCA of the process shown in figure 21.1 showed that $\overline{X}_1 = 5$, $\overline{X}_2 = 6$ and $\overline{X}_3 = 7$, then we would subtract these averages from the actual measurements. The sample from stream 1 at 8:00 becomes $8 - 5 = 3$ and $7 - 5 = 2$. The sample from stream 2 at 8:00 becomes $6 - 6 = 0$ and $9 - 6 = 3$. Table 21.1

Table 21-1-Transformed data from figure 21.1

Time		8:00			9:00			10:00		
Stream		1	2	3	1	2	3	1	2	3
Sample	1	3	0	0	0	1	3	3	-1	-2
	2	2	3	-2	2	1	2	3	-1	2
$\overline{X}$		1.5	1.5	-1.0	1.0	1.0	2.5	3.0	-1.0	0.0
R		1	3	2	2	0	1	0	0	4

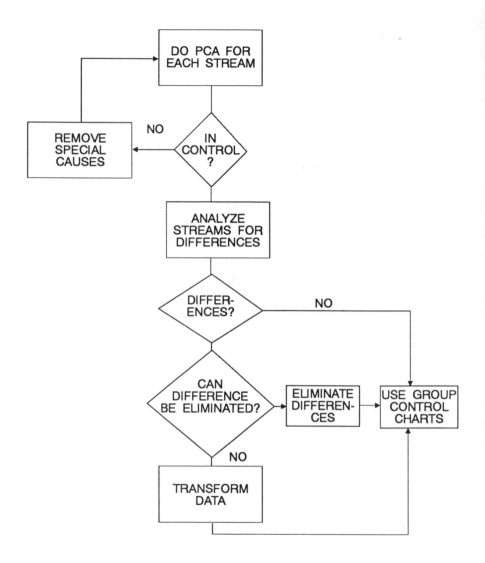

Figure 21-2-Implementing multiple stream SPC

shows the data from figure 21.1 after subtracting the stream averages from each value. Notice that the ranges are not changed by the subtraction process.

References

Boyd, D.F. (1950), "Applying the group chart for $\overline{X}$ and R," Industrial Quality Control, Nov. pp 22-25.

Burr, I.W. (1976), *Statistical quality control methods*, Marcel Dekker, New York, Section 7.5.3 and 7.5.4.

Nelson, L.S. (1986), "Control chart for multiple stream processes," Journal of Quality Technology, 18(4), pp. 255-256.

Ott, E.R. and Snee, R.D. (1973), "Identifying useful differences in a multiple-head machine," Journal of Quality Technology, 5(2), pp. 47-57.

Chapter 22

PROCESS CONTROL PLANNING

OBJECTIVES
After completing this section you will know how to

- Identify the key process elements
- Prepare the process control plan
- Prepare contingency plans
- Perform process improvement planning

The methodology presented here is highly structured and easily adapted to processes of all kinds. It can be used for both manufacturing and non-manufacturing processes.

Identifying key process elements
In the past identification of key process elements was left to "experts" who selected the most important control items through a subjective approach. The results were mixed; some experts chose a very small number of items, others a large number. A major shortcoming was that any questions about the control elements was often taken as a personal affront by the expert, who felt that his or her judgement was being called into question. The rationale behind the choices was seldom explicit and it is likely that different experts used different criteria for selection; one expert might emphasize the function of the product, another the cost of inspection, and another might look to the process capability and likelihood of problems. Process control was often a secondary concern, with the major focus being on detecting non-conforming products.

The situation was even worse for non-manufacturing businesses and administrative processes. In these industries the concept of "process" was unheard of, so process control was totally alien. With few exceptions, the individual was blamed when something went wrong.

In the modern organization teams, rather than individuals, are usually given the job of selecting items for control using SPC and other quality improvement tools. Unlike individuals working alone, team members must be prepared to explain their choices with cogent and persuasive logic. This can be facilitated if a structured approach is used to select the process control items. The method described in this section is a simplified version of quality function deployment (QFD). QFD has been used for years to "deploy" the voice of the customer throughout the entire business. We will use QFD for exactly the same reason: to extend the voice of the customer to the process control plan. The reader is reminded that there are both internal and external customers. The external customer receives the final product or service and resides outside of the company. The internal customer receives an *interim* product or service and resides within the company. A given process may have several internal customers, such as the next process, the quality department, and material handling. The wants of all internal customers should be considered in setting up the process control plan. The rendition of QFD used in this book will involve building a simple "house of quality" as shown in figure 22.1. The steps taken in creating the house of quality are:

1. Use brainstorming to create a list of process elements and customers for the process.
2. Survey the customers for the process to determine what they want from the process. Have the customers rank each want as either high, average or low. Record the customer's responses as rows in the "customer wants" section of the house of quality, using the customer's own words and phrases as much as possible. Record the score for the customer importance values (CIVs) in the CIV column of the house of quality. The scoring system shown in figure 22.1, high = 5, etc. has been used successfully in other QFD applications, but of course you may modify it if you choose. If several customer's have different CIVs for a given row, have the team determine the CIV to record in the house of quality by consensus. Usually the highest CIV is used; it's usually better to give some customers more than they need than to give someone less than they need.
3. Record the process elements in the columns of the house of quality. Complete the correlation matrix, the "roof" on the house of quality. The correlation matrix shows the relationship between each process element and every other process element. Again, use the high, average and low system to identify the strength of the correlation. If there is no correlation, leave the box blank and record a score of zero. If there is *negative correlation* (i.e., increasing one element will result in decreasing another) record a minus sign in front of the score. Unlike other parts of the house of quality, the

217

High	5
Average	3
Low	1

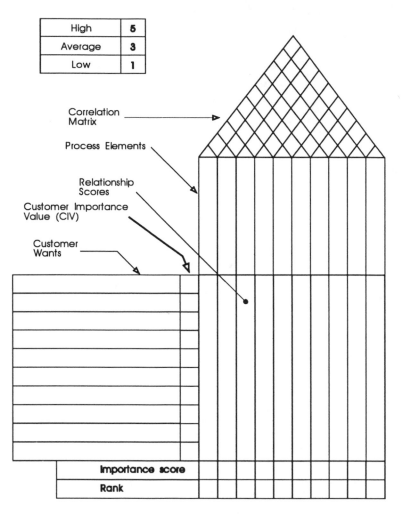

Correlation Matrix

Process Elements

Relationship Scores

Customer Importance Value (CIV)

Customer Wants

Importance score

Rank

Figure 22-1-The House of Quality

values in the roof can often be determined with hard data. Scatterplots are helpful for this purpose. The correlation matrix will be used to minimize the cost of control and to determine "trade-offs."
4. By consensus, determine the relationship score for each customer want and process element. Use the high, average and low scoring system.
5. Determine the importance scores for each process element. This is done by multiplying the CIV for each row by the relationship scores for the pro-

cess element column and adding the results for all rows. A process element that has a high relationship with many customer wants will receive a high importance score.

6. Rank order the process elements according to their importance scores.

At this point the team will have an objective indication of the importance of each process element. However, it is likely that members of the team will disagree with the objective assessment. The final rankings should be determined by discussion and consensus. The objective analysis will be extremely helpful in these discussions. Obviously, the end result of all of this is an indication of which process elements are the most important in terms of meeting the wants of the customer. This information will be used in the next phase in creating the process control plan.

Preparing the process control plan

The team should begin this phase by creating a flowchart of the process using the process elements determined in creating the house of quality. The flowchart will show how the process elements relate to one another and it will help in the selection of control points. It will also show the point of delivery to the customer.

For any given process there are a number of different types of process elements. Some process elements are internal to the process, others external. The rotation speed of a drill is an internal process element, while the humidity in the building is external. Some process elements, while important, are easy to fix at a given value so that they do not change unless deliberate action is taken. We will call these "fixed" elements. Other process elements vary of their own accord and must be watched, we call these "variable" elements. The drill rotation speed can be set in advance, but the line voltage for the drill press may vary, which causes the drill speed to change in spite of its initial setting (a good example of how the correlation matrix might be useful.) Figure 22.2 provides a planning guide based on the internal/external and fixed/variable classification scheme. Of course, other classification schemes may be more suitable on a given project and you are encouraged to develop the approach that best serves your needs. For convenience each class if identified with a roman numeral; I = fixed internal, II = fixed external, III = variable internal and IV = variable external.

In selecting the appropriate method of control for each process element, pay particular attention to those process elements which received high importance rankings in the house of quality analysis. In some cases you might find that an important process element is very expensive to control. When this happens, look

	INTERNAL	EXTERNAL
FIXED	I: Setup approval; periodic audits; preventive maintainance.	II: Audit; certification.
VARIABLE	III: Control charts; foolproof product; foolproof process; sort output.	IV: Supplier SPC; receiving inspection; supplier sorting; foolproof product; foolproof process.

Figure 22-2-Process Control Planning Guide

at the correlation matrix for possible assistance. The process element may be correlated with other process elements that are less costly to control. The correlation matrix will also help you to minimize the number of control charts. It is usually unnecessary to keep control charts on several variables that are correlated with one another. In these cases it may be possible to select the process element that is least expensive to monitor as the control variable.

As figure 22.2 indicates, control charts are not always the best method of controlling a given process element. In fact, control charts are seldom the method of choice. When process elements are important we would prefer that they *not vary at all*! Only when this can not be accomplished economically do we resort to the use of control charts to monitor the element's variation. Control charts may be thought of as a control mechanism of last resort. Control charts are useful only when the element being monitored can be expected to exhibit measurable and "random-looking" variation when the process is properly controlled. A process element that always checks 10 if everything is okay is not a good candidate for control charting. Nor is one that checks 10 or 12, but never anything else. Ideally, the measurements being monitored with variables control charts will be capable of taking on any value, i.e., the data will be continuous. Discrete measurement data can be used if it's not *too* discrete; indeed, all real-world data is somewhat discrete. As a rule of thumb, at least 10 different values should appear in the data set and no one value should comprise more than 20% of the data set. When the measurement data becomes too discrete for SPC, monitor it with checksheets or simple time-ordered plots (run charts.)

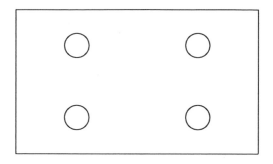

Figure 22-3-Gearbox Mounting Plate for SPC

Of course, the above discussion applies to measurement data. Attribute control charts (volume one, chapter 10) can be used to monitor process elements that are discrete counts.

Any process control plan must include instructions on what action to take if problems appear. This is particularly important where control charts are being used for process control. Unlike process control procedures like audits or setup approvals, it is not always apparent just what is wrong when a control chart indicates a problem. The investigation of special causes of variation usually consists of a number of predetermined actions (such as checking the fixture or checking a cutting tool), followed by notifying someone if the items checked don't reveal the source of the problem. Don't forget to verify that the arithmetic was done correctly and that the point was plotted in the correct position on the control chart.

The reader may have noticed that figure 22.2 includes "sort output" in a couple of places. Sorting the output implies that the process is not capable of meeting the customer's requirements. However, even if sorting is taking place, SPC is still advisable. SPC will help assure that things don't get any *worse*. SPC will also reveal *improvements* that may otherwise be overlooked. The improvements may result in a process that is good enough to eliminate the need for sorting.

Example of process control planning
An SPC team is considering the part shown in figure 22.3. For illustration purposes, the process is a very simple one. It is usually a good idea for SPC teams to start with a simple process to get a feel for the way the methodology works.

Table 22-1-What Customer Wants in Gearbox Plates

ID	Customer Wants	CIV
A	Fit not too tight	5
B	Fit not too sloppy	5
C	Pattern not too close to edge	3
D	Pattern not too far from edge	3
E	Holes round	3
F	No burrs in holes	1
G	No burrs on edges of plate	1

In fact, even when dealing with extremely complicated processes, it is best to break the process down into simple subprocesses.

The first step in process control planning is to flowchart the process. Using the flowchart, identify the suppliers, process elements, and customers for the process. Prepare a list of the customer wants and the CIV for each want. Table 22.1 shows what the customer wants from the process producing the gearbox

Table 22-2-Gearbox Plate Manufacturing Process

ID	Process Elements	Class
1	Drill bit sizes	I
2	Initial setup of fixture	I
3	Feed rate	I
4	Drill speed	I
5	Coolant age	I
6	Coolant flow rate	I
7	Coolant nozzle position	I
8	Part placed in fixture correctly	III
9	Material hardness	IV
10	Deburring tool	I
11	Hole size	III
12	Hole location	III

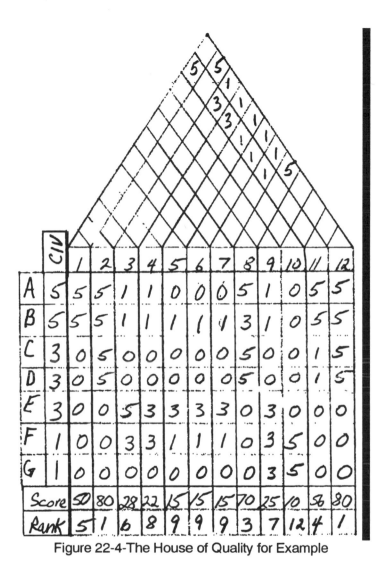

Figure 22-4-The House of Quality for Example

mounting plate. Each want is given an identification letter (A-G) and the CIVs are shown.

Table 22.2 shows the process elements. Each process element is given an identification number (1-12). The element is classified using the criteria in the process control planning guide in figure 22.2, the classification is shown with a roman numeral in table 22.2.

A house of quality is created using the customer wants as rows and the process elements as columns, as indicated by figure 22.1. The result for our example is shown in figure 22.4. A score and ranking result for each process element, based on the CIVs and the relationship between the process element and the customer wants.

How should these scores and rankings be used? First and foremost, do not think of the scores and rankings as absolutes. They merely provide information to be carefully considered when preparing the process control plan. The scores for process elements #2 and #12 are the highest, both are 80. This indicates that the initial setup of the fixture and the hole locations are important process elements. The roof of the house of quality contains a 5 at the intersection of elements 2 and 12, indicating they are highly correlated with one another. However, the house of quality also indicates that hole location is highly correlated with element 8, part placement in the fixture. Element 2 is a class I item, indicating that it should be checked at setup approval and with periodic audits. Since it is so important, relatively frequent audits should be considered. Elements 8 and 12 are category III items. Element 8, part placement in the fixture, is a poor candidate for SPC; foolproofing would probably be the best way to approach the control of this element. Element 12, hole location, is a good candidate for a control chart. However, if the process setup and foolproofing are good enough, it may be that the hole location is guaranteed; if so, the SPC sampling frequency and sample sizes could be greatly reduced or, perhaps, the control chart can be completely eliminated.

What about the process elements with low ranks, should they be ignored? Of course not. Although the most important process elements are given the greatest amount of attention, all of the process elements have an impact on quality and cost, so all must be considered. For example, although the deburring tool is the least important element, the process control plan should at least assure that the correct deburring tool is provided to the operator.

Observe that drawing the house of quality can be done quite easily with pencil and paper. Too often, SPC teams get themselves bogged down with artistic considerations that have no bearing on the ultimate goal of improving the process. The house of quality shown in figure 22.4 was drawn up in about thirty minutes by one person. The discussions that go into creating the house of quality take quite a bit longer, but these discussions are worth the effort because they lead to improved understanding of the things that affect quality.

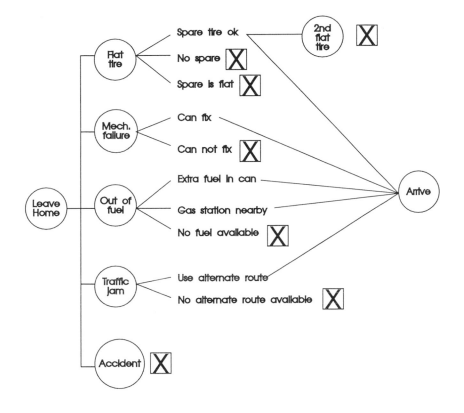

Figure 22-5-Sample Contingency Planning Diagram

Contingency planning

All processes produce two different types of outcomes: those we want and those we don't want. In process control planning, it is important that both type of outcomes be carefully considered. The appropriate tool for dealing with undesirable outcomes is the contingency planning diagram. Preparation of this diagram involves five steps.

1. Use brainstorming to determine all possible undesirable outcomes.
2. Determine the events or sequence of events that would result in each undesirable outcome.
3. Prepare plans that prevent each undesirable outcome or reduce the likelihood to acceptably low levels.
4. Prepare exigency plans to deal with undesirable outcomes that occur in spite of everything you do.
5. Prepare a contingency planning diagram that graphically summarizes the results of the above four steps.

Figure 22.5 shows a contingency planning diagram for a person trying to get to work on time.

Process improvement planning

The "C" in SPC stands for "control." But control implies maintaining the current status of the process. In SPC this means that any special cause that changes the current level of performance will be investigated. However, the process itself will not be improved by this approach. More must be done.

The first goal of the SPC team should be to understand the process and bring it into a state of statistical control. A state of statistical control is reached when special causes rarely appear and they are quickly identified and corrected when they do appear. After reaching this state, process improvement planning can begin. It is usually not a good idea to begin process improvement planning until statistical control is reached because the level of the team's process knowledge is inadequate. In fact in can be argued that when the process is out of control there really isn't a "process" per se, there are multiple processes. If you don't know what is causing the process to change "all by itself," it is presumptuous to believe that you can deliberately change the process in the way you want. Besides, once you isolate the special causes you might have a process that is perfectly acceptable without additional investments. It is not unheard of to have improvement of two or three orders of magnitude with no money spent other than the expense of SPC team meetings and training.

If you reach a state of statistical control and the process is still not acceptable, a rigorous quality improvement program may be worthwhile. Again, experience indicates that these programs are usually done best by teams rather than by individuals working alone. Creative thinking is necessary. Here are some questions to consider:

❏ Can this process be eliminated?
❏ Can this process be combined with another process?

- ❑ Can one or more process steps be eliminated?
- ❑ Can one or more process steps be combined with other steps?
- ❑ Can the process steps themselves be simplified?
- ❑ Can scheduling be improved?
- ❑ Can the process flow be improved?

Of course, many of the tools used in routine SPC, such as process flowcharts, brainstorming, cause and effect diagrams and checksheets can also be used in process improvement planning.

Appendix of Tables

Index

Table 1 - Factors for control charts for variables $\overline{X}$, $\overline{Y}$, s R: Normal universe factors for computing central lines and 3σ control limits

Observations in Sample, n	Chart for Averages					Chart for Standard Deviations							Chart for Ranges						
	Factors for Control Limits			Factors for Central Line		Factors for Control Limits				Factors for Central Line			Factors for Control Limits						
	A	A_2	A_3	c_4	$1/c_4$	B_3	B_4	B_5	B_6	d_2	$1/d_2$	d_3	D_1	D_2	D_3	D_4			
2	2.121	1.880	2.659	0.7979	1.2533	0	3.267	0	2.606	1.128	0.8865	0.853	0	3.686	0	3.267			
3	1.732	1.023	1.954	0.8862	1.1284	0	2.568	0	2.276	1.693	0.5907	0.888	0	4.358	0	2.574			
4	1.500	0.729	1.628	0.9213	1.0854	0	2.266	0	2.088	2.059	0.4857	0.880	0	4.698	0	2.282			
5	1.342	0.577	1.427	0.9400	1.0638	0	2.089	0	1.964	2.326	0.4299	0.864	0	4.918	0	2.114			
6	1.225	0.483	1.287	0.9515	1.0510	0.030	1.970	0.029	1.874	2.534	0.3946	0.848	0	5.078	0	2.004			
7	1.134	0.419	1.182	0.9594	1.0423	0.118	1.882	0.113	1.806	2.704	0.3698	0.833	0.204	5.204	0.076	1.924			
8	1.061	0.373	1.099	0.9650	1.0363	0.185	1.815	0.179	1.751	2.847	0.3512	0.820	0.388	5.306	0.136	1.864			
9	1.000	0.337	1.032	0.9693	1.0317	0.239	1.761	0.232	1.707	2.970	0.3367	0.808	0.547	5.393	0.184	1.816			
10	0.949	0.308	0.975	0.9727	1.0281	0.284	1.716	0.276	1.669	3.078	0.3249	0.797	0.687	5.469	0.223	1.777			
11	0.905	0.285	0.927	0.9754	1.0252	0.321	1.679	0.313	1.637	3.173	0.3152	0.787	0.811	5.535	0.256	1.744			
12	0.866	0.266	0.886	0.9776	1.0229	0.354	1.646	0.346	1.610	3.258	0.3069	0.778	0.922	5.594	0.283	1.717			
13	0.832	0.249	0.850	0.9794	1.0210	0.382	1.618	0.374	1.585	3.336	0.2998	0.770	1.025	5.647	0.307	1.693			
14	0.802	0.235	0.817	0.9810	1.0194	0.406	1.594	0.399	1.563	3.407	0.2935	0.763	1.118	5.696	0.328	1.672			
15	0.775	0.223	0.789	0.9823	1.0180	0.428	1.572	0.421	1.544	3.472	0.2880	0.756	1.203	5.741	0.347	1.653			
16	0.750	0.212	0.763	0.9835	1.0168	0.448	1.552	0.440	1.526	3.532	0.2831	0.750	1.282	5.782	0.363	1.637			
17	0.728	0.203	0.739	0.9845	1.0157	0.466	1.534	0.458	1.511	3.588	0.2787	0.744	1.356	5.820	0.378	1.622			
18	0.707	0.194	0.718	0.9854	1.0148	0.482	1.518	0.475	1.496	3.640	0.2747	0.739	1.424	5.856	0.391	1.608			
19	0.688	0.187	0.698	0.9862	1.0140	0.497	1.503	0.490	1.483	3.689	0.2711	0.734	1.487	5.891	0.403	1.597			
20	0.671	0.180	0.680	0.9869	1.0133	0.510	1.490	0.504	1.470	3.735	0.2677	0.729	1.549	5.921	0.415	1.585			
21	0.655	0.173	0.663	0.9876	1.0126	0.523	1.477	0.516	1.459	3.778	0.2647	0.724	1.605	5.951	0.425	1.575			
22	0.640	0.167	0.647	0.9882	1.0119	0.534	1.466	0.528	1.448	3.819	0.2618	0.720	1.659	5.979	0.434	1.566			
23	0.626	0.162	0.633	0.9887	1.0114	0.545	1.455	0.539	1.438	3.858	0.2592	0.716	1.710	6.006	0.443	1.557			
24	0.612	0.157	0.619	0.9892	1.0109	0.555	1.445	0.549	1.429	3.895	0.2567	0.712	1.759	6.031	0.451	1.548			
25	0.600	0.153	0.606	0.9896	1.0105	0.565	1.435	0.559	1.420	3.931	0.2544	0.708	1.806	6.056	0.459	1.541			

Table 2 -- Cumulative normal distribution -- values of p

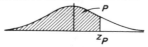

Values of P corresponding to z_p for the normal curve.

z is the standard normal variable.   The value of P for $-z_p$ equals one minus the value of P for $+z_p$,
e.g., the P for -1.62 equals $1 - .9474 = .0526$.

z_p	.00	.01	.02	.03	.04	.05	.06	.07	.08	.09
.0	.5000	.5040	.5080	.5120	.5160	.5199	.5239	.5279	.5319	.5359
.1	.5398	.5438	.5478	.5517	.5557	.5596	.5636	.5675	.5714	.5753
.2	.5793	.5832	.5871	.5910	.5948	.5987	.6026	.6064	.6103	.6141
.3	.6179	.6217	.6255	.6293	.6331	.6368	.6406	.6443	.6480	.6517
.4	.6554	.6591	.6628	.6664	.6700	.6736	.6772	.6808	.6844	.6879
.5	.6915	.6950	.6985	.7019	.7054	.7088	.7123	.7157	.7190	.7224
.6	.7257	.7291	.7324	.7357	.7389	.7422	.7454	.7486	.7517	.7549
.7	.7580	.7611	.7642	.7673	.7704	.7734	.7764	.7794	.7823	.7852
.8	.7881	.7910	.7939	.7967	.7995	.8023	.8051	.8078	.8106	.8133
.9	.8159	.8186	.8212	.8238	.8264	.8289	.8315	.8340	.8365	.8389
1.0	.8413	.8438	.8461	.8485	.8508	.8531	.8554	.8577	.8599	.8621
1.1	.8643	.8665	.8686	.8708	.8729	.8749	.8770	.8790	.8810	.8830
1.2	.8849	.8869	.8888	.8907	.8925	.8944	.8962	.8980	.8997	.9015
1.3	.9032	.9049	.9066	.9082	.9099	.9115	.9131	.9147	.9162	.9177
1.4	.9192	.9207	.9222	.9236	.9251	.9265	.9279	.9292	.9306	.9319
1.5	.9332	.9345	.9357	.9370	.9382	.9394	.9406	.9418	.9429	.9441
1.6	.9452	.9463	.9474	.9484	.9495	.9505	.9515	.9525	.9535	.9545
1.7	.9554	.9564	.9573	.9582	.9591	.9599	.9608	.9616	.9625	.9633
1.8	.9641	.9649	.9656	.9664	.9671	.9678	.9686	.9693	.9699	.9706
1.9	.9713	.9719	.9726	.9732	.9738	.9744	.9750	.9756	.9761	.9767
2.0	.9772	.9778	.9783	.9788	.9793	.9798	.9803	.9808	.9812	.9817
2.1	.9821	.9826	.9830	.9834	.9838	.9842	.9846	.9850	.9854	.9857
2.2	.9861	.9864	.9868	.9871	.9875	.9878	.9881	.9884	.9887	.9890
2.3	.9893	.9896	.9898	.9901	.9904	.9906	.9909	.9911	.9913	.9916
2.4	.9918	.9920	.9922	.9925	.9927	.9929	.9931	.9932	.9934	.9936
2.5	.9938	.9940	.9941	.9943	.9945	.9946	.9948	.9949	.9951	.9952
2.6	.9953	.9955	.9956	.9957	.9959	.9960	.9961	.9962	.9963	.9964
2.7	.9965	.9966	.9967	.9968	.9969	.9970	.9971	.9972	.9973	.9974
2.8	.9974	.9975	.9976	.9977	.9977	.9978	.9979	.9979	.9980	.9981
2.9	.9981	.9982	.9982	.9983	.9984	.9984	.9985	.9985	.9986	.9986
3.0	.9987	.9987	.9987	.9988	.9988	.9989	.9989	.9989	.9990	.9990
3.1	.9990	.9991	.9991	.9991	.9992	.9992	.9992	.9992	.9993	.9993
3.2	.9993	.9993	.9994	.9994	.9994	.9994	.9994	.9995	.9995	.9995
3.3	.9995	.9995	.9995	.9996	.9996	.9996	.9996	.9996	.9996	.9997
3.4	.9997	.9997	.9997	.9997	.9997	.9997	.9997	.9997	.9997	.9998

Table 3 -- Equivalent Guassian Deviates (EGD)

	0.00	0.01	0.02	0.03	0.04	0.05	0.06	0.07	0.08	0.09
0.0		2.33	2.05	1.88	1.75	1.65	1.56	1.48	1.41	1.34
0.1	1.28	1.23	1.18	1.13	1.08	1.04	0.99	0.95	0.92	0.88
0.2	0.84	0.81	0.77	0.74	0.71	0.67	0.64	0.61	0.58	0.55
0.3	0.52	0.50	0.47	0.44	0.41	0.38	0.36	0.33	0.31	0.28
0.4	0.25	0.23	0.20	0.18	0.15	0.13	0.10	0.08	0.05	0.02
0.5	0.00	0.02	0.05	0.08	0.10	0.13	0.15	0.18	0.20	0.23
0.6	0.25	0.28	0.31	0.33	0.36	0.38	0.41	0.44	0.47	0.50
0.7	0.52	0.55	0.58	0.61	0.64	0.67	0.71	0.74	0.77	0.81
0.8	0.84	0.88	0.92	0.95	0.99	1.04	1.08	1.13	1.18	1.23
0.9	1.28	1.34	1.41	1.48	1.56	1.65	1.75	1.88	2.05	2.33

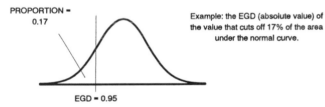

PROPORTION = 0.17

EGD = 0.95

Example: the EGD (absolute value) of the value that cuts off 17% of the area under the normal curve.

Table 4 -- Folded normal distributions

EXAMPLE: $\mu_f/\sigma_f = 1.7$

t_f IS IN σ_f UNITS

μ_f/σ_f → t_f ↓	1.3236	1.35	1.40	1.45	1.50	1.55	1.60	1.65	1.70	1.75	1.80	1.85	1.90	1.95	2.00	2.05	2.10	2.15
0.0	.0000	.0000	.0000	.0000	.0000	.0000	.0000	.0000	.0000	.0000	.0000	.0000	.0000	.0000	.0000	.0000	.0000	.0000
0.1	.0481	.0463	.0428	.0393	.0360	.0328	.0299	.0271	.0245	.0221	.0199	.0179	.0161	.0144	.0129	.0115	.0102	.0091
0.2	.0960	.0924	.0855	.0786	.0720	.0658	.0599	.0544	.0492	.0445	.0401	.0361	.0324	.0291	.0260	.0232	.0207	.0184
0.3	.1435	.1383	.1280	.1179	.1082	.0989	.0902	.0820	.0744	.0674	.0609	.0549	.0494	.0444	.0398	.0356	.0318	.0284
0.4	.1905	.1837	.1703	.1572	.1444	.1323	.1209	.1102	.1002	.0910	.0824	.0745	.0672	.0605	.0544	.0488	.0437	.0391
0.5	.2369	.2286	.2123	.1963	.1809	.1661	.1522	.1391	.1269	.1155	.1049	.0951	.0861	.0778	.0702	.0632	.0568	.0509
0.6	.2924	.2727	.2539	.2354	.2174	.2003	.1841	.1688	.1545	.1411	.1287	.1171	.1064	.0964	.0873	.0789	.0712	.0641
0.7	.3270	.3161	.2950	.2742	.2542	.2349	.2167	.1995	.1832	.1680	.1538	.1405	.1281	.1166	.1060	.0962	.0871	.0788
0.8	.3704	.3585	.3355	.3129	.2910	.2700	.2500	.2310	.2131	.1962	.1803	.1654	.1515	.1386	.1265	.1153	.1049	.0952
0.9	.4125	.3998	.3753	.3512	.3279	.3054	.2840	.2635	.2441	.2258	.2084	.1921	.1767	.1623	.1488	.1363	.1245	.1136
1.0	.4534	.4400	.4144	.3892	.3648	.3412	.3186	.2969	.2763	.2567	.2381	.2204	.2037	.1880	.1732	.1593	.1462	.1340
1.1	.4927	.4789	.4526	.4267	.4015	.3772	.3537	.3312	.3096	.2889	.2692	.2504	.2326	.2156	.1995	.1844	.1700	.1566
1.2	.5305	.5165	.4898	.4636	.4381	.4133	.3893	.3662	.3439	.3224	.3018	.2820	.2631	.2451	.2279	.2115	.1960	.1813
1.3	.5668	.5526	.5260	.4998	.4743	.4494	.4252	.4018	.3790	.3570	.3357	.3152	.2954	.2764	.2582	.2407	.2241	.2082
1.4	.6013	.5873	.5610	.5352	.5100	.4853	.4612	.4377	.4148	.3924	.3707	.3496	.3292	.3094	.2903	.2719	.2543	.2373
1.5	.6341	.6204	.5947	.5696	.5450	.5209	.4972	.4739	.4510	.4286	.4066	.3852	.3642	.3439	.3241	.3049	.2863	.2684
1.6	.6652	.6519	.6272	.6031	.5793	.5559	.5328	.5100	.4874	.4651	.4432	.4216	.4004	.3796	.3593	.3395	.3202	.3014
1.7	.6945	.6818	.6583	.6353	.6127	.5903	.5680	.5458	.5238	.5019	.4801	.4586	.4373	.4163	.3957	.3754	.3555	.3361
1.8	.7221	.7100	.6879	.6663	.6449	.6237	.6024	.5811	.5593	.5385	.5172	.4960	.4748	.4538	.4330	.4124	.3922	.3722
1.9	.7479	.7366	.7160	.6959	.6760	.6560	.6360	.6157	.5953	.5747	.5541	.5333	.5124	.4916	.4709	.4502	.4298	.4095
2.0	.7720	.7615	.7426	.7241	.7057	.6872	.6684	.6493	.6300	.6103	.5904	.5703	.5500	.5295	.5090	.4885	.4680	.4476
2.1	.7945	.7848	.7676	.7508	.7340	.7169	.6995	.6818	.6636	.6450	.6260	.6066	.5870	.5671	.5471	.5268	.5065	.4862
2.2	.8152	.8065	.7910	.7759	.7607	.7452	.7292	.7128	.6959	.6784	.6605	.6421	.6233	.6041	.5847	.5649	.5450	.5249
2.3	.8344	.8266	.8128	.7994	.7858	.7718	.7573	.7423	.7267	.7104	.6937	.6763	.6585	.6402	.6215	.6024	.5830	.5634
2.4	.8520	.8451	.8331	.8213	.8093	.7968	.7833	.7701	.7553	.7409	.7253	.7092	.6924	.6751	.6573	.6390	.6203	.6012

Table 4 -- Folded normal distributions (continued)

t_f \ μ_f/σ_f	1.3236	1.35	1.40	1.45	1.50	1.55	1.60	1.65	1.70	1.75	1.80	1.85	1.90	1.95	2.00	2.05	2.10	2.15
2.5	.8682	.8621	.8518	.8416	.8310	.8200	.8084	.7962	.7832	.7696	.7553	.7403	.7247	.7085	.6917	.6743	.6565	.6382
2.6	.8830	.8778	.8689	.8602	.8511	.8415	.8313	.8204	.8087	.7964	.7834	.7697	.7553	.7402	.7245	.7082	.6913	.6739
2.7	.8964	.8920	.8846	.8773	.8695	.8612	.8523	.8426	.8323	.8213	.8095	.7971	.7839	.7700	.7555	.7403	.7245	.7031
2.8	.9086	.9049	.8989	.8928	.8862	.8792	.8714	.8630	.8539	.8441	.8336	.8224	.8105	.7978	.7845	.7705	.7558	.7405
2.9	.9196	.9166	.9118	.9068	.9014	.8954	.8883	.8815	.8736	.8650	.8557	.8456	.8349	.8235	.8114	.7986	.7851	.7709
3.0	.9295	.9272	.9234	.9194	.9150	.9100	.9044	.8992	.8913	.8838	.8756	.8668	.8572	.8470	.8361	.8245	.8122	.7992
3.1	.9383	.9366	.9338	.9307	.9271	.9230	.9183	.9131	.9072	.9007	.8936	.8858	.8774	.8684	.8586	.8482	.8371	.8254
3.2	.9463	.9450	.9430	.9407	.9379	.9345	.9307	.9263	.9213	.9157	.9096	.9029	.8955	.8875	.8789	.8697	.8598	.8492
3.3	.9533	.9525	.9512	.9495	.9473	.9447	.9415	.9379	.9337	.9290	.9237	.9180	.9116	.9047	.8971	.8890	.8802	.8708
3.4	.9596	.9592	.9584	.9573	.9556	.9535	.9510	.9480	.9445	.9406	.9361	.9312	.9257	.9198	.9132	.9061	.8984	.8901
3.5	.9651	.9650	.9647	.9640	.9628	.9612	.9592	.9568	.9539	.9506	.9469	.9427	.9381	.9330	.9274	.9212	.9145	.9073
3.6	.9700	.9702	.9702	.9699	.9690	.9678	.9663	.9643	.9620	.9593	.9562	.9527	.9488	.9445	.9397	.9344	.9287	.9224
3.7	.9743	.9746	.9750	.9749	.9744	.9735	.9723	.9707	.9688	.9666	.9641	.9612	.9580	.9543	.9503	.9458	.9409	.9355
3.8	.9780	.9785	.9791	.9792	.9789	.9783	.9774	.9762	.9747	.9729	.9709	.9684	.9657	.9627	.9593	.9556	.9514	.9469
3.9	.9813	.9819	.9826	.9829	.9828	.9823	.9816	.9807	.9795	.9781	.9764	.9745	.9723	.9698	.9670	.9639	.9604	.9566
4.0	.9841	.9848	.9856	.9860	.9860	.9857	.9852	.9845	.9836	.9825	.9811	.9796	.9778	.9758	.9735	.9709	.9680	.9648
4.1	.9865	.9873	.9882	.9886	.9887	.9885	.9882	.9876	.9869	.9861	.9850	.9838	.9823	.9807	.9788	.9767	.9743	.9717
4.2	.9887	.9894	.9903	.9907	.9909	.9908	.9906	.9902	.9897	.9890	.9882	.9872	.9860	.9847	.9832	.9815	.9796	.9774
4.3	.9905	.9912	.9921	.9925	.9927	.9927	.9926	.9923	.9919	.9914	.9907	.9900	.9891	.9880	.9868	.9855	.9839	.9822
4.4	.9920	.9928	.9936	.9940	.9942	.9943	.9942	.9940	.9937	.9933	.9928	.9922	.9915	.9907	.9897	.9887	.9874	.9860
4.5	.9933	.9940	.9948	.9952	.9955	.9955	.9955	.9953	.9951	.9948	.9945	.9940	.9935	.9928	.9921	.9912	.9902	.9891
4.6	.9944	.9951	.9958	.9962	.9964	.9965	.9965	.9964	.9963	.9960	.9958	.9954	.9950	.9945	.9939	.9933	.9925	.9916
4.7	.9954	.9960	.9967	.9970	.9972	.9973	.9973	.9973	.9972	.9970	.9968	.9965	.9962	.9958	.9954	.9949	.9943	.9936
4.8	.9962	.9968	.9973	.9977	.9978	.9979	.9980	.9980	.9978	.9977	.9976	.9974	.9972	.9969	.9965	.9961	.9957	.9951
4.9	.9969	.9974	.9979	.9982	.9983	.9984	.9985	.9984	.9984	.9983	.9982	.9980	.9979	.9977	.9974	.9971	.9968	.9964
5.0	.9974	.9979	.9984	.9986	.9987	.9988	.9988	.9988	.9988	.9987	.9987	.9986	.9984	.9983	.9981	.9979	.9976	.9973
5.1	.9979	.9983	.9987	.9989	.9990	.9991	.9991	.9991	.9991	.9991	.9990	.9990	.9988	.9987	.9986	.9984	.9982	.9980
5.2	.9983	.9987	.9990	.9992	.9993	.9993	.9994	.9994	.9993	.9993	.9993	.9992	.9992	.9991	.9990	.9988	.9987	.9985
5.3	.9986	.9989	.9992	.9994	.9995	.9995	.9995	.9995	.9995	.9995	.9995	.9994	.9994	.9993	.9993	.9992	.9991	.9989
5.4	.9989	.9992	.9994	.9995	.9996	.9996	.9997	.9997	.9997	.9996	.9996	.9996	.9996	.9995	.9995	.9994	.9993	.9992
5.5	.9991	.9993	.9995	.9996	.9997	.9997	.9997	.9998	.9998	.9997	.9997	.9997	.9997	.9998	.9996	.9996	.9995	.9995
5.6	.9993	.9995	.9997	.9997	.9998	.9998	.9998	.9998	.9998	.9998	.9998	.9998	.9998	.9998	.9997	.9997	.9997	.9996
5.7	.9994	.9996	.9997	.9998	.9998	.9999	.9999	.9999	.9999	.9999	.9999	.9999	.9999	.9999	.9998	.9998	.9998	.9998
5.8	.9995	.9997	.9998	.9999	.9999	.9999	.9999	.9999	.9999	.9999	.9999	.9999	.9999	.9999	.9999	.9999	.9998	.9998
5.9	.9996	.9998	.9999	.9999	.9999	.9999	.9999	.9999	.9999	.9999	.9999	.9999	.9999	.9999	.9999	.9999	.9999	.9999
6.0	.9997	.9998	.9999	.9999	.9999	1.0000	1.0000	1.0000	1.0000	1.0000	1.0000	1.0000	1.0000	1.0000	.9999	.9999	.9999	.9999
6.1	.9998	.9999	.9999	.9999	1.0000										1.0000	1.0000	.9999	.9999
6.2	.9998	.9999	.9999	1.0000													1.0000	1.0000
6.3	.9999	.9999	.9999															
6.4	.9999	.9999	1.0000															
6.5	.9999	1.0000																
6.6	.9999																	
6.7	.9999																	
6.8	1.0000																	

Source: Journal of Quality Technology (12)4. Reprinted by permission of ASQC.

Table 4 -- Folded normal distributions (continued)

EXAMPLE: $\mu_f/\sigma_f = 1.7$

t_f IS IN σ_f UNITS

t_f

μ_f/σ_f \ t_f	2.20	2.25	2.30	2.35	2.40	2.45	2.50	2.55	2.60	2.65	2.70	2.75	2.80	2.85	2.90	2.95	3.00
0.0	.0000	.0000	.0000	.0000	.0000	.0000	.0000	.0000	.0000	.0000	.0000	.0000	.0000	.0000	.0000	.0000	.0000
0.1	.0081	.0071	.0063	.0056	.0049	.0043	.0038	.0033	.0029	.0025	.0022	.0019	.0017	.0014	.0012	.0011	.0009
0.2	.0164	.0145	.0129	.0114	.0100	.0088	.0078	.0068	.0060	.0052	.0045	.0039	.0034	.0030	.0026	.0022	.0019
0.3	.0253	.0224	.0199	.0176	.0156	.0137	.0121	.0106	.0092	.0082	.0071	.0062	.0054	.0047	.0041	.0035	.0030
0.4	.0349	.0311	.0277	.0246	.0218	.0193	.0170	.0150	.0132	.0116	.0102	.0089	.0078	.0068	.0059	.0051	.0044
0.5	.0456	.0408	.0364	.0324	.0288	.0256	.0227	.0201	.0177	.0156	.0137	.0120	.0106	.0092	.0080	.0070	.0061
0.6	.0576	.0517	.0463	.0414	.0370	.0330	.0293	.0260	.0231	.0204	.0180	.0159	.0140	.0122	.0107	.0094	.0082
0.7	.0711	.0641	.0577	.0518	.0464	.0415	.0371	.0331	.0294	.0261	.0232	.0205	.0181	.0160	.0140	.0123	.0108
0.8	.0863	.0782	.0706	.0637	.0573	.0515	.0462	.0414	.0370	.0330	.0294	.0261	.0232	.0205	.0181	.0160	.0140
0.9	.1035	.0941	.0854	.0773	.0699	.0631	.0569	.0512	.0459	.0412	.0368	.0329	.0293	.0260	.0231	.0204	.0181
1.0	.1226	.1120	.1021	.0929	.0844	.0765	.0693	.0626	.0564	.0508	.0456	.0409	.0366	.0327	.0292	.0259	.0230
1.1	.1439	.1320	.1209	.1106	.1009	.0919	.0836	.0758	.0687	.0621	.0561	.0505	.0454	.0407	.0365	.0326	.0291
1.2	.1674	.1543	.1420	.1304	.1195	.1094	.0999	.0911	.0829	.0753	.0682	.0617	.0557	.0502	.0452	.0406	.0363
1.3	.1932	.1789	.1653	.1525	.1404	.1291	.1184	.1085	.0991	.0904	.0823	.0748	.0679	.0614	.0555	.0500	.0450
1.4	.2211	.2057	.1909	.1769	.1637	.1511	.1392	.1281	.1176	.1077	.0985	.0899	.0819	.0745	.0676	.0612	.0553
1.5	.2512	.2347	.2188	.2036	.1892	.1754	.1624	.1500	.1383	.1273	.1169	.1072	.0981	.0895	.0816	.0742	.0674
1.6	.2833	.2658	.2489	.2326	.2170	.2021	.1879	.1743	.1614	.1492	.1376	.1267	.1164	.1068	.0977	.0893	.0814
1.7	.3172	.2988	.2810	.2637	.2471	.2311	.2157	.2009	.1869	.1734	.1607	.1486	.1371	.1263	.1161	.1065	.0975
1.8	.3527	.3336	.3150	.2968	.2792	.2622	.2458	.2299	.2147	.2001	.1861	.1728	.1601	.1481	.1367	.1259	.1158
1.9	.3895	.3699	.3506	.3317	.3133	.2953	.2779	.2611	.2447	.2290	.2139	.1994	.1856	.1723	.1597	.1478	.1364
2.0	.4274	.4073	.3876	.3681	.3490	.3303	.3120	.2942	.2769	.2602	.2440	.2284	.2134	.1989	.1851	.1720	.1594
2.1	.4659	.4457	.4256	.4057	.3861	.3668	.3478	.3292	.3111	.2934	.2762	.2596	.2434	.2279	.2129	.1986	.1849
2.2	.5047	.4845	.4643	.4442	.4243	.4045	.3850	.3658	.3470	.3285	.3104	.2928	.2757	.2591	.2430	.2275	.2127
2.3	.5435	.5235	.5034	.4833	.4632	.4432	.4233	.4037	.3842	.3651	.3463	.3279	.3099	.2923	.2753	.2587	.2427
2.4	.5819	.5623	.5424	.5225	.5025	.4824	.4624	.4424	.4226	.4030	.3836	.3646	.3458	.3275	.3095	.2920	.2750

Table 4 -- Folded normal distributions (continued)

Column headings are values of μ_f/σ_f; row labels are t_f.

t_f	3.00	2.95	2.90	2.85	2.80	2.75	2.70	2.65	2.60	2.55	2.50	2.45	2.40	2.35	2.30	2.25	2.20
2.5	.3092	.3272	.3455	.3642	.3832	.4025	.4221	.4419	.4618	.4817	.5013	.5218	.5417	.5615	.5811	.6004	.6195
2.6	.3452	.3639	.3829	.4022	.4217	.4414	.4613	.4813	.5013	.5212	.5408	.5609	.5805	.5995	.6189	.6377	.6560
2.7	.3827	.4019	.4214	.4411	.4610	.4809	.5009	.5209	.5408	.5605	.5801	.5995	.6186	.6373	.6557	.6736	.6911
2.8	.4212	.4409	.4608	.4807	.5006	.5206	.5405	.5603	.5799	.5992	.6183	.6371	.6555	.6735	.6911	.7081	.7246
2.9	.4606	.4805	.5005	.5204	.5403	.5601	.5797	.5991	.6182	.6370	.6554	.6735	.6911	.7081	.7247	.7407	.7561
3.0	.5003	.5203	.5401	.5599	.5795	.5989	.6174	.6359	.6554	.6735	.6911	.7082	.7249	.7410	.7565	.7714	.7856
3.1	.5401	.5598	.5794	.5989	.6180	.6369	.6552	.6735	.6911	.7083	.7250	.7412	.7568	.7717	.7861	.7993	.8129
3.2	.5794	.5983	.6180	.6368	.6554	.6735	.6910	.7084	.7252	.7414	.7570	.7721	.7865	.8004	.8136	.8261	.8380
3.3	.6179	.6368	.6554	.6735	.6912	.7085	.7250	.7415	.7572	.7724	.7869	.8008	.8141	.8267	.8387	.8500	.8607
3.4	.6554	.6735	.6913	.7086	.7254	.7417	.7572	.7726	.7872	.8011	.8145	.8272	.8393	.8507	.8615	.8717	.8812
3.5	.6913	.7086	.7255	.7418	.7576	.7728	.7871	.8014	.8148	.8276	.8398	.8513	.8622	.8724	.8820	.8911	.8995
3.6	.7235	.7419	.7577	.7729	.7876	.8016	.8148	.8279	.8401	.8517	.8627	.8730	.8827	.8918	.9003	.9082	.9156
3.7	.7578	.7730	.7877	.8018	.8153	.8282	.8402	.8521	.8631	.8734	.8832	.8924	.9010	.9090	.9164	.9233	.9297
3.8	.7878	.8019	.8155	.8284	.8407	.8523	.8630	.8738	.8836	.8929	.9015	.9096	.9171	.9240	.9305	.9364	.9419
3.9	.8156	.8285	.8408	.8525	.8636	.8741	.8836	.8932	.9019	.9100	.9175	.9246	.9311	.9371	.9427	.9477	.9524
4.0	.8410	.8527	.8638	.8743	.8842	.8935	.9020	.9104	.9180	.9251	.9316	.9377	.9433	.9484	.9531	.9574	.9613
4.1	.8639	.8745	.8844	.8937	.9025	.9107	.9181	.9254	.9320	.9381	.9437	.9489	.9536	.9580	.9619	.9655	.9688
4.2	.8845	.8939	.9027	.9109	.9185	.9257	.9320	.9384	.9441	.9493	.9541	.9576	.9624	.9661	.9693	.9723	.9750
4.3	.9023	.9110	.9187	.9259	.9325	.9387	.9442	.9496	.9544	.9588	.9628	.9665	.9698	.9728	.9756	.9780	.9802
4.4	.9189	.9260	.9327	.9389	.9446	.9498	.9544	.9591	.9631	.9668	.9702	.9732	.9760	.9784	.9807	.9827	.9844
4.5	.9328	.9390	.9447	.9500	.9549	.9593	.9632	.9671	.9705	.9735	.9763	.9788	.9810	.9830	.9848	.9864	.9879
4.6	.9449	.9502	.9550	.9595	.9636	.9673	.9705	.9737	.9765	.9790	.9813	.9834	.9851	.9868	.9882	.9895	.9906
4.7	.9551	.9596	.9637	.9674	.9708	.9739	.9766	.9792	.9815	.9836	.9854	.9870	.9885	.9898	.9909	.9919	.9928
4.8	.9638	.9675	.9709	.9740	.9769	.9794	.9816	.9837	.9856	.9872	.9887	.9900	.9911	.9922	.9930	.9938	.9945
4.9	.9710	.9741	.9770	.9795	.9818	.9839	.9857	.9874	.9888	.9901	.9913	.9923	.9932	.9940	.9947	.9954	.9959
5.0	.9770	.9796	.9819	.9839	.9858	.9875	.9889	.9903	.9914	.9925	.9934	.9942	.9949	.9955	.9960	.9965	.9969
5.1	.9819	.9840	.9859	.9875	.9890	.9903	.9915	.9926	.9935	.9943	.9950	.9956	.9962	.9966	.9971	.9974	.9977
5.2	.9859	.9876	.9891	.9904	.9916	.9926	.9935	.9944	.9951	.9957	.9963	.9968	.9972	.9975	.9978	.9981	.9983
5.3	.9891	.9905	.9917	.9927	.9936	.9944	.9951	.9958	.9963	.9968	.9972	.9976	.9979	.9982	.9984	.9986	.9988
5.4	.9917	.9927	.9937	.9945	.9952	.9958	.9964	.9969	.9973	.9976	.9980	.9982	.9985	.9987	.9988	.9990	.9991
5.5	.9937	.9945	.9952	.9959	.9964	.9969	.9973	.9977	.9980	.9983	.9985	.9987	.9989	.9990	.9992	.9993	.9994
5.6	.9953	.9959	.9965	.9969	.9973	.9977	.9980	.9983	.9986	.9988	.9989	.9991	.9992	.9993	.9994	.9995	.9996
5.7	.9965	.9970	.9974	.9977	.9981	.9983	.9986	.9988	.9990	.9991	.9992	.9993	.9994	.9995	.9996	.9996	.9997
5.8	.9974	.9978	.9981	.9984	.9986	.9988	.9990	.9991	.9993	.9994	.9995	.9995	.9996	.9997	.9997	.9998	.9998
5.9	.9981	.9984	.9986	.9988	.9990	.9991	.9993	.9994	.9995	.9996	.9996	.9997	.9997	.9998	.9998	.9999	.9999
6.0	.9986	.9988	.9990	.9992	.9993	.9994	.9995	.9996	.9996	.9997	.9997	.9998	.9998	.9999	.9999	.9999	.9999
6.1	.9990	.9992	.9993	.9994	.9995	.9996	.9996	.9997	.9997	.9998	.9998	.9998	.9999	.9999	.9999	.9999	.9999
6.2	.9993	.9994	.9995	.9996	.9996	.9997	.9998	.9998	.9998	.9999	.9999	.9999	.9999	.9999	.9999	.9999	1.0000
6.3	.9995	.9996	.9997	.9997	.9998	.9998	.9998	.9999	.9999	.9999	.9999	.9999	.9999	1.0000	1.0000	1.0000	
6.4	.9997	.9997	.9998	.9998	.9999	.9999	.9999	.9999	.9999	.9999	.9999	.9999	1.0000				
6.5	.9998	.9998	.9999	.9999	.9999	.9999	.9999	.9999	.9999	1.0000	1.0000	1.0000					
6.6	.9998	.9999	.9999	.9999	.9999	.9999	1.0000	1.0000	1.0000								
6.7	.9999	.9999	.9999	.9999	.9999	1.0000											
6.8	.9999	.9999	.9999	1.0000	1.0000												
6.9	1.0000	1.0000	1.0000														

Table 5 -- Factors for short run control charts for individuals, $\overline{X}$ and R charts

g	1 (R based on moving range of 2)				2				3				4				5			
	A_{2F}	D_{4F}	A_{2S}	D_{4S}	A_{2F}	D_{4F}	A_{2S}	D_{4S}	A_{2F}	D_{4F}	A_{2S}	D_{4S}	A_{2F}	D_{4F}	A_{2S}	D_{4S}	A_{2F}	D_{4F}	A_{2S}	D_{4S}
1	NA	NA	236.5	128	NA	NA	167	128	NA	NA	8.21	14	NA	NA	3.05	13	NA	NA	1.8	5.1
2	12.0	2.0	20.8	16	8.49	2.0	15.70	15.6	1.57	1.9	2.72	7.1	0.83	1.9	1.44	3.5	0.58	1.7	1.00	3.2
3	6.8	2.7	9.6	15	4.78	2.7	6.76	14.7	1.35	2.3	1.90	4.5	0.81	1.9	1.14	3.2	0.59	1.8	0.83	2.8
4	5.1	3.3	6.6	8.1	3.62	3.3	4.68	8.1	1.26	2.4	1.62	3.7	0.79	2.1	1.01	2.9	0.59	1.9	0.76	2.6
5	4.4	3.3	5.4	6.3	3.12	3.3	3.82	6.3	1.20	2.4	1.47	3.4	0.78	2.1	0.95	2.8	0.59	2.0	0.72	2.5
6	4.0	3.3	4.7	5.4	2.83	3.3	3.34	5.4	1.17	2.5	1.39	3.3	0.77	2.2	0.91	2.7	0.59	2.0	0.70	2.4
7	3.7	3.3	4.3	5.0	2.65	3.3	3.06	5.0	1.14	2.5	1.32	3.2	0.76	2.2	0.88	2.6	0.59	2.0	0.68	2.4
8	3.6	3.3	4.1	4.7	2.53	3.3	2.87	4.7	1.13	2.5	1.28	3.1	0.76	2.2	0.86	2.6	0.59	2.0	0.66	2.3
9	3.5	3.3	3.9	4.5	2.45	3.3	2.74	4.5	1.12	2.5	1.25	3.0	0.76	2.2	0.85	2.5	0.59	2.0	0.65	2.3
10	3.3	3.3	3.7	4.5	2.37	3.3	2.62	4.5	1.10	2.5	1.22	3.0	0.75	2.2	0.83	2.5	0.58	2.0	0.65	2.3
15	3.1	3.5	3.3	4.1	2.18	3.5	2.33	4.1	1.08	2.5	1.15	2.9	0.75	2.3	0.80	2.4	0.58	2.1	0.62	2.2
20	3.0	3.5	3.1	4.0	2.11	3.5	2.21	4.0	1.07	2.6	1.12	2.8	0.74	2.3	0.78	2.4	0.58	2.1	0.61	2.2
25	2.9	3.5	3.0	3.8	2.05	3.5	2.14	3.8	1.06	2.6	1.10	2.7	0.74	2.3	0.77	2.4	0.58	2.1	0.60	2.2

Numbers enclosed in bold boxes represent the recommended minimum number of subgroups for starting a control chart.

Table 6 -- Significant number of consecutive highest or lowest values from one
stream of a multiple-stream process
On average a run of the length shown would appear no more than 1 time in 100.

# Streams, k	2	3	4	5	6	7	8	9	10	11	12
Significant run, r	7	5	5	4	4	4	4	4	3	3	3

Index